2025

HOROSCOPES

Week-by-week predictions for every zodiac sign

PATSY BENNETT

ROCKPOOL

THE MOON'S PHASES FOR THE YEAR

The moon's phases, including eclipses, new moons and full moons, can all affect your mood. All of these events are explained and listed in the book, enabling you to plan ahead with the full knowledge you're moving in synchronicity with the sun and the moon. On the following pages are the moon's phases for 2025 for both the southern and northern hemispheres.

JANUARY

S	M	T	W	T	F	S
			1	2	3	4
5	6	7	8	9	10	11
12	13	14	15	16	17	18
19	20	21	22	23	24	25
26	27	28	29	30	31	

FEBRUARY

S	M	T	W	T	F	S
						1
2	3	4	5	6	7	8
9	10	11	12	13	14	15
16	17	18	19	20	21	22
23	24	25	26	27	28	

MARCH

S	M	T	W	T	F	S
						1
2	3	4	5	6	7	8
9	10	11	12	13	14	15
16	17	18	19	20	21	22
23	24	25	26	27	28	29
30	31					

APRIL

S	M	T	W	T	F	S
		1	2	3	4	5
6	7	8	9	10	11	12
13	14	15	16	17	18	19
20	21	22	23	24	25	26
27	28	29	30			

MAY

S	M	T	W	T	F	S
				1	2	3
4	5	6	7	8	9	10
11	12	13	14	15	16	17
18	19	20	21	22	23	24
25	26	27	28	29	30	31

JUNE

S	M	T	W	T	F	S
1	2	3	4	5	6	7
8	9	10	11	12	13	14
15	16	17	18	19	20	21
22	23	24	25	26	27	28
29	30					

2025 SOUTHERN HEMISPHERE MOON PHASES

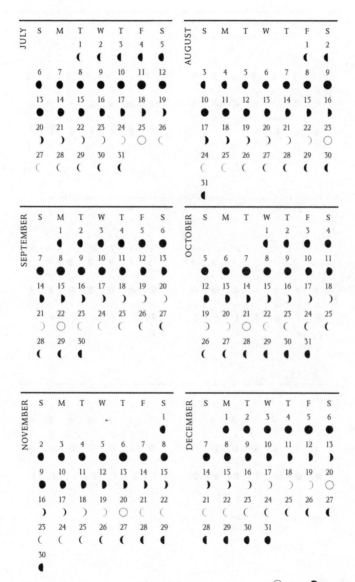

○ New moon ● Full moon

2025 NORTHERN HEMISPHERE MOON PHASES

JANUARY

S	M	T	W	T	F	S
			1	2	3	4
5	6	7	8	9	10	11
12	13	14	15	16	17	18
19	20	21	22	23	24	25
26	27	28	29	30	31	

FEBRUARY

S	M	T	W	T	F	S
						1
2	3	4	5	6	7	8
9	10	11	12	13	14	15
16	17	18	19	20	21	22
23	24	25	26	27	28	

MARCH

S	M	T	W	T	F	S
						1
2	3	4	5	6	7	8
9	10	11	12	13	14	15
16	17	18	19	20	21	22
23	24	25	26	27	28	29
30	31					

APRIL

S	M	T	W	T	F	S
		1	2	3	4	5
6	7	8	9	10	11	12
13	14	15	16	17	18	19
20	21	22	23	24	25	26
27	28	29	30			

MAY

S	M	T	W	T	F	S
				1	2	3
4	5	6	7	8	9	10
11	12	13	14	15	16	17
18	19	20	21	22	23	24
25	26	27	28	29	30	31

JUNE

S	M	T	W	T	F	S
1	2	3	4	5	6	7
8	9	10	11	12	13	14
15	16	17	18	19	20	21
22	23	24	25	26	27	28
29	30					

2025 NORTHERN HEMISPHERE MOON PHASES

JULY

S	M	T	W	T	F	S
		1	2	3	4	5
6	7	8	9	10	11	12
13	14	15	16	17	18	19
20	21	22	23	24	25	26
27	28	29	30	31		

AUGUST

S	M	T	W	T	F	S
					1	2
3	4	5	6	7	8	9
10	11	12	13	14	15	16
17	18	19	20	21	22	23
24	25	26	27	28	29	30
31						

SEPTEMBER

S	M	T	W	T	F	S
	1	2	3	4	5	6
7	8	9	10	11	12	13
14	15	16	17	18	19	20
21	22	23	24	25	26	27
28	29	30				

OCTOBER

S	M	T	W	T	F	S
			1	2	3	4
5	6	7	8	9	10	11
12	13	14	15	16	17	18
19	20	21	22	23	24	25
26	27	28	29	30	31	

NOVEMBER

S	M	T	W	T	F	S
						1
2	3	4	5	6	7	8
9	10	11	12	13	14	15
16	17	18	19	20	21	22
23	24	25	26	27	28	29
30						

DECEMBER

S	M	T	W	T	F	S
	1	2	3	4	5	6
7	8	9	10	11	12	13
14	15	16	17	18	19	20
21	22	23	24	25	26	27
28	29	30	31			

◯ New moon ● Full moon

Patsy Bennett, a rare combination of astrologer and psychic medium, contributes horoscopes to magazines internationally and in Australia and has appeared on several live daytime TV and radio shows. She is also a speaker and provides astrology and psychic consultations, and she holds astrology and psychic development workshops in Byron Bay, Australia, where she lives.

Patsy runs www.astrocast.com.au, www.patsybennett.com, facebook @patsybennettpsychicastrology and instagram @patsybennettastrology.

FURTHER INFORMATION

For an in-depth personal astrology chart reading contact Patsy Bennett at patsybennettastrology@gmail.com.

Further astronomical data can be obtained from the following:

* Michelsen, Neil F. and Pottenger, Rique, *The American Ephemeris for the 21st Century 2000–2050 at Midnight*, ACS Publications, 1997.

A Rockpool book
PO Box 252
Summer Hill
NSW 2130
Australia

rockpoolpublishing.com
Follow us! f @ rockpoolpublishing
Tag your images with #rockpoolpublishing

ISBN: 9781922785916

Published in 2024 by Rockpool Publishing
Copyright text © Patsy Bennett 2024
Copyright design © Rockpool Publishing
2024

Design and typesetting by Sara Lindberg, Rockpool Publishing
Edited by Lisa Macken

Printed and bound in China
10 9 8 7 6 5 4 3 2 1

All dates in this book are set to Greenwich Mean Time (GMT).
Astrological interpretations take into account all aspects and the sign the sun and planets are in on each day and are not taken out of context.

CONTENTS

INTRODUCTION

There is so much to be excited about in 2025, especially the opportunity to transform aspects of your life you have outgrown. In tandem, this will be an excellent year for self-development and improved relationships. The transformations you make in your life are likely to be changes you'll welcome.

Consider in your own time how you'd like to see your life progress in 2025 and make tracks to ensure your dreams happen. It may sound like a pipe dream, but with the necessary focus on practicalities, and together with inspiration and motivation, you could truly make a dream come true.

This horoscope book is a guide for you, with weekly horoscopes highlighting your options and the areas of your life that will gain focus or thrive. There is a round-up of the predominant themes for each month, divided into the following important areas of your life: finances, health, love life, career and home life. As you'll gain an appreciation of those areas that will thrive, and how they will thrive, you'll gain advance information about where best to focus your attention.

The weeks in this horoscope book run from Thursdays to Wednesdays simply because of the way the year falls, ending as it does on a Wednesday on 31 December. By following the sun, moon and stars you'll discover a fresh rhythm in your life that encourages you to make the most of your full potential, enables you to work proactively with your positive traits and sidelines your negative characteristics.

Be sure to approach the retrograde phases with patience and the will to learn, and as a result you'll find life much easier and will gain the chance to slow down and avoid feeling pressured, finding time to enjoy a slower pace during the retrograde phases and especially the Mercury retrogrades.

Above all, be confident that being guided doesn't mean you must act or live your life in a particular way. This horoscope book is intended as a means to bring your best traits forward so you can live your life to the fullest. I hope you have a wonderful year.

To find out more about the daily astrological phenomena I use to make weekly predictions, you'll find the *2025 Astrology Diary* invaluable.

MERCURY, VENUS AND MARS RETROGRADE PERIODS IN 2025

Mercury retrograde phases
15 March to 7 April
18 July to 11 August
9 November to 29 November

Venus retrograde phase
2 March to 13 April

Mars retrograde phase
1 January to 24 February

January

WEEK 1: 1–8 JANUARY

Some beautiful astrological aspects point to an ideal time to move your plans forward. You may receive an unexpected ego boost, such as a financial improvement. However, if you're negotiating or making agreements, ensure you are careful to obtain all the facts to avoid making mistakes. This may also be a particularly romantic or sociable time, and a health or personal matter may deserve extra attention.

WEEK 2: 9–15 JANUARY

You'll appreciate the opportunity to enjoy time out. If you're working these will be busy times, but there's also the chance to enjoy the promise a new year brings. It's a good week to focus on optimum health, especially towards 9 January. Lovely developments will bring a more comfortable vibe into your domestic or daily life. Just avoid making mistakes by planning well ahead.

WEEK 3: 16–22 JANUARY

You are in line to see a marked improvement in your work or status and may even be surprised by developments. However, you'll benefit from a healthy break to avoid fatigue. You may need to reassess a situation or change your perspective. Avoid attempting a broad sweep; be selective and focused. The sun's alignment with Pluto could create intensity, so be sure to take things one step at a time.

WEEK 4: 23–29 JANUARY

Trust your instincts, as these are likely to be spot on. A debt may be repaid, and you'll appreciate that an issue from your past can be remedied. You'll also enjoy a boost in morale or even status. The Aquarian new moon on 29 January could kick-start a fresh phase in your relationship with a group, friend or organisation. For some, this may signal a new chapter in your career or general direction.

FINANCES

If you're back at work you'll find this a lucrative week, as the harmonious angle between the sun in your 10th house and Saturn in your 12th will be productive – that is, unless you overspent during the festive season or if you're still overspending now at the start of the new year! Domestic, family or work matters will require focus to avoid over-expenditure. You're likely to enjoy socialising, so consider setting yourself a budget there as well.

HEALTH

Fresh air, a change of environment or the chance to take a holiday will appeal, and you'll enjoy the benefits of focusing on your health. Your sign's ruler Mars in the nurturing sign of Cancer will encourage you to take time out at home and bring a health focus to your home life. Consider slowing down if possible when you can, as overexertion could force you to take a break from your usual routine.

LOVE LIFE

Your sign's ruler Mars will be retrograde until the end of February, bringing a risk that you are not your usual full-of-beans self. This will take its toll on your love life unless you create the space to self-nurture. Luckily, Chiron in your sign will encourage you to express yourself, and you may find that talking, dancing and walking together with that someone special assumes a therapeutic and positive aspect in your love life.

CAREER

Pluto in your career sector for the entire year promises a transformative process in this key aspect of your life. You'll gain insight already this week about where you'd like to place your attention. Review your personal responsibilities versus money-making ventures; you may need to make a difficult choice. However, if you are innovative and look outside the square at your options you could make ingenious changes that encompass both areas.

HOME LIFE

Mars retrograde in your home sector suggests you will rethink aspects of your home life or a family commitment. This may be due, for example, to a change of direction or status because of work commitments. Developments may add tension to some of your decisions, so be sure to make important choices with the benefit of expert advice rather than being impulsive with long-term domestic decisions. You'll enjoy a reunion.

February

WEEK 1: 30 JANUARY–5 FEBRUARY

You'll meet someone or hear from someone you have a predestined connection with, be this in connection with work or romance. Singles may meet a lovely character. A new direction will be significant. Key domestic and personal decisions will merit a little focus so you are clear about the long-term implications. A decision around a trip or financial matter will come down to principles and values.

WEEK 2: 6–12 FEBRUARY

You may be surprised by developments at work or regarding an agreement. Consider news carefully as it may represent a turning point. A trip or visit could be a catalyst for change. A fresh phase will begin with the full moon on 12 February, enabling you to move ahead with domestic and work-related schedules. Just avoid pre-empting matters and making assumptions.

WEEK 3: 13–19 FEBRUARY

This will be a particularly passionate week, but if an argument is brewing you must avoid conflict. To head off a stalemate, stick with the facts. Chance encounters are likely to be enjoyable: you may meet up with all kinds of interesting and unusual characters. If you're working this will be a productive time, but you must ensure you're tactful for the best results.

WEEK 4: 20–26 FEBRUARY

Research may be necessary before you make decisions about an agreement if circumstances cause confusion now. For many, though, events will bring clarity or a breakthrough, especially in connection with a friend, group or organisation. Avoid looking only at the past; consider all of the opportunities coming your way. A work option may be ideal. It's a good week to improve your health.

FINANCES

Be prepared for the out of the ordinary this month financially! This is a good time to be innovative. Venus in your sign will put focus not only on love but also on money, and you may be surprised by financial developments mid-month. A matter to do with your past or work is likely to be a focus and a karmic connection could bring ideal results, but this will depend on the integrity with which you have managed finances in the past.

HEALTH

Mars ends it retrograde phase at the end of the month, so if you've been feeling lacklustre you'll begin to regain your energy and mojo. Avoid feeling this will happen overnight, as it will take some time – for some even until the end of April – before you feel you're back on par. The key word regarding health, vitality and well-being in February is patience. Be sure to support your health with all the means you know, beginning with a good diet.

LOVE LIFE

The conjunction of the moon's north node, Venus and Neptune at the beginning of the month points to key developments regarding someone you hold dear to your heart. If you're single you may meet someone truly marvellous, and if you're in a relationship you'll be making important decisions in February, so be sure you're happy with the direction your choices take you. With Venus in Aries there's no doubt love will be a theme, so take the initiative!

CAREER

February offers you the chance to move forward with key career choices; for some, these will have been on the table already in May last year. You'll gain the chance now to move them ahead at a rapid pace. You'll see vital matters in the spotlight mid-month, around the full moon on 12 February, which will bring to centre stage your personal and domestic priorities and shine a light on what must be done work-wise to secure these.

HOME LIFE

The full moon in Leo on 12 February points to personal, family or domestic matters coming to a head, kick-starting a fresh phase in your domestic life or family circle. You may discover that a property or financial agreement will require an adjustment on your part and it will be to your benefit to find ways to work methodically towards a harmonious outcome, especially if your energy levels have been low or health matters restrict your options.

March

WEEK 1: 27 FEBRUARY–5 MARCH

A fresh work initiative or project could be ideal, but you must gain all the facts before committing to it. You may begin to experience more security, especially financially, even if a mystery arises at first. As Venus turns retrograde on 2 March it'll be in your interest to complete agreements beforehand to avoid having to restructure them.

WEEK 2: 6–12 MARCH

This is a great time for discussions, as you're likely to be able to make well-informed decisions and especially as you get closer to the lunar eclipse on 14 March. Aim to build a solid rapport with people who can help you. An agreement can be made domestically, at work or in your health schedule that could be binding.

WEEK 3: 13–19 MARCH

You're likely to make a fresh arrangement either at work or with an organisation that may come about via specific news, which contains a surprising element or comes from out of the blue. Check all the facts if you are making commitments, as mistakes could be made because you may be particularly idealistic at this time. However, it's probable you manage to make a binding agreement you're happy with.

WEEK 4: 20–26 MARCH / WEEK 5: 27 MARCH–2 APRIL

WEEK 4: this week's strongly Neptunian vibe could create a mystery surrounding a work, personal or spiritual matter. Meetings, chats and get-togethers are likely to be uplifting if you have the time to indulge in people's romantic ideals. Keep your own communications as clear as possible, especially where information is imprecise and facts must be clarified. The sun in your sign for the next four weeks will boost your energy levels. **WEEK 5:** the Aries solar eclipse on 29 March will motivate you to express your values and ideas more, enabling you to implement plans. A fresh understanding of yourself or of someone else will arise as you find ways to establish better relationships, especially if you were born at the end of March or early April. You may enjoy a reunion and may even hear from an old flame or ex-colleague.

FINANCES

March is a good month to review finances and consider innovative ways to build wealth and curb spending. Take the time early on in the month to reconfigure financial matters, and if you have important paperwork to complete try to do so before Venus turns retrograde on 2 March and at the least before Mercury turns retrograde on the 15th. News early in the month either to do with work or regarding a past investment will require careful analysis.

HEALTH

The sun will enter Aries at the equinox on 21 March, which will help boost energy levels, but with Venus and Mercury (from the 15th) retrograde you must be careful with communications to avoid having to go over old ground and feeling as though you're backtracking in various ways, which will drain your energy. The solar eclipse in your sign on the 29th provides the chance to truly turn a corner in your life, so be prepared to be mentally and emotionally bold.

LOVE LIFE

Venus retrograde in your sign will be taking you through a nostalgic phase over the next six weeks. You may find yourself being drawn to an ex, or at the least reviewing or rearranging some of your agreements in a key partnership. You will also find this is an introspective time in which you gain insight into yourself and your motivations for being in particular relationships. If some aspects of your love life are disheartening, bear in mind this is a temporary phase and take heart.

CAREER

March's eclipse season will kick-start an entirely fresh phase in your work life or daily routine. By the end of March you'll have gained the opportunity to move forward more determinedly with your plans, but you must be prepared for situations mid-month that may bring a surprise your way. For many this will be a positive development, but nothing can be taken for granted in an eclipse month so it's best to be thorough with your decision-making.

HOME LIFE

The aspect between the sun and Mars on 7 March points to a positive time to invest in your domestic life and home. You may be drawn to repairing your décor or even restructuring your home through remodelling and investing in the garden or bringing aspects of landscaping into your home through colour choice and plants. However, you must avoid overcommitting to certain domestic matters as otherwise you'll feel a financial or personal strain towards the month's end.

April

WEEK 1: 3–9 APRIL

You may be pleasantly surprised by the outcome of the week. Some developments may seem unusual or be unexpected, but they could lead somewhere exciting. You may hear key news from the past regarding work or your home life that boosts your circumstances, so be sure to take the initiative in one or all of these areas.

WEEK 2: 10–16 APRIL

The entry of Neptune in Aries points to an increased focus on the arts, spirituality, romance, film and music. You will enjoy infusing your life with these qualities now but you must be sure to keep your feet on the ground to avoid having unrealistic expectations. The full moon on 13 April signals a fresh phase in a key relationship, and for some a fresh daily, work or health schedule.

WEEK 3: 17–23 APRIL

It's a mixed bag this week, so for some Aries developments could be ideal and especially relating to work, health and someone special. A reunion or news from the past will be refreshing and you'll gain the opportunity to indulge in your creative side. Romance may be particularly captivating. You must, however, avoid wishful thinking and making rash decisions or you'll experience the need for a course correction.

WEEK 4: 24–30 APRIL

You'll enjoy a reunion or return to an old haunt. There is certainly a nostalgic atmosphere to the week; nevertheless the arts, music, spiritual development and favourite aspects of your working life can flourish. The new moon on 27 April points to an excellent time to turn a corner financially, but you must find a balance between over- and underindulgence.

FINANCES

You'll manage to get more of a handle on your work and finances this month. You may discover that certain domestic matters can begin to work increasingly in your favour. It will certainly be in your interest to take steps to organise your finances as this could change your circumstances considerably and potentially bring money your way. What's more, the full moon at the end of the month will spotlight decisions that could bring you more security.

HEALTH

If you've had a niggling health concern this is a good month to find out more about the best ways to manage your circumstances. It's also a good month to discover the power of positive thought; you may find you automatically feel more optimistic through a change of routine, which will improve your mental health. Spiritually minded Aries will find this month that your ability to meditate, visualise or develop your intuition is heightened.

LOVE LIFE

Venus retrograde until 13 April and the presence of Neptune in Aries will contribute to a romantic month. A nostalgic phase or trip down memory lane will reconnect you with circumstances that occurred late in June last year or earlier. The conjunction of Venus, Saturn, the moon's north node, Mercury and Neptune all point to a sense of predestiny or the unavoidable. If you're careful with your choices you could catapult your love life into a new cycle.

CAREER

You may discover new ways to work and earn money; for example, if you've been working at home or have a very slow-paced career then April will see your horizons broaden and also a faster pace after mid-month. You may even experience a change of environment, so if things have been slow look out for new opportunities and options to improve this important part of your life. Just avoid making rash decisions around the 20th.

HOME LIFE

This is a good month to look at ways your hard work can pay off in your home life, family and personal investments. Projects you begin at the start of the month will produce fantastic results, especially if you have already put considerable hard work into your ideas and ventures. Developments mid to late month could also mean that some of your decisions regarding your daily schedule will mean changes in your personal life and at home.

May

WEEK 1: 1–7 MAY

There is a romantic quality to the week's developments, and you may particularly enjoy a favourite activity or interest. Just avoid seeing life idealistically, and you must avoid conflict. Your involvement with a group or organisation will show change and you'll gain the chance to re-evaluate it over the coming months. It's a good week for a health appointment and to offer or ask for help if it's needed.

WEEK 2: 8–14 MAY

This is a good week to stride ahead with your plans and make concrete changes that could benefit your financial circumstances. The full moon in Scorpio on 12 May promises to bring considerable change your way but may also bring out tempers and tantrums unless you're careful to avoid anger and outbursts, either in yourself or others.

WEEK 3: 15–21 MAY

You'll enjoy a change of routine or a surprise this weekend. You may be drawn to investing in yourself or something different. Events now could provide you with an increased sense of stability or security, so be sure to investigate ways that you could improve your circumstances as your efforts are likely to pay off.

WEEK 4: 22–28 MAY

Your sign's ruler Mars makes a harmonious aspect with Venus, and this spells a busy but also potentially productive week. However, you must avoid overexerting yourself. The new moon on 27 May suggests that a meeting or trip will provide you with food for thought, as a reunion or the prospect of beginning a fresh chapter will prove enticing. It's vital to get a key financial decision right.

FINANCES

You may experience a surprise or unusual financial boost. Be sure to attend to paperwork as you may be owed something from the past. The new moon on 27 May will help you kick-start a fresh financial chapter, and you may be surprised towards the end of the month by some of the financial avenues that open up for you. However, you must avoid placing stock in activities and ventures that don't resonate with your values and principles.

HEALTH

You tend to overexert yourself, so be sure and especially in the third week of the month to schedule in relaxation time. Some health gurus will tell you that happiness is the key to holistic health, and happiness certainly does boost a sense of well-being and self-esteem. Consider this month whether your activities, including your work and financial investments, provide you with a sense of happiness and, if they don't, May is the month to change this.

LOVE LIFE

The Scorpio full moon on 12 May will bring passion into your love life, so if you've felt more recently that this has been missing then rest assured this full moon will reignite it. For some people this may even be in unforeseen ways or through a chance meeting with someone unexpected. Couples will enjoy the therapeutic aspects of a more passionate love life; however, the full moon will also incite anger so it's best to avoid contentious topics mid-month.

CAREER

To be happy career-wise you need to pursue goals or at least feel you are useful to someone. You'll find out in May whether the direction you're taking in your daily work life does still feel fulfilling. If however you decide that some aspects of your daily working life are hard work and you have no sense of accomplishment you'll be looking for something different. The good news is you are likely to find it.

HOME LIFE

May is ideal for putting extra energy into your home life, domestic circumstances and a property as your efforts will be fruitful, especially towards the end of the month. The harmonious aspect between Venus and Mars will provide you with the motivation and energy to invest in yourself and those you love, especially at home. This will be an ideal time for working on a property or improving the décor, and also on your relationships at home.

June

WEEK 1: 29 MAY–4 JUNE

A clever and exciting plan or trip that merits careful scheduling could progress, so take the initiative and put building blocks in place that can provide you with structure. Talks – for some mostly to do with finances and for others work – will be productive. A focus on beauty and health will raise morale. Someone may need your help, and if you need advice it will be available.

WEEK 2: 5–11 JUNE

The full moon on 11 June will usher in a new phase in which you'll feel all the more inclined to be adventurous. A negotiation, work, key person or long-distance travel will figure in your decisions. First, though, important news or a trip will merit careful analysis to avoid mistakes being made as you make changes in the big picture.

WEEK 3: 12–18 JUNE

Negotiations and talks could be more significant than meets the eye. Health schedules and work will present new options to gain a deeper understanding of yourself or someone close. The changing face of your personal life and favourite pastimes will pose new logistics but will also gradually provide more stability. Weigh up your options at work and regarding your status in general, as a surprise may arise.

WEEK 4: 19–25 JUNE / WEEK 5: 26 JUNE–2 JULY

WEEK 4: the new moon on 25 June will promote inspired ideas and stimulate far-reaching plans. However, it may also reawaken fears or favourite dreams you've recently shelved. Be practical and then let your mind soar, as you'll gain the chance to put great ideas into action. For some this new moon will promote travel, writing and creativity. Just avoid arguments where possible. **WEEK 5:** this will be an excellent week to take the initiative at work, as your efforts are likely to succeed. It all comes down to your communication abilities, so be sure to be super clear as otherwise you may be surprised by some of the miscommunications that occur. You may enjoy a reunion or news from the past.

FINANCES

June will involve the necessity of considering various changes regarding some of the financial arrangements you've already set up. You could make some impressive gains financially, but this will depend on being both realistic and practical and having already built a solid financial platform for yourself. Working Aries may be surprised by developments, especially around 1 and 5 June. Be careful with financial considerations on the 19th and during the last week of the month.

HEALTH

Mars, your ruling planet, will be in your health sector from 17 June onwards, helping to improve your energy levels. Until that time you're likely to be busy, which will involve personal, creative or family matters and the chance to boost your health and well-being and especially during the first week of the month. You'll appreciate the chance to broaden your horizons in June, finding a trip or being in a beautiful place revitalising.

LOVE LIFE

There will be a degree of soul searching and research involved with changes you undertake in your personal life, but as long as you've researched your options and keep those you love in the loop you're likely to succeed. Your home will be a nexus of activity, and if you're diplomatic and look for collaboration and co-operation this will be a nurturing month. Just be sure around the solstice to avoid raking up arguments that would preferably be solved.

CAREER

You're likely to be busy, especially if you work in the property, construction, communications or travel industries. It's a good month for all Aries to brush up your communication skills. If you've always intended to learn how to be more sympathetic or empathic towards those you work with, be these colleagues, clients or employers, this will be a good month to deepen your understanding of the many different ways we communicate and not only verbally.

HOME LIFE

Mercury in your fourth house of home, property and family from 9 June, followed by Jupiter the next day, will improve your communications, making this an excellent month to boost domestic relationships. The sun at the solstice brings a sense of potential, but it will be vital at this time to avoid arguments as they are likely to spring seemingly from nowhere. The new moon on the 25th will be an excellent time to turn a corner with a domestic or personal matter.

July

WEEK 1: 3–9 JULY

You'll enjoy an impromptu get-together or an unusual event and investing time in yourself and your well-being. Avoid allowing a difference of opinion to lead to conflict. You may be drawn to making an out of the ordinary investment or will experience unexpected financial developments. For some these will be due, for example, to a change of status because of a fresh work situation.

WEEK 2: 10–16 JULY

The full moon on 10 July will spotlight important collaborations and investments, not only regarding your work and status but also those that have a knock-on effect with your home life and family. Both Venus and Uranus will boost your communication skills and create a sense of financial progress, so this is a good time to move forward with your most treasured projects. You may enjoy an unexpected get-together or development at home.

WEEK 3: 17–23 JULY

Try to get important conversations on the table before Mercury turns retrograde on 18 July. You could make great financial progress and with a creative project this week, but you must be careful not to overwork or overestimate other people's communication abilities. You may need to go over old ground with a work or financial matter, so be prepared to be patient.

WEEK 4: 24–30 JULY

The new moon on 24 July will kick-start a refreshing cycle in your family and domestic life, and this could also signal changes property-wise. You could make a great deal of progress at work and with creative projects, so take the initiative. You'll enjoy a sense of accomplishment or at least the certainty that a venture is plausible, so this is an excellent time to make tracks with your activities.

FINANCES

Early in July you may be drawn to reviewing your finances from a perspective of better investment and research into organisations that could help you to improve your financial circumstances. The Capricorn full moon on 10 July will spotlight practical ways to invest your money and especially in property and your career and favourite ventures. You may experience an unexpected financial boost towards the 11th but you must be careful mid-month to ensure past arrangements still work for you.

HEALTH

July will be a good month to review some of your health practices and especially if you feel that your vitality has been diminishing in recent weeks. Be prepared to seek expert advice towards 19 July. Beware of overdoing work or chores, as you will otherwise feel tired by the end of the month and niggling health issues or bad habits could re-emerge. If you're travelling, take time out and prepare in advance to avoid stress.

LOVE LIFE

This is a lovely month for you to enjoy being outgoing and sociable, and travel will be a drawcard. Your curiosity will get the better of you when it comes to travelling to somewhere different or unusual. In your love life this also means you're going to be more gregarious, both as a couple and if you're single. Just be sure towards the end of the month that you keep communications clear as you will otherwise be prone to misunderstandings.

CAREER

This is a progressive and busy month, so careful attention to good communications will certainly put you in a strong position. Try to get important business communications on the table by 18 July when Mercury will turn retrograde to avoid delays. You are likely then for the rest of the month to be in a strong position to review and revise any aspect of your career that you'd like to amend.

HOME LIFE

The full moon on 10 July will spotlight your extracurricular activities such as a wish for travel and/or a legal, study or overseas matter. Any of these will have a bearing on your home life or a property. You'll gain insight into the best way forward regarding your work and personal investments and may also be ready to commit to a particular course of action regarding your home life.

August

WEEK 1: 31 JULY–6 AUGUST

Developments will bring your deeper emotions to the surface, especially with news and circumstances connected with domestic-, property- or family-related matters. Take your time to unwind; seek the facts and avoid making assumptions and especially regarding work, health and travel. Be prepared to do the legwork and undertake adequate research, and pay special attention to good communication skills for the best results.

WEEK 2: 7–13 AUGUST

As your sign's ruler enters Libra you're better prepared to see both sides to stories over the next six weeks. At first you may feel so ready to do anything for the sake of peace that you miss important developments that could boost your status, work and finances, so be sure to remain proactive and take on a challenge rather than simply giving in.

WEEK 3: 14–20 AUGUST

This is an excellent week to get ahead at work and gain direction with your longer-term career plans. Take the initiative and discuss your big-picture plans with collaborators and those you share resources or duties with, such as around domestic concerns. This is also a good week to focus on your health and well-being, as your efforts are likely to be successful.

WEEK 4: 21–27 AUGUST

A work project or change in your family life will become more feasible, as the new moon on 23 August will show just where you could put your ideas to good use in practical ways. However, if you discover flaws in your planning this week then see these as the chance to fine-tune or correct your plans. A financial matter will become clearer as you work on long-term strategies.

FINANCES

This is a super go-ahead month for you regarding finances and your status. You could truly make some invaluable changes to both areas, especially during the second week of the month. Be sure to research your options carefully as an unexpected, unusual or once in a lifetime opportunity may arise that could boost your financial circumstances. However, the new moon on 23 August may spotlight areas you'll need to fine-tune financially.

HEALTH

August is an important month health-wise, as you'll gain the chance to decide how best to look after yourself: whether to continue to work hard towards a goal you have perhaps outgrown or whether to embrace a fresh, more holistic and wholesome daily routine that enables you to grow and enjoy life more. The favourable aspect between the sun and Chiron on 19 August will be particularly conducive for improving your health schedules.

LOVE LIFE

Mars in your seventh house of relationships will ramp up the feistiness in a partner, but could also bring a sense of peace to you. You're liable to wish to be a mediator and peacemaker and look for the best path forward for both you and your partner. If you're single a little innovation will help you locate someone compatible, especially around 9 and 16 August. Couples will enjoy ramping up romance at home, especially mid-month.

CAREER

Hard work pays off and you could once again see concrete results for your endeavours in August, especially around the Mars–Uranus trine on 8 and 20 August. You may, however, be surprised by developments early in August that could boost your status and/or finances. The full moon on the 9th will spotlight career options, and you may tend to feel you're going backwards even though a new door opens in unexpected ways.

HOME LIFE

Mercury retrograde in your home sector until 11 August will encourage you to remodel various aspects of your home life, be these structural (think repairs) or in domestic relationships. You may feel nostalgic but must avoid allowing this temporary feeling to dictate your actions. By September you'll be feeling different again as an unavoidable family- or property-related matter will move forward towards the 20th if you wish to make changes.

September

WEEK 1: 28 AUGUST–3 SEPTEMBER

As Saturn leaves your sign your attention is likely to turn to the past and to reconsidering some of your work and health practices over the coming months. This is certainly a good week to focus on your health and well-being practices to ensure you're happy with their efficacy. You'll enjoy a reunion but must be careful with communications next week to avoid misunderstandings.

WEEK 2: 4–10 SEPTEMBER

Get set to turn a corner in connection with a past project, work or health. You may enjoy a reunion. Information could be inspiring, but if events this week appear confusing then prepare to be a little patient and avoid making rash decisions. Take an innovative approach to welcoming a new daily schedule. Romance could come a-knocking at your door.

WEEK 3: 11–17 SEPTEMBER

You'll appreciate the opportunity to reconnect with someone either at work or regarding a health interest. Your sign's ruler Mars will align opposite Chiron, the asteroid planet that represents healing. Take a moment to focus on your health or that of someone close. If there is an issue at work find ways to 'heal' this too. Luckily, communications are likely to go relatively well this week.

WEEK 4: 18–24 SEPTEMBER / WEEK 5: 25 SEPTEMBER–1 OCTOBER

WEEK 4: let your inner artist out! If you're musical, inventive or romantic or you love luxury you'll enjoy including more of these qualities in your life. A fun, dynamic approach to your favourite projects could boost circumstances, so take the initiative. However, a change of routine or at work may require some adaptation, but as a result your creativity and relationships could blossom. **WEEK 5:** you're likely still to be in the throes of potential for change as last week's aspects between the sun, Pluto and Uranus continue to resonate. You have a wonderful opportunity to step into new circumstances either at work, socially or in your personal life, so do take the initiative. However, this week, as with last week, it's important to avoid arguments as this could overshadow otherwise positive potential.

FINANCES

As Uranus begins a five-month retrograde phase you may undergo considerable financial changes, both during the first and last weeks of the month. The good news is you'll gain the next few months to get on top of any fresh financial conditions or circumstances that begin now. Just be sure to avoid making impulsive decisions, especially around 7 and 24 September and at the very end of the month.

HEALTH

The start of the month is ideal for working out a strong daily health practice. For some Aries the total lunar eclipse on 7 September and developments mid-month will spotlight a health circumstance that will benefit from more research and guidance: a health circumstance either of your own or that of someone close. September is certainly a good month to instigate fresh dietary and fitness schedules to better suit your current circumstances.

LOVE LIFE

Your sign's ruler Mars travelling through your seventh and eighth houses will bring more activity in your love life, including more passion. However, a partner may appear feistier than usual, especially around 5 September and the last week of the month, so avoid arguments at these times as they are likely to escalate quickly. For singles, September is a fiery month: not only in the passion stakes but arguments could ignite over nothing, so be sure to maintain an even keel.

CAREER

The total lunar eclipse on 7 September will spotlight an important connection. For many Aries this will point to a new daily work routine or a fresh schedule regarding your daily chores. Someone you know from your past may be instrumental in helping move a project along. The solar eclipse on the 21st will add to a changing picture in your daily and work routine. A fresh arrangement or agreement could be fortuitous and may build around the 24th.

HOME LIFE

The first week of the month will provide opportunities to move a domestic project forward. If, however, you encounter opposition or arguments it will be in your interest to look at how best to serve your long-term goals rather than get caught in temporary disagreements. Arrangements you make towards 21 September at work or changes in your daily routine could have a positive knock-on effect to your home or a property.

October

WEEK 1: 2–8 OCTOBER

It's in your interest to be careful with communications this week. A health-related activity or change of routine may challenge you to work that little bit harder. News from a business or personal partner will draw on your resources. You could excel, so be patient this week. You'll enjoy a reunion or return to an old haunt this weekend.

WEEK 2: 9–15 OCTOBER

Key decisions and financial arrangements can be made that could change the face of some of your work and daily routines. If you're unsure of who and what to commit to, ensure you research your circumstances and gain expert help if necessary. You'll relish the chance to invest in yourself, your quality of life and those you love the most.

WEEK 3: 16–22 OCTOBER

The new moon on 21 October will kick-start a fresh phase in a business or personal partnership. You may be in a position to negotiate the terms of an agreement that affect your home, family or property. Someone is likely to ask for your help, and if you need help you'll be happy to accept a hand. This is a good week to look for therapeutic ways to improve your daily life.

WEEK 4: 23–29 OCTOBER

This will be an excellent week to take the initiative with your various collaborations and shared projects, both at home and at work, as the stars will help you make progress. Towards mid next week you may receive unexpected financial or personal news, which will be ideal for some Aries and especially in relation to work and/or health. You'll enjoy a reunion.

FINANCES

A key financial or work decision towards 11 October will merit careful focus. Any change you make in your usual daily routine will also affect your finances; however, with careful consideration and a big-picture, long-term outlook you could make a great deal of progress both financially and at work in October. Be sure to invest in yourself as this is what will ensure your finances are secure and safe and they could also improve.

HEALTH

Both the Mercury–Chiron opposition on 3 October and the Venus–Saturn opposition on the 11th will bring to mind important health, well-being and relationship matters that will deserve a patient approach. You may be drawn to reconnecting with a health or beauty practitioner you trust to help you. Be sure to consider the big-picture outcome of the decisions you make health-wise, as this is an ideal time to step into fresh and therapeutic territory and is not to be missed.

LOVE LIFE

At the start of October, if you or your partner feel a little vulnerable or misunderstood be sure to avoid exacerbating circumstances by being super clear and avoiding taking other people's moods personally. Developments around 13 October and the new moon on the 21st will bring a great deal of focus onto your love life, and a partner may feel amorous in the last half of the month. Singles may attract others more than usual, which you will appreciate.

CAREER

You'll appreciate the opportunity to work increasingly towards creating a daily and financial circumstance that better suits you in your current circumstances. You may even find once you have all your ducks in a row that things already start falling in place towards the end of October. The final week of the month will be conducive to rapid progress in your career, especially regarding collaborations and creative projects. If you're unsure of your path be sure to trust your gut.

HOME LIFE

Home can sometimes become a battlefield in those cases where communications fall apart, so it will be important and especially at the start of the month and mid-month to pay careful attention to what your family, partner or housemate is trying to say. You yourself may have important matters to discuss. Be sure to choose your words carefully to avoid giving offence, especially mid-month.

November

WEEK 1: 30 OCTOBER–5 NOVEMBER

This is a good time to build stability and security in your life, especially in key relationships as you or someone close may be feeling vulnerable or sensitive. If events seem restrictive, consider practicalities first then everything else will flow from there. The Taurus full moon supermoon on 5 November will spotlight the need for a fresh approach to someone close and also to a financial arrangement.

WEEK 2: 6–12 NOVEMBER

Both Mercury and Jupiter turn retrograde this week. Try to get important paperwork, especially to do with work and finances, on the table before Sunday if possible to avoid delays further down the line. It will be a good opportunity over the coming weeks to review finances if necessary. As Venus enters the sign of passionate Scorpio expect your love life to sizzle, but you must avoid arguments this weekend.

WEEK 3: 13–19 NOVEMBER

This is an excellent week for getting ahead both at work and home, as your efforts are likely to succeed. If you need collaboration it will be available, so be sure to ask for help if it's needed. You may receive good news to do with a collaboration at work. You'll enjoy socialising, with some early festive-season events being a drawcard.

WEEK 4: 20–26 NOVEMBER / WEEK 5: 27 NOVEMBER–3 DECEMBER

WEEK 4: get set to share a key asset in a new way over the coming days or weeks: you may change the way you share a duty or finances with someone close. A reunion and your interest in mysteries will blossom. You may be surprised by some financial news or will undertake an unusual transaction that could change your life. **WEEK 5:** a close relationship may change parameters as you take steps in a fresh direction in the relationship. Someone you love may surprise you with their news. Some Aries will have a surprise regarding finances that will merit further analysis or focus. It's certainly a lovely week to invest in your home life and family and celebrate the relationships you love.

FINANCES

The full moon and supermoon on 5 November will spotlight the importance of having your feet on the ground financially. It will also mark the end of a lengthy financial chapter. There will be a fated or family connection. The re-entry of Uranus into your finance sector from the 8th will bring the opportunity to review your circumstances and make changes. The new moon on the 20th will revitalise your finances even if it involves unexpected or unprecedented circumstances.

HEALTH

Chiron, known as the 'wounded healer' in Greek mythology, is in your sign and it makes a tough aspect with Jupiter this month and could bring long-standing health niggles into focus for some Aries. You may be drawn to reviewing your exercise and dietary requirements and may also benefit from seeking more opportunity to rest, especially after Mercury turns retrograde on 9 November and on the 2nd, 15th and 29th.

LOVE LIFE

In the bigger picture you have positive stars for romance, although your vulnerabilities may emerge at the start of the month. Someone you share duties and responsibilities with may have a surprise for you, and the more you approach the situation in practical terms and especially around 5 November the better will be the outcome. The entry of Venus into Scorpio will bring more passion into your love life from the 6th onwards, but you must avoid arguments as they could be more prevalent than usual.

CAREER

The full moon and supermoon on 5 November could mark the start of a fresh agreement at work. If you're under negotiation regarding contracts or new arrangements, try to get paperwork on the table by the 8th for the best results and to avoid having to redo agreements at a later date or experience delays. Nevertheless, you may undergo a boost in your career towards the 17th and 19th.

HOME LIFE

Mid-November will be an excellent time to focus on your home, family and domestic circumstances in the bigger arena. It's certainly a good month for redecoration and for reimagining the purpose of your home life: that is, as a restful space. You may enjoy receiving visitors or visiting someone yourself, which will be uplifting and especially mid-month. Towards the end of November you'll appreciate a sense of togetherness or contentment at home.

December

WEEK 1: 4–10 DECEMBER

You'll gain the chance to unwind, which will boost your energy levels. The supermoon on 4 December points to a fresh agreement or contract that could kick-start something new. For some this will involve travel, and for others study or spiritual or legal matters. Avoid complex communications so there are no upsets, especially early next week. Also avoid making rash decisions and check your plans align with your sense of purpose and direction.

WEEK 2: 11–17 DECEMBER

You'll appreciate the chance to be more realistic and practical about your endeavours, especially if some matters are up in the air or if you've been a little idealistic. You like a challenge so you'll get to prove your abilities, but if life is a little disorienting then ensure you take time out. Your sign's ruler Mars enters Capricorn, which may be inspiring as certain projects will take off.

WEEK 3: 18–24 DECEMBER

This is a great week to consider how you could bring more of what you love in life into your daily activities. The new moon on 20 December will usher in a more adventurous phase in which travel and exploration will appeal. There is a therapeutic, uplifting aspect to the week that may promote good health; however, you will not agree with everyone about everything so be careful with your interactions.

WEEK 4: 25–31 DECEMBER

Merry Christmas! a change of routine or impromptu developments will bring variety into life. However, you must be open to discussing differences of opinion to avoid a stalemate. Working Aries will be busy and may need to sort out mysteries or conundrums for the people who come your way. You'll enjoy a trip or another therapeutic development towards Sunday.

FINANCES

You're likely to be drawn to adventurous and upbeat activities this month and must ensure you have budgeted adequately to support your activities such as travel, sports and adventure. Mid-month and during the pre-Christmas week you may discover certain costs or responsibilities are heavier than you had hoped, so be sure to plan ahead. The tough aspects at the solstice between the sun and Saturn could bring about a need to rein in spending.

HEALTH

A positive aspect during the first week of December will encourage you to invest in your health and well-being through activities such as physical fitness and sports. This is a wonderful opportunity to revitalise your health and improve vitality. Just avoid overdoing things around the 8th and towards the solstice, as you may be inclined to overstretch yourself and burn the candle at both ends. Nevertheless, the help of a proficient health and well-being expert will be invaluable.

LOVE LIFE

The full moon and supermoon on 4 December will kick-start a new phase in a significant relationship or arrangement. For some this will mean a fresh start in your love life. You will be feeling adventurous throughout the month and there is no underestimating what you can achieve in your life now. However, it will be important to maintain a steady focus on good and balanced communication and relationship skills to avoid complexities. Singles will be particularly outgoing, which indicates the chance to socialise with dynamic and upbeat people.

CAREER

The entry of Mars in Capricorn mid-month will certainly help you move ahead in your career, although initially you may feel you must adjust some of your expectations regarding your projects and schedules in December. The new moon in Sagittarius on the 20th will certainly encourage you to thrive with certain projects and interests, but you must be sure that you're basing your expectations on realities.

HOME LIFE

A fortunate aspect involving Jupiter in your fourth house of home during the first week of the month will be excellent for moving forward aspects of your home or family life that have been slow to budge. As the month progresses you'll gain confidence regarding changes you have already been considering at home. The key to a happy home in December revolves around good communication skills and especially in the run-up to Christmas, when tensions may run high.

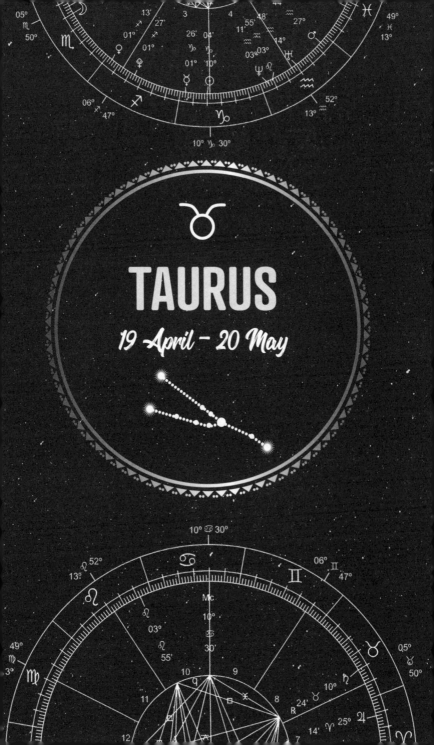

January

WEEK 1: 1–8 JANUARY

There are many aspects of the week you'll appreciate, such as a reunion and the chance to review projects if necessary at work. Finances may require focus if you're making work agreements, so keep an eye on details and ensure you haven't overlooked any bills or debts. This is a good time for making a commitment to a person or plan and for creating a solid foundation.

WEEK 2: 9–15 JANUARY

You'll appreciate the chance to resume your usual daily routine with the benefit of New Year's resolutions. You'll enjoy getting together with like-minded people and a break if you're on holiday. You'll need to be tactful and diplomatic with certain groups and organisations, if only to keep the peace. Someone may be a little forgetful, and if this is you then ensure you're practical first up and take time out.

WEEK 3: 16–22 JANUARY

You may be surprised by news or an impromptu get-together this week. A change of schedule or in your career direction will need careful adjustment. Be clear about your priorities and with communications and all else will fall into place. Aim to improve your understanding of circumstances and avoid taking things personally if an event or situation falls short of expectations.

WEEK 4: 23–29 JANUARY

Get set to consider new ways to work, forge ahead in life in general and find ways to boost your status. You may be inclined to try something new over the coming weeks and months. If you feel melancholic consider seeking upbeat company; you'll enjoy a lovely social or networking event. Avoid locking horns with someone with different ideas as conflict could escalate.

FINANCES

Jupiter, the planet of abundance, is still retrograde in your money zone, so if you feel that some financial matters are dragging be patient: they will begin to turn around after this month, even if only slowly at first. The good news is this gives you time to do any financial forensic work required such as research into the best way to move ahead financially based on past lessons.

HEALTH

There is a great deal of astrological focus on your health and well-being at the moment, and in particular on your energy levels. It's an excellent time to find ways to boost these, as you may otherwise feel drained and especially around 9 and 21 January. Luckily, the 22nd and the days towards the new moon in Aquarius on the 29th will be productive if you wish to look for fresh ways to boost your health.

LOVE LIFE

Uranus retrograde continues to bring innovation and surprises your way. Try as you might to smooth things out, you may seem to go two steps forward and three steps back. Luckily, Uranus will end its retrograde phase this month, although it may take another few weeks to feel that you're back in your stride. The good news is that Uranus also brings spontaneity and the chance to have fun, with key dates being 23, 26 and 30 January.

CAREER

The new moon on 29 January will turn a page for you in your career and general direction, even if developments feel a little intense. It's certainly a good month to take the initiative and make changes in your career if you feel the time is ripe for a new direction, promotion or fresh start. You can transform this important part of your life now, so be proactive.

HOME LIFE

You may need to decide between priorities: will you place your attention on your career and status in life, or on your home? Mars retrograde in your domestic sector may lead to you feeling your home life is lacklustre, so avoid making abrupt decisions based on this impression if it has developed fairly recently (since December last year). Things will improve. It's actually a great month to renovate, remodel or add a little luxury to your surroundings.

February

WEEK 1: 30 JANUARY–5 FEBRUARY

It's all about your communication skills: the key to success lies in approaching those you love and co-workers with a calm and enthusiastic attitude. Avoid over- and underestimating finances through overspending or underbudgeting. You'll enjoy key news or a trip or get-together. If you're considering a fresh direction at work or in your personal life be sure to take the initiative, as your efforts are likely to pay off.

WEEK 2: 6–12 FEBRUARY

Take the time this weekend to spruce up your environment and enjoy the company of like-minded people. The full moon in Leo on 12 February will bring certain conversations, relationships, agreements or family arrangements to your attention. Some people will be particularly supportive, while others may prove their loyalties lie elsewhere. Be prepared to adapt to unexpected news.

WEEK 3: 13–19 FEBRUARY

You'll enjoy the chance to relax so ensure you organise a treat, if only to break up a busy week. If you're immersed in work you're likely to achieve a goal. It's a great weekend for socialising, and a refreshing, more varied schedule will revitalise your health and mood. A trip or visit may appear to be hard work logistically but is likely to be fulfilling and transformative.

WEEK 4: 20–26 FEBRUARY

You'll gain further insight into developments in relation to work, and for some Taureans in relation to a friendship or collaboration. An agreement can be made, and someone may offer terms that you must agree with or agree to disagree; research will help you decide, and you may be surprised by what you find. News may have a therapeutic effect, making this a good week to improve your health.

FINANCES

Jupiter will end its retrograde phase in your money sector, which will help you make financial progress, and this is certainly a good month to renegotiate some of your agreements and put in place more feasible savings and investment plans. If you're prone to overspending then you're likely to experience a wake-up call this month, which will enable you to get on top of spending issues. A group, friend or organisation will be particularly helpful.

HEALTH

If you have not been making health your number one priority this will be a good month to do so: it's definitely time to look after your health. You are known to like the good things in life and can be prone to being sedentary, so consider an upbeat fitness regime. Just avoid minor bumps and scrapes around 4, 10 and 20 February. The Pisces new moon on the 28th will be ideal for reinstating holistic, spiritual awareness.

LOVE LIFE

February is a sociable and romantic month ideal for bringing more elements into your life that you love. If you're single you may meet someone strangely familiar but whom you've never actually met before. You may be inclined to look up an ex but must do a little soul searching first to determine if this feeling arises from nostalgia or genuine compatibility. The new moon in Pisces on 28 February signals the start of a fresh phase in a friendship or association.

CAREER

February could bring important changes in your career, and if you take the initiative you could make great progress. The start of the month will be particularly conducive to discussions at work to remedy or advance your position, both personally and financially. Be prepared to enter fresh territory and think outside the box about your various options for the best effect. Be careful with communications around 10, 11 and 20 February to avoid undoing all your hard work.

HOME LIFE

There will be a sense of coming full circle in some respect in a domestic circumstance. You may be surprised by news around the full moon on 12 February. Be prepared for the unexpected and to enter fresh territory if necessary. Nevertheless, much of your focus this month will be on your career and social life, so be prepared to devote time to your home as this is where much of your growth and fulfilment come from.

March

WEEK 1: 27 FEBRUARY–5 MARCH

A friend or organisation may inspire you to gain ground in your interests and activities. Be ready to make changes at work or in your health schedule. You may experience the need to backtrack with various agreements or arrangements so be sure to be patient, especially around 2 March. You may find this a particularly inspiring or eye-opening week romantically.

WEEK 2: 6–12 MARCH

You'll enjoy being creative and outgoing and your favourite projects could flourish. Take the initiative also with travel: you'll enjoy getting together with favourite friends or planning or taking a trip. This is a good week to enter into serious discussions and make an agreement or commitment at work or with a group, friend or organisation. An authority figure may be significant.

WEEK 3: 13–19 MARCH

You may hear key news from a friend, group or organisation. You may begin to approach your work, career or status from a fresh perspective as you gain a sense of purpose and more insight into your true priorities. An offer may come from out of the blue. You have the chance to smooth over relationships that have gone awry once the dust settles.

WEEK 4: 20–26 MARCH / WEEK 5: 27 MARCH–2 APRIL

WEEK 4: the conjunction of the sun and Neptune could bring an ideal development work-wise or regarding health and your appearance. You may be particularly drawn to socialising and romance will build. However, you may be forgetful or someone you rely on may be less reliable. Avoid confusion by double-checking facts and ask for clarity from a friend, group or work.
WEEK 5: this is a good week to consult loyal friends and organisations to sort out a financial or personal matter, but you must avoid arguments. A past matter may resurface. The solar eclipse on 29 March could kick-start a fresh work or daily schedule. You'll enjoy socialising and may meet someone special or with whom you share common goals.

FINANCES

Developments around 2 March will illuminate the state of your finances. If you discover there is a shortfall you will gain the upper hand, devising ways to cut out some of your unnecessary expenses such as certain luxuries. The eclipses will alter your work situation or routine mid-month. If you don't need to tighten your belt you must nevertheless watch overspending in March as you'll be liable to regret it.

HEALTH

The key to managing a good health and well-being schedule in March will revolve around being careful to manage your energy levels, especially with respect to work and travel. You may find feeling stressed produces lacklustre communications, angry outbursts or forgetfulness, so stress management and any modality that calms your nervous system will be beneficial. The true stress points will be on the 2nd, 15th and 26th.

LOVE LIFE

The eclipses this month will shine a light on the people around you, both in your social and personal lives. You may find that one particular relationship runs its course or, conversely, that you are drawn to making a commitment to someone special. You may enjoy an unexpected development that introduces a new circle. If you're single the eclipse on 14 March and the days and weeks thereafter could bring an unexpected meeting.

CAREER

A clever agreement could take you places, so be sure to consider and discuss your various work options. There is a great deal of focus on your career astrologically, and it is certainly a good time to invest in your skill sets. You may be drawn to studying or learning something new to stay on top of developments in your field. Mid- to late March will be particularly forward moving for you, so be sure to take the initiative.

HOME LIFE

You'll begin to feel that your home life contains more of the elements you enjoy and appreciate, and this will continue throughout the month when you'll feel at least some of your expectations of a happy home are met. However, if matters are still slow moving or frustrating in this area of your life take heart, because you'll be back on track next month and there'll be no holding you back from making positive changes.

April

WEEK 1: 3–9 APRIL

You can make agreements you're happy with now, and a meeting with someone authoritative could prove to be positive. News will place you in a clearer frame of mind about your options moving forward. A health or work matter is best approached philosophically. You'll find support if changes need to be made, and research and information will help you proceed.

WEEK 2: 10–16 APRIL

Keep your feet on the ground as you can make truly wonderful progress, especially with your big-picture goals, social life, career and personal life. News or a reunion on Friday could be pivotal. The full moon on 13 April points to a fresh chapter in your daily health routine and work. Avoid making rash decisions at home at this time and set the healthiest schedule possible.

WEEK 3: 17–23 APRIL

This will be a good week to deepen your connections or make a commitment with a friend or organisation. Decisions made now may well have an impact on your home life or vice versa, and the result will be the chance to enter fresh territory. Be brave, as your actions are likely to be successful, but you must avoid making rash or impulsive decisions and especially towards Monday.

WEEK 4: 24–30 APRIL

The new moon on 27 April will be in your sign and indicates the chance to restart aspects of your life you feel have become stuck. For some this will revolve more around your work and daily life and for others around your personal life and the need to break out of a circumstance that tests your patience. A meeting or news will determine your next step.

FINANCES

Jupiter in your finance sector promises a more favourable financial outlook towards the end of the month, as long as you avoid overspending. Key work-related decisions and financial matters from the past will have a bearing on your financial outlook and some of the arrangements you agree to are likely to be long-standing, so be sure to undergo adequate research to avoid making mistakes and especially in the last two weeks of the month.

HEALTH

The last two weeks of April are ideal for setting in place a thorough health routine. You'll gain the chance already early in April to secure a routine or schedule with a friend, group or organisation that will be particularly helpful in your quest for better health. The full moon on the 13th may spotlight exactly where to place your focus health-wise. Your energy levels are set to improve, so take heart if you've felt tired.

LOVE LIFE

There is a sense of pre-destiny or unavoidability around your love life this month. Whether you feel drawn to someone from your past or stuck in current circumstances, the new moon in your sign on 27 April will encourage you to turn a corner so the past has less of a hold on you and you get up to date with your true feelings and desires.

CAREER

Mid-month and towards 20 April will be an excellent time to forge ahead with your career with regard to your various relationships with groups and organisations. You may find you also gain the opportunity to make fresh agreements or contracts with certain people that could put you in a stronger position. However, certain considerations regarding your home life will need to be taken into account when you're making decisions about your career this month.

HOME LIFE

As Mars enters Leo on 18 April you're likely to feel a breath of fresh air at home and an increased sense of adventure. If you love travel this may be due to a change of environment. The second half of the month will be a good time to improve your domestic circumstances such as via improved home décor. You may feel more sociable than usual in April, inviting friends and colleagues into your home and visiting theirs.

May

WEEK 1: 1–7 MAY

You'll appreciate the opportunity to get together with friends or family and someone you find inspiring. A shared aspect of your life such as space at home or a duty will merit careful attention to avoid arguments. A new approach to your career, status or general direction in life will need considered analysis so you avoid making rash decisions. Romance could blossom, so make a date!

WEEK 2: 8–14 MAY

The Scorpio full moon on 12 May signals a fresh chapter in a business or personal partnership, especially if you were born before mid-May, and a change of schedule at work or regarding health if you were born later. This may come about suddenly or will involve considerable change. Avoid making snap decisions and consider practicalities first.

WEEK 3: 15–21 MAY

A lively reunion or impromptu event will change your usual routine this week, and where you may enjoy a more relaxed time or someone has other plans then rest assured your activities are likely to be enlivening. You may also experience the repayment of a debt or an improvement in health, so be positive!

WEEK 4: 22–28 MAY

You're all set to make considerable progress, especially at work and home, and may even be surprised by some of the goals you attain this week so be bold! a choice concerning finances or a close relationship will merit careful consideration, as you're about to begin a fresh chapter in either one or both of these areas. Ensure you look for upbeat solutions.

FINANCES

You'll welcome a financial improvement in mid- to late May that will improve your bank balance or credit. You may be surprised by an impromptu work or financial offer, but be sure to analyse the variants sufficiently to avoid making mistakes. The new moon on the 27th will provide you with insight into a viable path, so be sure to take note of what happens around this time as it could help you out of a situation that feels stuck.

HEALTH

You'll gain improved energy levels as the month progresses and may towards the third week of the month enjoy a welcome healthy break or good health news. As an earth sign you prefer to stick with the tried and trusted, as opposed to venturing into fresh territory health-wise. However, you may discover that a different approach to some of your fitness routines will help you feel more positive about making changes in the broader context of your life.

LOVE LIFE

The first week of May has romantic elements and you'll enjoy a reunion if you're single. Make a date, as romance will flourish in the first weekend of the month. The Scorpio full moon on the 12th will highlight a particular arrangement, and you may find that you must tweak this in your love life due to unexpected developments. Emotions are likely to be intense around this time, so avoid making emotionally based decisions you could come to regret.

CAREER

This is a good month to work towards the desired outcomes you're looking for work-wise, even if it involves having to go into fresh territory or undertake some difficult conversations. You may be surprised by developments mid- to late month or by your ability to innovate and push forward into your desired area. Be sure to be guided by your values and principles and keep an open mind about new territory that could be exciting.

HOME LIFE

This is a good month to make considerable progress in your personal life, with your family and home. You'll gain the motivation to see things through, especially during the second week of the month. You're likely to be entering fresh territory in your daily life, work routine or relationships, so the more you can concentrate on maintaining a sense of status quote at home the more energy you'll have to devote to these areas.

June

WEEK 1: 29 MAY–4 JUNE

Key financial decisions merit detailed analysis. Avoid taking risks or making investments without researching options. If you're unsure of someone ask where you stand, and be ready for the answer. This is a good week for a health or beauty appointment. Research and development, whether you're a student or teacher or working, will be productive so be sure to ask for advice.

WEEK 2: 5–11 JUNE

The entry of Venus in your sign will put your mind on money, love, the arts and romance. It's time to enjoy yourself, but at the same time a fresh way to explore and unify some of your commitments will appeal. The full moon on 11 June will highlight how to consolidate and integrate some of your ideas financially and in your personal life.

WEEK 3: 12–18 JUNE

You'll enjoy a get-together, trip or key conversation that provides you with perspective. You may also enjoy a return to an old haunt or a financial boost. If you feel your values are challenged this week, consider discussing your options with the people who support you as they will understand you. Events that are unusual or different could be disorienting, so avoid rushing into matters without forethought.

WEEK 4: 19–25 JUNE / WEEK 5: 26 JUNE–2 JULY

WEEK 4: it will be important for you to maintain your belief in your values, in all good things, as you could turn a corner as a result be this financially, at work or in your status in general. It all comes down to believing in yourself now. You may need to undergo some difficult conversations or financial transactions towards the new moon on 25 June, but if you maintain an optimistic and careful approach your actions are likely to succeed. **WEEK 5:** the key to a successful week revolves around good communication skills, especially in relation to your home life and work. There is still the likelihood that certain communications regarding work will require more effort than usual, but if you keep your feet on the ground and are methodical with the work that needs to be done you could make quite an impression.

FINANCES

The full moon on 11 June will spotlight some of your shared ventures that involve joint finances. It may be time to consider a fresh budget or way to share important financial commitments such as your taxes. You may receive a financial boost if you've managed your finances well in the past. If not, you're likely to discover that you must look at a new way to invest. Be sure to seek expert help if a conundrum arises.

HEALTH

A fortunate and constructive aspect between Mars and Chiron early in the month will help you make solid progress with your health, and if someone close such as a family member has been unwell this will also be a positive time to find out more about how to configure a daily health routine that promotes a strong constitution. The month's end will encourage you to also put in place a solid and supportive health routine for yourself.

LOVE LIFE

The full moon on 11 June will spotlight agreements and arrangements and this can include a spotlight on your love life, as there are no agreements and arrangements more important than those with your partner. If you're single you may reunite with an ex, and where you take that relationship will depend on the kind you desire. As there are therapeutic astrological aspects this June it is quite possible that you can overcome past differences.

CAREER

Pluto in your career sector offers you the potential to review and revise past work arrangements and move forward in constructive and innovative ways, so be sure to keep an open mind about where your career and long-term goals lie as the more adventurous you are the better for you. You may even achieve a fresh financial agreement around the full moon on 11 June and therefore must be prepared to negotiate if necessary.

HOME LIFE

Your home life will benefit from good communication skills on your part and an eye to creating a nurturing and healing environment. The new moon on 25 June will spotlight the need to communicate better both with family members and those in your domestic environment such as housemates, which will be therapeutic in the big picture with your relationships at home. You may find that your health benefits as the result of a spring clean.

July

WEEK 1: 3–9 JULY

You'll enjoy sharing time with like-minded people and may hear unexpectedly from someone or discover surprising news. A refreshingly different approach to your career and health will benefit you now. A discussion or financial transaction may be unexpected and it's best to overcome differences of opinion before they escalate. You're ready to turn a corner in a favourite activity or interest, which will bring more options your way.

WEEK 2: 10–16 JULY

This will be a good week to consider how you might bring more of what you love into your life. For example, if you love travel this is a good time to book a trip, and if you love study it's a good time to research a new course. Be prepared to leave your comfort zone; you are unlikely to make unfeasible choices. You'll enjoy a get-together towards the weekend and may experience an ego or financial boost.

WEEK 3: 17–23 JULY

You'll enjoy socialising or a get-together at home. If you have important domestic or personal arrangements you need to try to get these discussed before Friday, when Mercury turns retrograde and could delay some communications over the future weeks. This is a good week to consider your health and well-being and make these your priority. Avoid impulsiveness on Monday.

WEEK 4: 24–30 JULY

Meetings and get-togethers this week will boost your mood. You may be surprised by some developments that are out of the ordinary. The new moon on 24 July will kick-start a fresh phase at home for many Taureans and at work for some. It's an excellent week to be dynamic and proactive, especially in your career, so if you've been looking for work you're likely to make a breakthrough now.

FINANCES

The conjunction of Venus and Uranus in your second house of money is likely to bring an unexpected financial development early in the month. A debt may be paid to you or you will clear a debt yourself. You may benefit from a career or work improvement that leads to better pay. The new moon on 24 July will kick-start a fresh phase that could bring more abundance your way, but you must be sure to negotiate and innovate work-wise.

HEALTH

July is a lovely month to find ways to be more active physically, spiritually and mentally. The first week of the month will encourage you to look for courses that expand your mind or put in place a health timetable that could improve your energy levels. The aspect between the sun and Chiron on 19 July will encourage you to put your health first, if you didn't already at the start of the month.

LOVE LIFE

You are one of the zodiac's most intense signs and you're serious about your love life, so if you've been considering making a commitment to someone this is your month to transform your status, both in the world (think marriage or commitment) and at home. However, if you've been preoccupied with your career and financial status, consider how your love life either promotes your status or the opposite. If you need more support this is the month to find it.

CAREER

July is a good month to invest in and even alter your career course, especially early in the month and around the new moon on 24 July as you'll make tracks towards your desired outcome. You may be pleasantly surprised early in the month as new opportunities come your way so keep your eyes open, and if nothing eventuates then keep going: options later in July appear to be promising.

HOME LIFE

The new moon on 24 July will kick-start a fresh phase in your home life, so if you've been considering making important changes in this area of your life consider earlier in July how you'd like things to take shape so you're ready to take action after the new moon. You'll gain the chance to make considerable changes in structured, methodical ways. Just remember to think outside the box at your options to maximise opportunities.

August

WEEK 1: 31 JULY–6 AUGUST

While you're a practical person you can experience strong emotions, especially if you feel frustrated by people's inconsistencies. You'll do well to focus on your plans and avoid being derailed by the dramas of other people, especially towards Friday and the weekend. A trip, visit or news may be pivotal. Be sure to maintain your principles while avoiding conflict.

WEEK 2: 7–13 AUGUST

This will be an excellent week to make progress in a key area such as your career, health or personal life; you may even be pleasantly surprised by developments. Be sure to reach out for information or advice from a loyal friend or organisation if necessary. Tuesday's Venus–Jupiter conjunction will be a good time for meetings and get-togethers and could signal financial developments for some.

WEEK 3: 14–20 AUGUST

It's a great week to get a new idea or activity off the ground, especially concerning your health and work and domestic lives as you and those close to you may be more passionate about what you want from life. Someone you have a strong link with will be super helpful in this regard. Romance could blossom at the weekend, so be sure to organise a date!

WEEK 4: 21–27 AUGUST

The new moon on 23 August will kick-start a fresh phase in your personal or domestic life. This new moon will enable you to move ahead with a clearer idea of your position as a nurturer of those at home and those you love, finding out where you excel and where you could do better. You may be surprised by developments this weekend, and a can-do attitude will work well.

FINANCES

Your principles and values may come under pressure early in August. If you feel that your finances also come under pressure at this time it will be a sign to look for a fresh and even innovative way to manage your response to a changing world and to your ever-changing financial circumstances. The Venus–Jupiter conjunction on the 12th could spell a new agreement that indicates abundance.

HEALTH

This will be an excellent month to make upbeat changes in your daily routine, and you may be surprised by some of the health and fitness ideas that appeal to you now as they may be out of the ordinary. It's an excellent month to find ways to bring more peace, balance and harmony into your daily life, as this will truly enhance your potential and happiness. You may experience uplifting developments towards 20 August in particular.

LOVE LIFE

A change in your status is likely in August as you embrace new activities and interests. Some Taureans may be starting a fresh career path or will be changing status from single to married or vice versa. Be prepared to look outside the square at your love life as you could truly work towards bringing more nurturance and love into your relationship, especially around 12 and 16 August and the new moon on the 23rd.

CAREER

The full moon on 9 August comes just one day after a positive aspect between Mars and Uranus that could catapult you into fresh territory in your career. You may have a difficult decision to make, but as long as you research your options carefully you could make great progress career-wise in August and especially in the first two weeks and towards the 20th, so be sure to take the initiative with your plans.

HOME LIFE

Key news at the start of the month is likely to put a fresh perspective on your home life. If you're travelling or receiving visitors the change of environment will be inspiring and may motivate you to make long-overdue changes at home. The third week of August is conducive to creating the kind of atmosphere you want at home. Communications are likely to flow more as the month progresses, making changes all the more feasible.

September

WEEK 1: 28 AUGUST–3 SEPTEMBER

Keep an eye on communications this week as you may be prone to misunderstandings or will need to be adaptable regarding previously made arrangements. Avoid impulsive reactions to developments as this will merely add to complexities. You'll find a friend, colleague or expert particularly helpful, so be sure to reach out to them for support and information if necessary.

WEEK 2: 4–10 SEPTEMBER

You may be surprised by developments. The lunar eclipse on 7 September will be inspiring, but if an important decision is pending be sure to avoid making snap decisions and especially if there are too many elements to configure at once. An escalation of events domestically, at work, health-wise or with family may set the scene for new variables. An unavoidable link with someone could boost your mood. For some, this will be romantically.

WEEK 3: 11–17 SEPTEMBER

This is a lovely week for get-togethers and socialising. If you're working on your home, developments are likely to go well. Next week's events may point out where you could do with more support and a group, friend or organisation will be helpful, so be sure to reach out. Your expert advice may also be needed. Early next week is a good time for a health appointment.

WEEK 4: 18–24 SEPTEMBER / WEEK 5: 25 SEPTEMBER–1 OCTOBER

WEEK 4: you'll turn a corner in a personal, family or creative venture that may be connected with developments at work or in your status and will involve making a commitment. Advancements could be ideal in the big picture in both your personal life and status, but avoid feeling overwhelmed or overcommitting to complex ventures and making promises you can't keep. **WEEK 5:** there is a considerable amount of change on the horizon, and if you're not already aware of this then this week you're likely to see how your new status, routine or personal situation is likely to impact your daily life. The key to a smoothly running week lies in determining your priorities and sharpening your communication skills.

FINANCES

This will be a good month to consider where you invest your hard-earned money, and if you realise there are some holes in your money bucket you'll gain the opportunity to mend them. You are likely to be drawn to investing in yourself and especially your skill sets. You may enter a fresh chapter in your career, which will have a knock-on effect with your finances. Just be sure to avoid gambling on your future and instead look for a sure thing.

HEALTH

A strong focus on energy levels, vitality and your ability to be productive will produce a desire to improve your health. Mid-month you may discover certain of your habits are either constructive or destructive regarding your health and will gain the opportunity as a result to create a healthier schedule. Be sure to reach out to a health professional for advice or information if necessary, especially towards 16 and 30 September.

LOVE LIFE

If you're single the total lunar eclipse on 7 September and developments around the 10th and 16th will be an excellent time to make new connections with inspiring people. However, whether in a partnership or single you may discover this month that some of your ideas are almost in the realm of idealism, and a more practical approach to finding time for those you love would be more productive.

CAREER

Early in the month a fortunate aspect could boost your career and you may be surprised by developments that enable you to develop some of your skill sets to their highest level. The solar eclipse on 21 September could bring into being a fresh arrangement or contract that promises not only more stability but also more excitement, so do look for fresh horizons in September if you're ready for something new as the stars will support your efforts.

HOME LIFE

Mid-September will be an excellent time to invest your energy into making your home and immediate environment more welcoming and pleasant, as your efforts are likely to pay off. You may be drawn to inviting people to your home or visiting other people's homes, as family and friends congregate mid-month. Just be sure to avoid thorny topics to ensure interpersonal dynamics thrive, not only in mid-month but also towards the 30th.

October

WEEK 1: 2–8 OCTOBER

Your return to an old haunt or a reminder of the past may bring about unexpected feelings or circumstances. A favourite activity or a trip are likely to be enjoyable and could bring heightened experiences or long-term change. You'll appreciate the opportunity to reconnect with someone with whom you feel a deep affinity such as an old colleague or family member.

WEEK 2: 9–15 OCTOBER

A more varied work or daily schedule will appeal to you. You may need to make a tough call when weighing up work versus fun and/or family and may need to make a commitment that could determine several outcomes at once: for some Taureans at work and for others in your personal life. This is an excellent week to take ambitious strides ahead into new territory, so be brave.

WEEK 3: 16–22 OCTOBER

The new moon on 21 October will help revitalise your health and daily routine. You'll enjoy a therapeutic get-together or event. Someone may need your help, and if you need help or advice either at work or health-wise it will be available. Be prepared to see another person's point of view regarding your home, family or a property. News from a business or personal partner early in the week may be a surprise.

WEEK 4: 23–29 OCTOBER

This is an excellent week to move forward with agreements you have made with someone special, and also with a business or personal partnership and domestic matters. You may receive unexpected news towards the middle of next week that surprises you. It's a good week to focus on building a daily work and health routine you enjoy, even if initially there is a degree of challenge. Your efforts will be worthwhile.

FINANCES

Uranus retrograde for the next few months may bring about a sense that you must tread water financially for a while despite work developments demanding that you step up in your career. If you keep an eye on your big-picture financial goals you are likely to reach them as you progress and you may even be pleasantly surprised early in 2026 that all your hard work is resulting in positive financial progress.

HEALTH

October is an excellent month for improving health, and you may be drawn to resuming a past health practice that you know is beneficial for you. A health practitioner you trust will be particularly helpful. It's a good time to improve your appearance as a way to boost morale. If you experience a complex or very busy time towards 23 and 24 October, embrace the challenge to create an efficient and supportive daily health routine.

LOVE LIFE

Your sign's ruler Venus steps into Libra, the sign of love, peace and harmony, on 13 October, putting your focus on fun, romance, music, passion and love for the last two weeks of the month. It will be a wonderful time to invest in these aspects of life and promote a feeling of love in your life, as your partner will respond accordingly. If you're single you'll enjoy this lovely time for romance with a light-hearted touch.

CAREER

This continues to be a good month to make changes in your career and status. The super-powerful aspect between the sun, Uranus and Pluto will help you get things shipshape, even if at first you feel you're clearing the way ahead as opposed to making concrete progress. If progress does not present immediately this month it will do so early in 2026 if you remain positive and diligent about your plans and direction.

HOME LIFE

Your daily duties such as work responsibilities may clash with your domestic obligations early in October, which will provide you with the opportunity to decide where your major priorities and loyalties must lie. Avoid spreading yourself so thin that you cannot complete duties in either area. The new moon on 21 October may spotlight differences of opinion regarding domestic-, family- or property-related matters. Be sure to consider the long-term outlook for the best results.

November

WEEK 1: 30 OCTOBER–5 NOVEMBER

The supermoon on 5 November will be in your sign and will be particularly powerful if you were born before the second week of May. You're likely to kick-start a fresh chapter in your personal life, and if you were born later in May this supermoon will kick-start a fresh chapter in your daily routine. It's a good time to look for security and stability.

WEEK 2: 6–12 NOVEMBER

The re-entry of Uranus into your sign, where it will remain until April 2026, offers you the chance to re-examine aspects of your personal life. This is a romantic weekend and singles may meet someone unique. Couples will enjoy rekindling the passion in your life. Be sure to avoid arguments this weekend if possible. You or a partner may feel nostalgic and a return to an old haunt may appeal.

WEEK 3: 13–19 NOVEMBER

This is an excellent week to reconnect with those with whom you have lost contact, including those you share space with but with whom you have grown distant. It's a good month to repair both work and personal relationships, even if this seems daunting as you'll feel that you have in some way overcome a hurdle. This weekend is a good time to improve your health and appearance.

WEEK 4: 20–26 NOVEMBER / WEEK 5: 27 NOVEMBER–3 DECEMBER

WEEK 4: the new moon on 20 November points to the deepening of a key relationship. Some Taureans may feel ready for a change in status, career or direction, so get set for fresh horizons. However, some will receive unexpected news or must give unexpected news to a personal or business partner. Take things one step at a time for the best results. **WEEK 5:** you may feel a little restless this week, as unexpected news or developments could put you in a new frame of mind. News is likely from a business or personal partner. Working Taureans may begin a fresh work routine. Luckily, a trusted companion, friend or group will prove their weight in gold. Be practical for the best results.

FINANCES

The opposition between Uranus and Mars early in the month may bring unexpected developments financially, but if you've already built a solid financial platform then any news is unlikely to create too many problems for you. You do have the opportunity at the end of the month to negotiate or put in place fresh agreements that will steer your life in a different direction, so be sure to be super clear about the terms and conditions to avoid disappointment further down the track.

HEALTH

It's a good month to ensure your health schedule supports your physical and mental needs, as this is likely to be a busy time. The first week of November may present scenarios where you know you should improve your health, simply so that you have more energy. Some Taureans will be asked to help someone such as a family member. Mid-November will be particularly productive for looking after health, either your own or that of someone else.

LOVE LIFE

The supermoon on 5 November will be in Taurus and signals the start of a fresh chapter in your love life. This may initially present as fairly intense but will create the opportunity to build more stability in your personal life. Singles may meet someone mysteriously familiar towards 8 November and will certainly enjoy socialising. As Venus enters Scorpio, couples will appreciate a more passionate month. Unexpected news is likely around the 20th that may impact your partnership.

CAREER

The tense aspect between Venus and Pluto early in the month is likely to bring changes in your career expectations, if not in your career direction. Mercury will turn retrograde on 8 November so you must try to get important paperwork or negotiations on the table by that date to avoid having to redraft agreements at a later time. However, if you're unsure about negotiations you'll gain the opportunity to review your thoughts in November, enabling you to move ahead with more certainty in December.

HOME LIFE

This will be a good month to re-evaluate your long-term plans domestically as you're likely to experience considerable change in this important area of your life. Jupiter will turn retrograde on 11 November and the remaining three weeks of the month will be productive with regard to domestic reconstruction or repairs. Some Taureans may be in a position to contemplate a return to an old haunt via a trip or a move.

December

WEEK 1: 4–10 DECEMBER

Keep communications on an even keel and ensure you have the facts to avoid misunderstandings. You may be asked for help, and if you need support or advice it will be available. The full moon and supermoon on 4 December brings a fresh financial circumstance as a new agreement at work or in your personal life will mean change. If you're making long-term financial decisions ensure you adequately research your circumstances.

WEEK 2: 11–17 DECEMBER

Romance could blossom; however, you must avoid allowing someone's negative thoughts to influence your positive mindset. While you can excel through hard work, especially in your personal life, there is an indication that you could misjudge a circumstance. Key talks at work or regarding your status will bear fruit, but if your hard work is no longer fulfilling then get back to the nitty gritty of what you love at work.

WEEK 3: 18–24 DECEMBER

The new moon on 20 December will kick-start a fresh phase in a significant collaboration, either in your personal life or at work. There will be therapeutic aspects to relationship developments, even if at the time you experience some degree of vulnerability. It's best to be careful with communications around the solstice as tension in the air risks spilling over into relationship complexities.

WEEK 4: 25–31 DECEMBER

A strong draw to your past could paradoxically revitalise the present. A reunion or a little nostalgia will encourage you to re-evaluate circumstances, especially regarding a collaboration or long-standing loyalty. This is in general a lovely week to improve your health and vitality and a trip somewhere beautiful will be therapeutic, but you must take care with communications to avoid misunderstandings.

FINANCES

It's time for something new financially and you'll gain the opportunity to repair areas of confusion or manage debt in a productive way by considering a fresh approach to the finances that you share, such as joint domestic responsibilities and taxes. The supermoon on 4 December will encourage you to make different financial arrangements but you must avoid making rash decisions, so ensure you do adequate research.

HEALTH

Chiron in your 12th house of health makes a positive aspect to Mars early in December, signalling a good time to work towards a solid base for yourself health-wise. However, if you tend to be impulsive it's in your interest to avoid minor bumps and scrapes early in the month. If you need the help of an expert it will be available. A lovely trip or reunion towards Christmas and the new year will prove to be therapeutic.

LOVE LIFE

The beginning of the month is ideal for discussing important matters with someone you love, as discussions are likely to be productive. Avoid arguments around 8, 16 and 21 December as these may take you in circles, and it's possible that you or someone close grabs the wrong end of the stick and misunderstandings arise. The new moon on the 20th will be a good time to choose fun and therapeutic activities to revitalise your love life.

CAREER

Take the initiative early in the month with discussions with colleagues, business associates and employers, especially if you know already that certain circumstances will need to be addressed at some point. It's better to take the initiative rather than to seem lacking in interest. As the month progresses you're liable to regain a sense of belonging if not power in your career, but you must be careful with collaborations and teamwork even if you are in a position of authority.

HOME LIFE

This is a good month to invest wholeheartedly in your home life, and especially with regard to making changes or spending more time there. However, some lucky Taureans will be visiting a lovely environment and this will certainly encourage you to incorporate elements of luxury into your home on your return. Your joint responsibilities or shared space will merit a little focus towards the solstice to ensure everyone in your living environment is happy with arrangements.

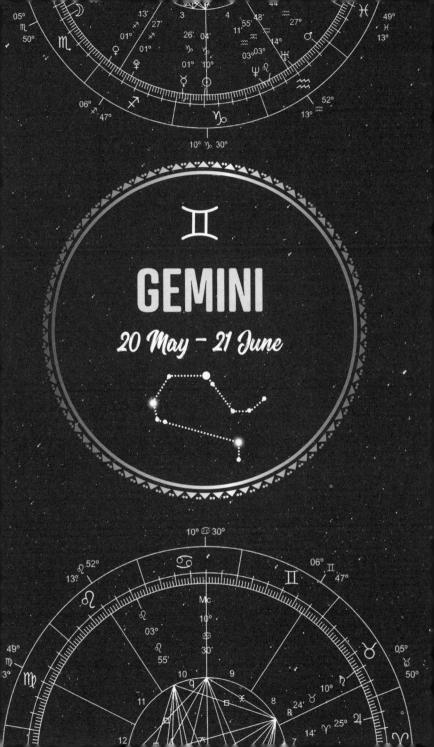

January

WEEK 1: 1–8 JANUARY

You'll discover a little more about whether your plans for 2025 will work, especially those that are long term and may involve considerable planning. You could move forward with a project that has made slow process. A grey area will require additional research. You may be surprised by news from a group, friend or organisation that could help you improve your circumstances.

WEEK 2: 9–15 JANUARY

You'll enjoy socialising and a varied daily routine. However, some outstanding chores will mean you must be a little more focused first on duties. Where you must make decisions, stick with the fundamentals and practicalities and the way ahead will be clearer, especially financially. You may enjoy a perfect opportunity to boost finances but must avoid overspending.

WEEK 3: 16–22 JANUARY

A change of perspective will mean that events in your life will change direction. News may be unexpected, and this will kick-start a fresh chapter. Your involvement with a friend or organisation may require careful handling. A collaboration or joint initiative could cause intense feelings, so be sure to think before you speak. Take your time to organise finances. A discussion or transaction could be a catalyst for better circumstances.

WEEK 4: 23–29 JANUARY

A fresh interest will begin to appeal and you may already get an inkling of events that could signal a turning point. News from a friend, group or organisation should be upbeat, but you must avoid making rash decisions. You'll enjoy a trip. Constructive talks with an organisation or regarding work will help you move ahead with your plans. Avoid arguments with someone you must get on with.

FINANCES

Jupiter in your sign provides you with the chance to review your finances and plan ahead as your finances become the main focus of what is and isn't possible this year, especially in relation to travel, work and your personal life. In early January you may still have a tendency to overindulge in post-seasonal celebrations, so be sure to pace yourself and especially if you're already in debt.

HEALTH

This will be an excellent year to get on top of any health worries you may have, as you'll find the relevant people who can help you retain good health. A partner or friend may act as a motivational force to encourage you to stay on top of good health practices. The year begins with a strong accent towards forging a personal understanding of how your mind, body and spirit function so that you're able to best nurture these vital aspects of yourself.

LOVE LIFE

Vestiges of the party season are likely to continue in January, at the start of the month at least, but then work demands kick in, focusing your attention there. Venus will highlight your ability to get on with various social circles, providing the ideal opportunity to socialise and network. Singles will be in your element but couples may find some aspects of your commitments get in the way of love, so be sure to find ways to keep the romance alive.

CAREER

Venus in Pisces will offer the chance to consider a powerfully romantic and ideal view of your career this year, but you must be careful to look at the work and your career in practical terms. Luckily, the Aquarian new moon on 29 January will offer the chance to alter how you see your status and career and to think outside the square about your options. Be sure to research options in readiness for change, if this is what you desire.

HOME LIFE

Your home will represent a haven for relaxation and sleep, as you're likely this month to be particularly busy either through work or having the wonderful chance to travel or at least be sociable. A change of pace towards the end of the month will enable you to view your home and its value in a new light, enabling you to invest more in this important aspect of your life through towards autumn.

February

WEEK 1: 30 JANUARY–5 FEBRUARY

A key get-together or news from a group or organisation may have an upbeat or ideal element. You'll appreciate receiving news that provides you with direction and insight into work or a project. You may be inclined to plan a trip. A legal or personal matter may require a little additional work. A financial project or the chance to remedy a past circumstance is best tackled carefully.

WEEK 2: 6–12 FEBRUARY

You can make a great deal of progress this week. A financial matter should be cleared up so you can deal with other matters that require more focus, such as work and personal agreements. For some, decisions will revolve around bigger-picture progress and how you can attain it. The full moon on 12 February spells a fresh chapter in a domestic circumstance that may require you to adjust your outlook.

WEEK 3: 13–19 FEBRUARY

A get-together will prove to be enjoyable, so be sure to organise a treat this Valentine's Day week. You may discover that some of your pastimes attract similarly minded people. A trip to a beautiful place will bring lovely people into your environment. You'll enjoy being in your element, with your work or social life creating an upbeat schedule. A chance meeting or a change of pace may involve a reunion. Avoid allowing someone's bad mood to affect yours.

WEEK 4: 20–26 FEBRUARY

Keep communications clear this week as you could truly excel in practical ways, both at work and financially. Just avoid rushing as mistakes could be made. Lovely news from a group or organisation could be ideal and will mean considerable change ahead. If you feel you will miss an opportunity, ensure you research ways to establish a good result regardless.

FINANCES

If you feel overworked and underpaid this is an excellent month to consider ways to remedy this situation. Jupiter ends its retrograde phase, providing you with the motivation to move things ahead that have been slow to grow. Financially, this is a good time to look at ways to invest more in yourself and your abilities and to find groups, structures or organisations that can help improve your finances.

HEALTH

Jupiter ends its retrograde phase in your sign, so if you've been feeling lacklustre over the past few weeks or months health-wise then circumstances are about to improve. In the process, though, there may be some ground to cover to ensure best practices are being followed, especially if you were born in May. At the very least your mood will improve during February, helping you to feel more optimistic and enthusiastic.

LOVE LIFE

This will once again be a sociable month, enabling you to meet all kinds of new people if you didn't already in January. A social meeting at the start of February could bring someone familiar into the love life of singles, someone you either knew previously or who seems familiar yet is a stranger. For couples, the start of February is ideal for a holiday, romantic renewal of vows or simply to enjoy a truly romantic time. The new moon on 28 February will once again enable you to meet someone new if you're single and to make a valid commitment if you're already in a relationship.

CAREER

The new moon on 28 February will enable you to turn an important corner in your career. This could come seemingly from out of the blue, but if you've been considering making changes in your career for some time and have been preparing for them there will be less of a surprise factor. You'll need to weigh up your aims and goals during February and decide how best to move forward in both practical and innovative ways, and avoid making unrealistic plans.

HOME LIFE

With so much focus on your favourite activities, the people you love and your activities your home may have a purely practical use at the start of the month. The full moon on 12 February spells a fresh chapter in a domestic circumstance that may require you to adjust your outlook. A surprise event or change in your usual daily or work routine suggests it's time to turn a corner, as there is an impact at home due to your status and personal growth.

March

WEEK 1: 27 FEBRUARY–5 MARCH

The Pisces new moon on 28 February signals the chance to broaden horizons. For some this will be via a trip and for others through work, study, spirituality or a relationship or legal matter. Be inspired but also be practical, as this particular new moon will predispose you to being super idealistic. Be careful to avoid arguments with a friend or organisation. You may be pleasantly surprised by a reunion.

WEEK 2: 6–12 MARCH

You'll feel more proactive and upbeat about your closest relationships, and the more positive energy you inject into your ventures the better you'll feel, especially socially and with people you'd like to build connections with. An agreement or negotiation could lead to a serious commitment. Ensure that talks you engage in are heading in the right direction for you, as commitments you make now will be long-standing.

WEEK 3: 13–19 MARCH

Your sign's ruler Mercury turns retrograde at the same time as the lunar eclipse, bringing into being a fresh understanding with someone. This will be either in your family, with an organisation, regarding a favourite project or at work. You may receive key news from a friend or organisation that puts some of your projects into perspective. A relationship can blossom if you take good care of communications.

WEEK 4: 20–26 MARCH / WEEK 5: 27 MARCH–2 APRIL

WEEK 4: you'll gain a better idea of whether an ambitious plan is practical or simply an unattainable dream. Some lucky Twins will be in the position to plan a holiday or ideal trip. An opportunity may arise regarding a friend or organisation. Romance could come a-knocking, so be sure to socialise if you're single and plan something special if you're a couple. **WEEK 5:** you'll be drawn to beginning a fresh chapter either in a career move or in your status. Travel, esoteric topics, self-development and, for some, legal matters will be in focus. A friend or organisation will prove helpful, so be sure to seek their advice. A financial circumstance is best tackled carefully. A personal or business agreement or work matter may seem predestined.

FINANCES

Considerable decision-making will be necessary, and as long as you've already undertaken research into the best path for you and those close to you, you could make some wonderful headway financially. As proactive Mars gains ground in your finance sector you'll be prepared to invest in aspects of life that make you happy, as opposed to constantly earning and saving. Just be careful to avoid overspending and making emotional investments, which you may come to regret.

HEALTH

You'll appreciate the opportunity to boost your fitness and health schedules: spending time in nature, walking or swimming, for example, will bring a sense of calm. You may be surprised by activities you never considered to be health practices that do in fact provide an uplifting effect, such as socialising. A group of like-minded people may be instrumental in providing or facilitating a deeper understanding of your mind/body/soul relationship, especially around the eclipses mid-month and on 29 March.

LOVE LIFE

This will be a turning-point month, as you'll be deciding which relationship you invest more into emotionally. You may be feeling particularly nostalgic or wish to reignite a past relationship, but you must ensure your emotions are not being driven by an idealistic version of the past as opposed to a realistic approach to the present. When you do you could find that your romantic life is truly at a peak, so it's an excellent time to invest in love.

CAREER

You can make a serious commitment to a valid career path in March, so be sure to take the initiative with your various plans and projects. The eclipse season can open doors for you and a development towards the end of March will certainly offer a fresh direction or investment opportunity, in yourself and your skill sets. Early March may already provide insight into a particular group or organisation you either wish to expand with or move away from.

HOME LIFE

The eclipse mid-month will spotlight changes at home, and much of your decision-making will come down to who you wish to spend more time with and how your decisions will impact your family and those you love. Try to get discussions on the table by 15 March, when your sign's ruler Mercury will turn retrograde and could delay discussions for several weeks. However, if you prefer to take decisions slowly the next two months will be ideal for reviewing your thoughts.

April

WEEK 1: 3–9 APRIL

The Venus–Uranus contact this week suggests surprise developments to do with work or health. You can certainly make great progress with your projects and will need to focus on the details of a collaboration or agreement to avoid unnecessarily intense talks further down the line. Mercury will end its retrograde phase, bringing key news or a meeting with a friend or organisation.

WEEK 2: 10–16 APRIL

You'll enjoy the chance for a reunion or impromptu get-together. If you've been drawn to travelling you'll appreciate the dreamy atmosphere, but you must be sure to keep an eye on details and avoid overtiring yourself. The Libra full moon on 13 April points to a key development regarding home or family. A group, friend or organisation may be particularly influential at this time.

WEEK 3: 17–23 APRIL

You're likely to hear news from a friend, group or organisation and this will provide you with clarity moving forward. If you've been planning to make a key legal or personal commitment, this is certainly a good week to do so. While you're one of the zodiac's best communicators, you must nevertheless be careful with communications on Sunday and Monday.

WEEK 4: 24–30 APRIL

You have the opportunity to make some serious decisions, and for some these will revolve around your social life or a group or organisation and for others around your career and status. The conjunction between Venus and the moon's north node also points to significant developments in your love life or domestic life that could alter your trajectory for some time to come.

FINANCES

Due to the serious nature of some of your decisions in April you're likely to make changes regarding your finances, such as your budget and investment strategy. A commitment could be positively transformative financially, bringing wealth your way. However, this will depend on meticulous hard work and your ability to keep your feet on the ground amid considerable change. Be sure to research your options and gain the help of an expert if necessary.

HEALTH

It's time to find more balance in your life, and this desire will fuel better health and well-being. If you achieve a sense of balance, peace and harmony from swimming, for example, this is something you will increasingly indulge in. If you're more predisposed towards spiritual development and enjoy meditation, this is where your attention will go. It's more than likely by the month's end that you'll have birthed a fresh health routine.

LOVE LIFE

You'll be drawn to making a significant commitment to someone special. For some this will be to a lover or partner and for others to a friend. You're likely to be drawn to the past and a nostalgic view of someone, so it's important in April to maintain perspective and consider your circumstances in light of the present, not the past, especially as a change in your usual routine or schedule may predispose you to a romantic outlook.

CAREER

Changes regarding your work, finances and groups of people you work with will be to your benefit. You may receive an unexpected offer or opportunity that enables you to improve your status, profile or work conditions. The conjunction of Venus, Saturn and the moon's north node after mid-month will provide you with direction. You could make rapid progress at this time but you must be careful with communications and avoid making promises you can't keep.

HOME LIFE

This will be an excellent month to work with friends, groups and organisations to enjoy a romantic, spiritual, artistic or dreamy approach to life. To do so you may visit their homes or they will visit yours. You may need to step into fresh territory domestically, but this is likely to be a success as long as you don't make any rash decisions, especially mid-month and towards 27 April.

May

WEEK 1: 1–7 MAY

You'll appreciate finding the time to focus on a favourite activity with favourite people, so be sure to organise something fun. You may enjoy being creative, musical and motivated by your projects. A disagreement is best avoided by basing talks on facts. If travel, study, a legal development or spiritual insight appeal to you, you may receive key news at the weekend.

WEEK 2: 8–14 MAY

The Scorpio full moon on 12 May will bring a change in your work or health routine or in your daily schedule. It's in your interest to be adaptable and consider first and foremost where your ultimate goals lie, so that your decision-making and the actions you take are meticulous. It's a good week to make progress at work and enjoy get-togethers with a friend or a group.

WEEK 3: 15–21 MAY

A chance meeting or favourable development at work will add to your self-esteem and bring you in touch with like-minded people. However, you must avoid locking horns with someone at work or in your personal life and would be far better to instead agree to disagree. Nevertheless, you'll enjoy a lovely reunion or good news from the past, a friend or expert.

WEEK 4: 22–28 MAY

The Gemini new moon on 27 May promises to kick-start a fresh chapter in May Twins' personal life and June Twins' work and health schedule. Key decisions or agreements can be made, so ensure you seek direction or advice if necessary. You'll enjoy travel, a fresh environment or the chance to learn something new. You'll also enjoy socialising and networking, and romance could flourish.

FINANCES

Consider this: do you have a financial arrangement that is outdated or holding you back? If so, this month will offer the opportunity to move forward. It may be an arrangement that is so long in the making that it would seem difficult to alter arrangements, yet by the end of the month you'll find that new opportunities and options open to you. The new moon in your sign on 27 May could already illuminate a fresh financial path.

HEALTH

The full moon in Scorpio on 12 May will spotlight which areas of your health may benefit from attention. If you've been underinvesting in your health you'll be motivated to do more. On the other hand, if your fitness practices have become all-consuming you'll regain perspective and find a way to channel excess energy into work and your personal life and not be consumed by constant concern over fitness. The new moon on 27 May suggests you'll enjoy boosting your appearance.

LOVE LIFE

The start of the month is ideal for deepening your connection with someone special, so be sure to organise an event or date. If you're single you'll enjoy socialising and spending time with like-minded people doing mutually enjoyable activities. The Gemini new moon on 27 May suggests you're ready to turn a corner in your personal life if you were born on or before the 27th and health-wise if you were born later. Both will boost your love life.

CAREER

The Scorpio full moon on 12 May will shine a light on your work and daily life, adding perspective to how you'd prefer your schedule to be. You'll make sound progress with a group or organisation so be prepared to take the initiative, and you may experience an unexpected development mid-month that takes you somewhere different. The new moon in your sign on the 27th points to the chance to reinvent yourself to a degree, especially in your career.

HOME LIFE

You can make a lot of progress in a domestic scenario, especially towards the end of the month. The key to making the right decisions revolves around acknowledging whether you have outgrown certain arrangements and agreements either with family, a property or your home, and whether you have it in you to finally push forward into something new. The arrival of the sun in Gemini just before the new moon on 27 May will illuminate your true feelings.

June

WEEK 1: 29 MAY–4 JUNE

A realistic and practical approach to your work and a partnership or collaboration will put you in a strong position. Avoid restricting your options too much; trust your intuition and values. A sensitive person or situation will merit careful handling to avoid getting stuck in conflict. Put your admirable communication skills to good use for the best effect.

WEEK 2: 5–11 JUNE

You love to talk, and a decision or contract can be reached in the coming days. Someone close or influential will be on your mind, on the phone or in your environment. Singles should mingle as you may meet someone optimistic towards the full moon on 11 June. However, you must be careful to avoid overspending. A considerable expense may arise, but some lucky Twins will be receiving a financial boost.

WEEK 3: 12–18 JUNE

It's a good week for health and beauty appointments, but you must be clear about details to avoid misunderstandings. You may receive a financial or ego boost. A key talk may mean you must dig deep to express yourself and your values. You may be surprised by your or someone else's reactions, so avoid impulsiveness and look for the steadiest way forward. Above all, avoid a battle of egos.

WEEK 4: 19–25 JUNE / WEEK 5: 26 JUNE–2 JULY

WEEK 4: the new moon on 25 June promises to revitalise your ideas, writing abilities and relationships, and you'll feel all the more adept at planning your projects and finances with the right priorities in mind. While certain communications and interactions may be challenging or unclear, if you focus on your strong communication abilities you'll be able to overcome miscommunications and correct mistakes.
WEEK 5: your sign's ruler Mercury enters Leo this week and this will revitalise your communications and social life. You'll appreciate the opportunity to spend time with like-minded people. You may experience a financial boost; however, you must avoid arguments and tension during the weekend. A trip will be transformative but you must avoid erratic drivers. You may receive unexpected news early next week.

FINANCES

Finances will take a considerable amount of focus in June, and the better your financial foundations are the more likely you will build solid progress. However, if you've been vague or haven't planned your finances carefully in the past you may discover a solution. Be prepared to navigate carefully financially as you may be liable to overspend. Mid-June may present a difficult financial transaction, so be sure to monitor finances closely then.

HEALTH

This is an excellent month to make tracks towards seeing your health and comfort as priorities, as the stars will help you with your efforts to formulate a solid and dependable health routine. Developments at home or with family will help buoy your mood. If you're travelling you'll find this a particularly therapeutic trip on many different levels. You'll enjoy touching base with those you feel you have a close spiritual or soul connection with.

LOVE LIFE

The key to a happy love life in June resides in good communication skills, which luckily you have. The full moon on the 11th will kick-start a fresh chapter in a key partnership, so if you're single and born before mid-June be sure to be adventurous if you're looking for a partner as you're likely to find someone significant this month. Couples could also enjoy a sense of reconnection unless your differences point to the need for separate paths.

CAREER

A group or organisation will be instrumental in inspiring you to review and potentially also change your career, taking you into new territory. However, you must ensure that you are in a strong enough financial position and especially in the run-up to the full moon on 11 June, as you may otherwise take steps you later come to regret. Be sure to sharpen your negotiation skills, especially if you were born after the 12th, as you may begin a fresh schedule or placement.

HOME LIFE

You may be surprised by developments at home or with property or family mid-June. The situation is best handled with care and support if someone needs your help. If you need a little support or advice regarding your domestic situation it will be available, so be sure to reach out. You may discover the merits of a nurturing home environment. You'll be drawn to doing some home repair and to improving any domestic relationships that need it.

July

WEEK 1: 3–9 JULY

As Venus and Uranus enter your sign your mind will turn to love, money, socialising and networking. You may prefer to focus on one activity or person, and romance can thrive now. You may be called in to work unexpectedly or must make an impromptu change in your usual routine. You may find that you reach a new understanding in a business or personal partnership as a door opens.

WEEK 2: 10–16 JULY

The full moon on 10 July will spotlight your shared ventures, including joint finances and shared space at home. This full moon offers the opportunity to find practical ways to make your shared responsibilities work for you. A particular obligation such as a financial or personal commitment may step to a new level. You'll enjoy socialising and may hear from an old friend or meet someone who seems strangely familiar.

WEEK 3: 17–23 JULY

Venus in your sign makes some tough astrological aspects this week that could bring difficult emotions to the surface. However, you'll enjoy a get-together or will receive good news that will buoy your mood. If you must make work or financial decisions ensure you obtain expert help if possible. Avoid overtiring yourself as you may be liable to live off your nerves now.

WEEK 4: 24–30 JULY

This is an excellent week to focus on your communication and negotiation skills, as you'll manage to get across some great ideas and also potentially make an agreement that could be financially beneficial. Your ability to collaborate will be key, so also boost your networking skills. A financial upturn is on the way for some lucky Geminis.

FINANCES

Jupiter, the planet associated with abundance but also with overspending, is in your money zone and makes a wonderful aspect with Venus early in July, indicating the opportunity to improve your finances but also the likelihood that you'll have large financial outlays to settle. There is a general groundswell of positivity in July for you, but if you're already in debt you would be wise to keep tabs on spending to avoid increasing that debt.

HEALTH

Geminis do tend to live off your nerves and it will certainly be in your interest to pace yourself throughout July, as you'll otherwise be tempted to burn the candle at both ends and especially towards the third and fourth weeks of the month. Aim to find ways to enjoy your daily life and slow down when possible, especially if you find yourself overwhelmed by chores and communications around 19 July.

LOVE LIFE

The entry of Venus and Uranus into your sign will bring a significant shift in your personal life over the coming weeks and months. You may already experience a need for freedom and adventure in your love life. You'll certainly enjoy socialising and networking early in the month and romance can flourish, both for singles and couples. Singles may meet someone from your past towards 12 July or someone you feel you have a predestined connection with.

CAREER

For many Geminis the entry of Venus and Uranus into your sign may initially impact your career and daily work life, as you're going to be craving something different and will be drawn to being restless for this reason. The favourable aspect between Venus and Pluto could bring a promotion or change in your daily routine around 7 July that can see your career and work flourish, so be prepared to discuss projects and ideas.

HOME LIFE

You may tend to underestimate the value of your home or a property in July, so be sure to remind yourself of the importance of this key area of your life and especially during the third and fourth weeks of the month. As you'll be busy at this time or in a different environment you may tend to make rash decisions regarding your home life that in fact would be to your detriment, so be sure to maintain perspective.

August

WEEK 1: 31 JULY–6 AUGUST

Take the time to gather your thoughts as you may feel inspired but also sensitive to the moods of other people, especially this weekend. You'll enjoy a trip or meeting this Friday but must avoid overspending if you're drawn to a little retail therapy this weekend. A difference of opinion or values will spotlight where you wish to place your energy moving forward, especially regarding your career and home life.

WEEK 2: 7–13 AUGUST

You'll enjoy a breath of fresh air this week and may be surprised by unexpected developments or news. It's an excellent week to try something different, both at work and domestically. You may also enjoy an ego or financial boost early next week. A tough decision regarding family or a friend or organisation is best taken with the full facts at hand.

WEEK 3: 14–20 AUGUST

A proactive, friendly and chatty approach this week will smooth out relationships and help you get ahead, both at work and home. If your health has been down in the dumps, get set for better energy levels by taking time out to rest and recuperate. You could enjoy a trip or visit with someone you feel a close connection with this weekend that will raise morale.

WEEK 4: 21–27 AUGUST

This week's developments will help you put in place a solid financial structure and organise a venture such as a creative or domestic project. If you tend to look at your projects idealistically you'll see the realities of circumstances more clearly. Communications are likely to go well next week if they're complex this week.

FINANCES

This will be a productive time to review your budget and finances as your efforts are likely to be successful, especially during the first three weeks of the month. If you're drawn to making considerable changes in your work or daily schedule consider your financial bottom line and stick with it, as you may otherwise be prone either to underspend or overspend in August.

HEALTH

You prefer to stay on top of your health by engaging in an active fitness routine. You may wish to embrace new modalities in August that enable you to enjoy a different workout or sport. Be sure to join clubs or make arrangements with friends to enjoy nature and the outdoors where possible. Mid-August is particularly conducive to boosting health and well-being, and this may also be in connection with your home life or a property.

LOVE LIFE

Mars in your fifth house of romance will encourage you to be more outgoing, seeking a romantic and pleasurable time. A lovely get-together during the weekend of 16 August is likely to bring you in touch with someone you truly admire. Singles may meet someone who seems strangely familiar yet you've never met before. Mid-August will be an excellent time for couples to reignite sensuality in your relationship. This may even be a particularly therapeutic time for you.

CAREER

This is a wonderful month to look at your big-picture career path from a fresh perspective, especially around the full moon on 9 August. You're likely to achieve an unexpected or unusual degree of change in your life in August, so you must be prepared to look at your options from many different perspectives to ensure the decisions you make are the correct ones for you now.

HOME LIFE

You'll gain the opportunity to make true headway both in your career and domestically. If you must choose between priorities, the energy you put into your domestic life or a property will be more obviously productive and especially once Mars enters Libra on 7 August. The following six weeks will be ideal for improving décor, a little updating of furniture or gardening. Mid-August will see developments at home or with family that may be therapeutic on some level.

September

WEEK 1: 28 AUGUST–3 SEPTEMBER

Your sign's ruler Mercury enters the sign of Virgo this week, which will encourage you to consider how best to bring about results and especially regarding a property and your personal or family life. You will not always agree with everyone and may be surprised by news that could include good financial developments or information from a group, friend or organisation.

WEEK 2: 4–10 SEPTEMBER

A new direction will appeal this week, and this may present first of all as an ideal project as it has all the qualities you love, including inspiration and excitement. A friend, group or organisation may prove particularly helpful. Travel, study, self-development, spirituality and the mysteries and adventures of life will all motivate you to embrace new projects.

WEEK 3: 11–17 SEPTEMBER

Being so active, you can easily fall into the trap of living off your nerves. This week, be sure to get the balance right between hard work and enjoyment and leave time for relaxation and sleep, otherwise you risk burning out. You'll relish the opportunity to enjoy some creature comforts at home. You'll need energy to make a serious commitment next week, so be sure to think things through.

WEEK 4: 18–24 SEPTEMBER / WEEK 5: 25 SEPTEMBER–1 OCTOBER

WEEK 4: the Virgo solar eclipse on 21 September will spotlight the opportunity to turn a corner in a travel-related project or venture that broadens your mind. Initially, you may be aware that a family or creative venture is moving into new territory. This weekend, key news or a trip or visit will bring a change of routine. Some communications may require additional tact so that you land the commitment you're looking for. **WEEK 5:** you'll gain a sense of making progress with a treasured project. For some this will mean a lovely sociable week and for others visible progress at work or with someone special. Be careful to ensure communications are as clear as they can be, especially towards mid next week, to avoid misunderstandings and mix-ups. If delays slow down your progress be sure to be patient.

FINANCES

Jupiter, the planet associated with abundance, makes a fortunate aspect to the Pisces lunar eclipse on 7 September and this could help you turn a corner financially and could even prospectively bring an abundant phase. However, a tough aspect to Mars suggests you avoid gambling; it is far better to invest in a sure outcome. In addition, the Mercury–Jupiter aspect at the end of the month indicates you need to keep an eye on transactions to avoid making mistakes then.

HEALTH

Mercury in Virgo, the sign of health and well-being, will encourage you to be proactive about your health in September. A change of routine or circumstance may mean you must alter your usual health schedule, which will merit careful attention. A return to an old haunt or the draw to a health routine that has been particularly constructive in the past could be productive health-wise, especially mid-month when you may be tempted to live off your nerves.

LOVE LIFE

Single Geminis may feel motivated to find someone who is a like-minded soul. Being in a friendship group or organisation is likely to inspire you to look for someone with similar interests. Get-togethers towards 10 September are likely to be particularly promising in this regard. Couples will enjoy reconnecting over shared interests such as family concerns. Travel will truly breathe fresh air into your relationship, so consider organising a short trip or longer holiday, which you'll appreciate.

CAREER

You're ready to turn a corner with regard to the groups and organisations you spend time with in your career. Important discussions and agreements could lead to new terms and conditions in your existing employment or to something completely different. You're ready to embrace something fresh and exciting in your life, so be sure to be proactive to create the outcomes you want such as approaching business partners or emailing your resumé to prospective employers.

HOME LIFE

The total lunar eclipse on 7 September could kick-start a fresh chapter concerning family or your home life. For some this will be in response to developments in your status in general or in your career in particular. It is certainly a good month to discuss long-term domestic plans with those they concern, as you could make some truly constructive decisions now. Luckily, Mercury in your fourth house of home and family will help you with negotiations and discussions.

October

WEEK 1: 2–8 OCTOBER

A change of dynamic at home or work or due to a change of pace is best approached patiently to avoid misunderstandings and mix-ups. It will be in your interest this week to avoid impulsiveness and erratic drivers, especially this weekend. Romance could truly blossom this weekend, and a family or creative project could also take off.

WEEK 2: 9–15 OCTOBER

This will be a romantic week, ideal to make a commitment to someone you admire or love. If you're single you may be surprised that you'd consider making a commitment to someone in the love stakes. For some Geminis, though, this week unfortunately spells the end of a liaison, especially if it has been on the cards for some time. Work-wise, be diligent to make way for new arrangements that take you into fresh territory.

WEEK 3: 16–22 OCTOBER

You'll appreciate the chance to turn a corner with a personal matter, and developments may require you to be more nurturing and caring. There is a healing or health-related aspect to developments this week ideal for connecting with a health professional or healing modality. This could be a romantic weekend, so be sure to organise a treat! Be careful with communications and avoid travel delays on Friday, though.

WEEK 4: 23–29 OCTOBER

This is an excellent week for socialising and networking and moving ahead with your projects, both at work and in your personal life. You may hear unexpected news or will change your usual routine mid next week. A fresh interest such as a sport or study project will appeal. This is an excellent time to gain insight into a health or beauty matter.

FINANCES

While you're not generally seen as the gambler of the zodiac (this would be more the domain of a Leo or Sagittarian) you do risk throwing caution to wind this month, especially mid-month and up to the new moon on 21 October. If you're considering a major financial investment it will be in your interest to consult experts to avoid inadvertent gambling. Keep an eye on expenditure also to avoid going into debt.

HEALTH

Your sign's ruler opposes Chiron on 3 October and the sun opposes Chiron on the 18th, bringing a focus to health and well-being both at the beginning and towards the end of the month. If you have been overexerting yourself you'll gain insight into the best ways to replenish energy levels. In addition, the new moon on the 21st will help you devise ways to create more peace, balance and harmony in your life, so be sure to take the initiative then to begin a fresh health regime.

LOVE LIFE

The first weekend of October is ideal for a reunion with someone you love as you're likely to enjoy your meeting: as long as you're both on the same page, because otherwise misunderstandings could arise. The Venus–Saturn opposition on 11 October will highlight the need to appraise a personal circumstance. You may be prepared to commit further to someone, or if a separation has been in the cards for a while this could be a parting of the ways.

CAREER

You'll appreciate the sense from mid-October onwards that your activities and interests have space to grow, and if you've put some of your career aspirations on hold more recently you'll gain the impetus to invest more in this important area of your life throughout the month. The conjunction of mercury and Mars on the 20th and their aspects to Saturn and Jupiter during the last week of the month could bring considerable progress at work. Be prepared to negotiate.

HOME LIFE

Where do you feel you belong? The answer to this question will help you make any important decisions that arise regarding your home life in October. However, with much of your focus on health, well-being, work and relationships your home life will assume a supporting role for you. That is, unless changes in your career and general direction mid-month dictate that your home life must adjust accordingly.

November

WEEK 1: 30 OCTOBER–5 NOVEMBER

Key decisions or agreements can be made and may engage new variables in your life, especially at work and with personal matters. Be adventurous but also tactful, as those close to you may be more sensitive than usual. The full moon and supermoon on 5 November will shine a light on your changing requirements at work and health-wise, and tending to your needs will be a priority.

WEEK 2: 6–12 NOVEMBER

Your sign's ruler Mercury will turn retrograde this week and it will be in your interest to complete paperwork and seek important agreement before it turns retrograde on 9 November, as this will avoid possible delays further down the line. However, if you'd prefer to review and reconsider some aspects of your agreements and work life the following few weeks will be ideal.

WEEK 3: 13–19 NOVEMBER

As the most flexible communicator of the zodiac, even you can sometimes experience difficult communications. While this will be a busy week full of meetings and socialising, it will nevertheless be in your interest to bring your best communication skills to the table. Some lucky Geminis may experience an improvement in your finances or at work, so take the initiative.

WEEK 4: 20–26 NOVEMBER / WEEK 5: 27 NOVEMBER–3 DECEMBER

WEEK 4: a fresh chapter at work is about to begin, and this could come about by deepening your relationship with a group or organisation. Your routine is likely to change and you may experience an unexpected or unusual change in your schedule. You're on track to create more variety and interest in your daily life, so look to add more of what you want to your schedule. **WEEK 5:** a lovely influence around you largely due to the people in your environment and the activities you undertake will be uplifting. This will increase your well-being and contentment. A trip or change of circumstance may be unexpected and will merit careful focus so you can adapt to your circumstances. You may be surprised by developments but they will not be outside your experience.

FINANCES

You can tend to gamble financially and early in November is a case in point, when you must avoid taking any more than a calculated risk as you stand to regret your actions. On the other hand, if you've researched your circumstances adequately and feel ready to make considerable changes financially your actions are likely to be therapeutic and could take you into a whole new and exciting chapter in your life.

HEALTH

It's time to be practical about your health and put in place schedules and programs that support your physical, mental, spiritual and emotional well-being. If you're fortunate to be able to take a holiday you'll enjoy the opportunity to create a fresh daily schedule that supports your health. The final week of the month will be particularly conducive to allowing yourself to enjoy your environment and the company of inspiring and fun people.

LOVE LIFE

You're known as the most accomplished communicator in the zodiac, yet even you can sometimes find discussions difficult and especially if they involve deep emotions. November could be an emotional month, so this is an opportunity for emotional growth. Displaying sensitivity to other people's feelings will help grease the wheels of your relationships, especially in the first week of the month when someone close to you may be feeling particularly vulnerable or wishes to discuss their feelings.

CAREER

The full moon and supermoon on 5 November spotlights your need for a fresh circumstance in your career and daily life. Try to put something new in action before the 8th, when Uranus will leave your sign for the next five months. This will bring the likelihood of change in your working day but is more likely to be in the shape of reviews, a return to an old routine or tweaked circumstances.

HOME LIFE

As the social butterfly of the zodiac and this being the run-up to the festive season, you're more likely to be socialising and working or enjoying yourself than focusing on your home life. That is, unless the changes occurring in your usual daily routine also impact your home life, in which case you'll find this a good month to re-evaluate where you live and your environment.

December

WEEK 1: 4–10 DECEMBER

You're under pressure with communications this week, so be super clear for the best results. The full moon and supermoon on 4 December is in your sign and signifies a fresh chapter in your personal life, especially if you were born before 3 June. If you were born later you're ready to turn a corner at work, health-wise or in your daily life. A fresh understanding or commitment may be needed.

WEEK 2: 11–17 DECEMBER

Being independent you like to feel you are free, so when your circumstances depend on the decisions of others you can feel frustrated. Take a moment this week to gain the information you need to feel more stable, and be patient with other people's arrangements. You're a good communicator, so be sure to be super clear with facts, details and arrangements to avoid confusion.

WEEK 3: 18–24 DECEMBER

The new moon on 20 December signals the opportunity to turn a corner in a significant work or personal relationship, especially if you were born on 18 or 19 June. Be proactive and positive but wary to avoid unnecessary arguments, especially around the solstice when mistakes and misunderstandings are likely. This aside, you'll enjoy some therapeutic developments that bring a sense of completion as you approach the end of the year.

WEEK 4: 25–31 DECEMBER

You're known for your gift of the gab, but even you can find communications complex. This week avoid mix-ups, or you could be disappointed. If you're working this week your hard work will have unexpected gains, even if it's inconvenient due to the festive time of year. A business or personal partnership could thrive this week, so be sure to take positive steps to improve relationships you value.

FINANCES

Some Geminis will find important financial transactions or decisions will need to be made early in the month already. As long as you've done your research you could be in line for a considerable financial boost, so be sure to take the initiative and do adequate research. However, you may need to review or reappraise some of your financial investments or expectations, especially with regard to a group, friend or organisation.

HEALTH

If health has been an area you'd like to improve, the first two weeks of the month will be ideal to do just that. You may be drawn to a particular group or organisation that matches your idea of healthy activities. You may also be drawn to developing your innate abilities such as psychic skills or spiritual development. A change of routine will take you into an environment where you may be surprised by its uplifting effects.

LOVE LIFE

It's time to turn a corner in your love life, especially if you were born before 3 June. Be super clear with communications, especially in the first week of the month. For all Geminis the more supportive you are of a partner the better, as they may require help or a deeper connection early in the month. Avoid stubbornness, especially around the 8th. Singles may discover that someone you thought was a true friend may have different goals.

CAREER

If you were born after 3 June the supermoon on 4 December will kick-start a fresh phase for you in your career or at least in your daily routine. You'll gain the chance to put in place a more creative and constructive work schedule or plan. You're communicating well, especially in the second week of the month, and if you bear in mind that others may find this week in particular slightly difficult communications-wise you will excel.

HOME LIFE

The demands of your daily life and circumstances may ask that you reconsider how you see your home life, and initially some obligations or structures you've already set up may no longer align with what you actually need. For some this will present new options to alter considerably how you go about things so your activities at home and the location of your home become the priority.

January

WEEK 1: 1–8 JANUARY

This is an excellent time to make plans with someone you love, such as a partner or family. It's also a good time for talks, especially regarding domestic or shared matters. Romance could blossom, so plan a treat as you're likely to enjoy it. If you're considering new investments or organising a career or health matter ensure you read the fine print to avoid making mistakes.

WEEK 2: 9–15 JANUARY

It's a good week to boost health and appearance and a change of environment will be inspiring. You'll relish music, romance and the arts, so be sure to take the initiative in these areas. The Cancer full moon on 13 January could bring a pleasant surprise, but if the opposite arises avoid jumping to conclusions. A change of pace may require you to be super patient.

WEEK 3: 16–22 JANUARY

Romance could thrive but you must ensure you're on the same page to avoid a disagreement. An improvement in your work or personal situation may ask that you be better organised or research circumstances. Good communication skills will boost your situation but some conversations will be intense or bring out your sensitivities, especially mid next week, so be sure to retain perspective.

WEEK 4: 23–29 JANUARY

The new moon on 29 January marks a turning point in a joint venture. Your duties, finances or commitments will be shared differently in the coming weeks. A fresh chapter may begin with an agreement. You must avoid making impulsive decisions, especially financially. Be creative and willing to look outside the square at your options, and look for solutions rather than perpetuate problems. A lovely trip, venture or project could be motivational. You'll enjoy an impromptu get-together.

FINANCES

You'll gain the opportunity in January to get on top of debts accumulated over the holiday season, which will help you feel less behind. However, if you find that certain financial commitments are unavoidable it's vital you look for professional or expert help to find ways to budget more effectively. The full moon on the 13th will spotlight whether the need to re-evaluate your budget is important.

HEALTH

A friend, group or organisation will be helpful regarding your general health and well-being, so be sure to seek out like-minded people you can walk, run, do yoga or train with or who inspire you. Mars in your sign from 6 January will bring a sense of urgency regarding some of your projects, yet as Mars will be retrograde the pace will be slower than usual so be sure to practise the art of patience and find ways to dispel frustration and annoyance. A zen approach to life will be invaluable.

LOVE LIFE

As Mars re-enters your sign it may bring into focus developments from early November that may require you to re-evaluate how you feel. You may reunite with someone special or return to a favourite place. Early January may involve intense feelings, so be prepared to pace yourself and avoid being caught in someone else's dramas, especially around the 3rd. The full moon on the 13th will kick-start a fresh cycle in your personal life, one that will prove therapeutic and even surprising.

CAREER

You may experience an ideal circumstance career-wise and could make great progress, as long as you know where you're heading and what you want out of this aspect of your life. If not you may find January a little confusing or disorienting. Keep an eye on where your interests take you career-wise around the full moon on 13 January, as it will highlight where you feel passionate about your activities and which ones leave you cold.

HOME LIFE

You'll achieve a sense of purpose or belonging at home in January, even if this means you must leave it temporarily such as to go on holiday or visit family. You'll gain a renewed sense of place, and direction as a result. Certain aspects of your home life you share with others such as family or housemates are likely to alter mid-month, which will provide the opportunity to include more of those aspects of your home life you cherish.

February

WEEK 1: 30 JANUARY–5 FEBRUARY

This is a therapeutic week, so be sure to take the initiative with changes you know are for the better in all areas of your life. You'll enjoy socialising and may receive key news from a friend, group or organisation. A work matter will merit attention to avoid making decisions that could backfire in the future. Circumstances could be ideal, but you must check they align with your big-picture plans.

WEEK 2: 6–12 FEBRUARY

Serious decisions regarding your status and general direction are best taken carefully as you may be seeing life through rose-coloured glasses at the moment. Romance, music and the arts can thrive under these stars, but you must be careful with important decisions. The full moon suggests a fresh approach to communications will be successful, and you may be drawn to investing in a new device. A fresh approach to finances may also appeal.

WEEK 3: 13–19 FEBRUARY

This is an excellent week to develop deeper relationships with those you love, so be sure to take the initiative. Keep practicalities in mind and the rest will fall in place at work. A get-together or change of environment or atmosphere will prove illuminating in many ways, so be ready to accept invitations or go to events as these could be enjoyable as well as motivating.

WEEK 4: 20–26 FEBRUARY

Recent developments and their ramifications will begin to fall in place, giving you the heads-up in real terms and especially regarding an overseas, personal, spiritual or study matter. Take action and avoid distractions. A decision could impact considerably on your circumstances, so if you need to get legal advice it will be useful. Ensure you do your research as agreements this week will be binding.

FINANCES

Be prepared to get the lowdown financially when making key decisions to do with your work or status, as you may tend to be a little idealistic. Take nothing for granted with regard to financial decision-making, especially in areas you share such as joint finances and legal arrangements. You may receive a good strong financial offer through work or a legal matter or venture, but unless you look at it from all angles you may be prone to making mistakes.

HEALTH

Mars retrograde in your sign will continue to drain your energy levels, so it's important in February to maintain a strong fitness regime and keep an eye on your diet, especially if you know certain foods don't agree with you. Early and mid-February will be particularly conducive to improving your energy levels, so be sure to actively improve your health and fitness then. This will be a good month for spiritual self-development, so take the initiative.

LOVE LIFE

The month will begin with intense or even potentially life-changing circumstances precipitated by the new moon on 28 February. You'll gain the chance to reconfigure some of your romantic commitments and discuss your future with someone important to you. Singles may find that this month is decisive with regard to your status. If you're single and looking for a valued partner be sure to begin that search in earnest this month, as it's likely you'll find them.

CAREER

Significant developments are likely, especially if you're already clear about your direction. You may meet someone influential or who inadvertently changes the course of your career. Be prepared to take the initiative both at the start of the month and mid-month, as your efforts in this area will be worthwhile. Also be sure to sharpen your networking and negotiation skills to make the most of an opportunity to advance.

HOME LIFE

Karmic and soul connections are important to you, and this month more so than ever. Key decisions will merit consideration for your family and those you love to ensure everyone is on the same page. Your home and family are the nexus of your existence, so take this into account when making your choices and especially at the full moon on 12 February and at the new moon on the 28th.

March

WEEK 1: 27 FEBRUARY–5 MARCH

You'll relish the impression that life's many developments can represent more stability and security and, at the very least, you'll see hints of it. You could see a fresh start with a shared area such as your work or home. If you're studying, planning a trip or broadening your horizons in another way this week will be inspiring. Just avoid getting stuck in the past and be prepared to embrace new opportunities.

WEEK 2: 6–12 MARCH

Take positive steps with a business or personal matter, as you could open doors and experience an upbeat change in dynamics. A trip or change of pace will feel inspiring, so be sure to indulge in a little travel even if only for a breath of fresh air. You could negotiate a key agreement at work or regarding a legal, study or travel venture. Be sure to take the initiative.

WEEK 3: 13–19 MARCH

You may be drawn to two different aspects of yourself: the outgoing, romantic you and the other practical, realistic self who is keen to avoid making mistakes. A balance between the two will work to your advantage now. A get-together has a bittersweet quality, as it may involve a parting or reunion. If you're unsure about financial agreements, obtain expert advice. A career matter or project could blossom.

WEEK 4: 20–26 MARCH / WEEK 5: 27 MARCH–2 APRIL

WEEK 4: a careful and detailed appraisal of paperwork, plans and communications will bring you closer to a goal. You may receive an ideal offer or the chance to broaden your horizons at work but you may need to reassess whether your ideas are practical or idealistic. Romance is on the cards, and if you've been considering making a commitment this could be it! **WEEK 5:** you may be drawn to commencing an exciting project that brings your skill set into play. You'll enjoy a trip somewhere wonderful but must avoid delays by planning ahead. It's a great time to consider including more activities you love into your life, and you'll enjoy a reunion or bonding over a favourite pastime. If study appeals to you, you may meet an influential teacher.

FINANCES

The key to ensuring your finances remain healthy is to be well informed, and the better informed you are the better in March. You could make great progress financially so be positive, but also sure to do adequate research and especially regarding long-term investments. Avoid short-gap remedies to debt or short-term investments for now as you may find these too restrictive in the long term. The solar eclipse on 29 March will kick-start a fresh phase in your career that could improve your income, so be sure to be proactive in the lead-up.

HEALTH

You'll appreciate the sense that your energy levels are gradually improving, especially if you felt they were flagging over the last few months. You'll continue to gain a sense of vitality, and by early May if not before will feel you're back to your usual self. This is certainly a good time to invest in your health and well-being, as your efforts are going to pay off. Consider talking to various professionals if you feel you need some expert advice, as they will prove helpful.

LOVE LIFE

This will be a key month in your love life. If you're single and have been considering a new approach to romance or making a commitment, this month you're likely to undergo key developments that take you closer to a fresh understanding of yourself and your relationships. The last two weeks of the month will be particularly indicative of the changes to come during the year in this key aspect of your life.

CAREER

If you've been planning a fresh course for yourself in 2025 this is an excellent month to make things happen. Be sure to take advantage of developments that open fresh doors for you in your career. However, you must be prepared to let the past go and investigate new avenues, otherwise you're likely to get stuck. The eclipse season will contribute to different opportunities, so be sure to jump in.

HOME LIFE

The total lunar eclipse on 14 March will fall in your domestic sector, bringing the high likelihood of considerable change in your domestic life or family. This may occur due to the impact of changes in your status or career. For many, though, changes at home may affect your career so you must be sure to plan as best you can so that developments at home do not adversely impact your professionalism. You may receive key news and an unexpectedly positive development regarding a friend or organisation that proves particularly helpful.

April

WEEK 1: 3–9 APRIL

Mars makes a wonderful aspect with Saturn, so this is an excellent time to put form to your ideas and especially concerning arrangements and plans you share with others. You'll gain the chance to experience a therapeutic trip or project and a surprise will keep you on your toes. Venus meeting with stable Saturn suggests you're ready to make an agreement, especially concerning work, but you must avoid rushing into matters without forethought.

WEEK 2: 10–16 APRIL

A fortunate astrological aspect makes for positive progress, especially if you've already put in some groundwork regarding your career general direction and finances. You may receive an unexpected offer from a group, friend or organisation. An agreement can be made regarding your big-picture progress as key news or a meeting arise. Just avoid making rash decisions regarding health and well-being.

WEEK 3: 17–23 APRIL

You'll be entering fresh financial territory this week and could make serious headway both at work and with your various projects and ventures that will not only boost your bank account, but also your self-esteem. Developments may be life changing, so the commitments and agreements you make must be clear so you don't regret actions taken now.

WEEK 4: 24–30 APRIL

This is an excellent week to find ways to spend more time on your favourite pastimes and with the people you love and admire. If you didn't already experience changes in your career or status last week these may arise now. It's likely that you experience an ego or financial boost. The new moon on 27 April will encourage you to treat yourself and others to some of life's luxuries.

FINANCES

This is an excellent time to make cleverly researched financial and personal investments, as your efforts are likely to be successful. However, if you're drawn into fresh territory it will be vital that you explore your options in more detail and/or obtain expert advice. You may be drawn to a fresh perspective from a financial point of view regarding your home or a family or creative project.

HEALTH

You have a great deal of opportunity to broaden your horizons in April and enjoy adventure and a refreshing change of routine, and all of this will have a positive effect on your morale and therefore on your health. However, certain matters that will be legal in nature for some Cancerians may feel disorienting, so it will be important to find health and well-being modalities that keep you grounded and positive.

LOVE LIFE

This is likely to be a fairly passionate month, especially towards the end of April, and while this could be enjoyable you must avoid arguments and a battle of egos with someone you love as this could create a long-standing rift. Earlier in the month it will therefore be in your interest to carefully consider any talks concerning joint finances or duties and, if you're in a new relationship, boundaries. It's better to have your cards on the table.

CAREER

The alignment of Venus, Saturn, the moon's north node, Mercury and Neptune all point to your ability to innovate and bring more desired elements into your career and ventures. You may be increasingly drawn to a philosophical, spiritual but also idealistic approach to some of your ventures, so it's very important to maintain perspective and avoid making rash decisions. When you do you could make unprecedented progress, so take the initiative.

HOME LIFE

The full moon on 13 April falls in your domestic and family sectors. In both cases this full moon points to the end of one particular chapter regarding your home or family and therefore the beginning of a new chapter. There may well be a predestined or unavoidable circumstance that comes into play during April if it hasn't already, such as an age-related circumstance of someone in your home or career changes that dictate your circumstances.

May

WEEK 1: 1–7 MAY

You're imaginative and spiritual, and this week you'll enjoy letting your spirit soar and may be inspired by a person or event. Success will lie in careful research rather than making snap decisions at work. You may begin a fresh chapter in a collaboration or duty, and if you can get the details worked out before the weekend you'll relax all the more this weekend.

WEEK 2: 8–14 MAY

Get set to turn a corner in your personal life or with family or creative projects. If you're single be sure to make the effort to socialise as you may meet someone charismatic. The Scorpio full moon on 12 May will spotlight some of your plans and ideas as you turn a corner with those you love. You may bump into someone unexpectedly if you're single or hear from an ex.

WEEK 3: 15–21 MAY

A change of pace this weekend will certainly prove revitalising, whether you enjoy socialising, a fresh environment or pushing the boat out in a new direction. You'll also enjoy truly unwinding in different ways and an impromptu get-together. It's a great week to look for ways to improve your health and career and status, so be sure to take the initiative.

WEEK 4: 22–28 MAY

The new moon on 27 May signals a fresh health or work schedule and also the chance to rearrange how you share duties and responsibilities with someone either at work or in your personal life. This is likely to be a super sociable week and especially this weekend, and you'll appreciate the opportunity to reconnect with people close to your heart. You may bump into someone unexpectedly.

FINANCES

Mars in your finance sector will contribute to an improved outlook financially, especially mid-month and towards 22 May when your hard work could produce a financial boost in your bank account. However, with Mars in your finance sector you must be careful to avoid spending money faster than you make it, as you could regret impulse spending. You'll be drawn to investing in your social life towards the end of the month.

HEALTH

A lovely aspect between Jupiter and Chiron mid- to late May will encourage you to look for ways to improve your health and well-being. If you've been waiting for health news it's likely to come towards the 15th. Mid-May will also be a good time to consider a fresh health routine or treat yourself to a new wardrobe or look, as your efforts are likely to be successful, pleasing and effective.

LOVE LIFE

The Scorpio full moon on 12 May will place your attention on your love life, and if you're single you may bump into someone intriguing and passionate towards mid-May. Couples' attention will go to one another with a view to rekindling passion. The new moon on the 27th will help to revitalise aspects of the life you share with someone special and may bring the need to return to an old haunt. Singles may bump into an ex.

CAREER

You could land an ideal contract or project at work, so be sure to look out for opportunities and be inspired as new and worthwhile ventures could come your way in the first week of the month and also towards the end of May. Mid-month provides once again the chance to pitch for work projects, so be sure to communicate well with colleagues and organisations and be proactive and outgoing.

HOME LIFE

You'll gain traction in May on where you'd like to see your home life deliver more of what you consider a sense of purpose in your life. In the process you may need to undergo a tough decision or clear aspects of your past so you can move forward. Be sure to evaluate how you wish to invest in your home life, as sentimentality will otherwise keep you rooted in the past.

June

WEEK 1: 29 MAY–4 JUNE

This is a good time to build stability in your life and especially at work and with health and family. If some events seem restrictive, then consider practicalities first and everything will flow from there. If you're looking for work or are considering a fresh health schedule, seek the help of an expert or organisation.

WEEK 2: 5–11 JUNE

You'll enjoy socialising this weekend. As both Mercury and Jupiter enter your sign, this week you'll gain a taste of things to come. The full moon on 11 June will spotlight key developments either at work or a change in your daily routine. The more you can configure a situation that suits you the better for you, but you must factor into the situation the parameters of your work demands.

WEEK 3: 12–18 JUNE

A lovely aspect suggests you can deepen your understanding of someone and enjoy creativity and music. A changeable atmosphere may lead to indecision about activities and which events should be undertaken for the best results, but you needn't put the cat among the pigeons: just trust your instincts. A meeting, reunion or domestic development will be poignant. You can make great progress at work or health-wise, so take the initiative.

WEEK 4: 19–25 JUNE / WEEK 5: 26 JUNE–2 JULY

WEEK 4: the Cancer new moon on 25 June signifies a fresh chapter, especially if it's your birthday then or just before. You can turn a corner in an area that's been challenging. Romance could blossom, and this is also a good time to improve your appearance. If your birthday is after Wednesday a fresh chapter at work or regarding your health, status or career is on the way. Be clear about your intentions. **WEEK 5:** the sun and Jupiter in your sign will bring out your optimism, but also your idealism. If you've recently experienced or this week experience a disappointment, consider whether you would benefit from adjusting expectations to reality. You're in line for good financial or work news and will enjoy socialising and networking this weekend, so be sure to reach out.

FINANCES

The finances you share with someone, for example, a partner or housemate, or money in the common purse such as your taxes will be under the spotlight in June. The better you're able to collaborate with those you share financial duties or responsibilities with the better for you. Good communication skills, especially towards the end of June, will be necessary to avoid miscommunications at work and regarding your duties and obligations.

HEALTH

The presence of Mercury and Jupiter in your sign for much of the month and the sun from 21 June onwards will buoy your mood and create the perfect circumstances for improved health and well-being. However, you may be liable to overwork or overestimate what you are capable of doing this month, so be sure to pace yourself as otherwise you may find by the end of June that you need time out.

LOVE LIFE

The lead-up to the full moon on 11 June is likely to be fairly intense, and you're most likely to experience this in your personal life and collaborations. Luckily, Mercury in your sign from the 9th will help you communicate well, but you may feel more emotional than usual and talks could spiral as a result. Be sure to work gently with good communication skills and you'll overcome hurdles and could pave the way for a better relationship.

CAREER

You'll gain the opportunity to step into a fresh understanding of your position career-wise, especially if you're aiming for status. Someone in a position of authority will have their say, and good communication skills on your part will be rewarded. Be prepared to adapt to a fresh schedule as this will help you navigate some of the month's unexpected developments, especially mid-June. Beforehand, circumstances around the 9th will give you an idea of how best to tackle the month's developments.

HOME LIFE

Your home life is a source of nurturance and you do look for support when you're under pressure. As this month will present the opportunity to breathe fresh air into your work, health and status, your home life will assume an important presence as a place of refuge and sustenance. Find ways to both support those you love at home and ask for support if you need it. You may be pleasantly surprised by the result.

July

WEEK 1: 3–9 JULY

You may experience unusual or unexpected developments. You'll enjoy the chance to do something different, but equally will enjoy relaxing with someone special. A fresh daily schedule or work timetable will be exciting, but if it's a little confronting ensure you take the time to discuss your options with experts who can help, as developments will gain momentum.

WEEK 2: 10–16 JULY

You'll appreciate the opportunity to improve your daily routine through activities such as socialising, greater focus on your health and varying your schedule so you experience more fun in your life. You'll appreciate a return to an old haunt or positive news from work or financially. You'll experience a sense of purpose or predestiny in a personal or work context, which will be motivating.

WEEK 3: 17–23 JULY

While you're one of the strongest signs of the zodiac you can fall into the pitfall of hasty decision-making. This will be a true risk this week, especially in connection with your home life, work and where you derive a sense of belonging and meaning in your life. You'll enjoy a fun reunion towards the weekend but must avoid clashing with others early next week.

WEEK 4: 24–30 JULY

The new moon on 24 July signals a new chapter in your personal or financial life. You may succeed at a job or gain status, and work will bring results or the chance to turn a corner. Right when you may be feeling it's time to be a little ruthless or reckless you'll discover that, in fact, diligence will pay off, so avoid doing anything hasty and your patience will be rewarded.

FINANCES

You're likely to experience an improvement in finances during the third week of the month, as long as you avoid making hasty financial decisions and impulse buys. The new moon on 24 July could precipitate the need to make an important decision that would have long-term repercussions financially, so be prepared to seek expert advice if needed. A change in finances is likely to be tied with developments at work or in your status in general.

HEALTH

You'll enjoy improving your appearance and investing in both your looks and wardrobe. You may even consider a fresh way to boost your energy levels and health and seek a variety of options. However, during the final week of July you may feel that your health and wellness routine needs either to return to a tried and trusted schedule or that you need to regain vitality. Be sure to obtain expert advice if in doubt.

LOVE LIFE

The full moon on 10 July will spotlight your love life, and if you're looking for a commitment from someone special this could be a good time to ask. You may enjoy a reunion or reconnection with your past that feels exciting. It's a good time for couples to renew their vows, and if you're single to find ways to meet dependable yet also fun characters to be with.

CAREER

This is a good month to decide where you would like to see your career heading, as you'll gain the motivation to make the necessary changes both at work and in your personal life to pursue your chosen path. This will include potentially altering your daily schedule, including your health routine, to accommodate the activities you prefer to follow career-wise. You may receive an unexpected offer towards 23 July so be sure to put out feelers.

HOME LIFE

There is a strong sense of sentimentality in connection with your domestic life in July, so if important domestic decisions will alter your long-term outlook it will be important to ensure that decisions you make that affect your family or property are not based on nostalgia, as this would hold you back. Consider instead in practical yet inspired ways how to change aspects of your home life that no longer resonate with you.

August

WEEK 1: 31 JULY–6 AUGUST

A journey of discovery may take you into uncharted territory. Be sure to give yourself and others the benefit of the doubt, but also be prepared to move a treasured venture forward. If you experience a little confusion with a particular arrangement, consider focusing on building rapport as you'll gain ground as a result. A key get-together or news will spotlight a proactive way forward with a financial or personal matter.

WEEK 2: 7–13 AUGUST

The Venus–Jupiter conjunction in Cancer will place your attention on what and who you truly desire in your life, especially if you were born early in July. All Cancerians may be drawn to making a key commitment, either in your personal life or at work. You will also be prepared to take dynamic steps in your domestic life that could alter your status, so you must choose wisely.

WEEK 3: 14–20 AUGUST

This is an excellent week to get things done, especially at home and with colleagues. Initiate talks that can take you closer to your goals at work. It's also a good time to consider how much you spend on your home life or family. Talks or negotiations could help you configure a fresh budget that creates a sense of security. A proactive approach to health will boost your mood.

WEEK 4: 21–27 AUGUST

This is the week to go for your goals with full confidence that you can succeed. The Virgo new moon on 23 August will help boost your projects. You may find that you're ahead, but if you experience the reverse an agreement can be made in the shape of career support or finances. Some Cancerians will be ready to make a romantic commitment.

FINANCES

You may receive key financial news early in the month that will provide you with the incentive to review your finances and improve them, or strengthen your resolve to keep going with the arrangements you've already made. A little confusion early in the month to do either with work or money will provide clarity. Mid-August is an excellent time to discuss finances, and you may experience a personal or career boost then or towards the end of the month.

HEALTH

The conjunction of Venus and Jupiter in your sign on 12 August will put your focus on beauty, abundance and energy levels all month. You may gain in all these areas and mid-month feel particularly on track health-wise. It's certainly a good month to consider joining groups or organisations that have your health and well-being at the core of their activities, especially towards the 19th. A trip may be particularly therapeutic at this time, so consider organising a holiday.

LOVE LIFE

Venus in your sign until the 25th will certainly bring the focus to your love life in August. However, the month may open on a slightly tense note and is likely to encourage you to improve your communication abilities. Jupiter will conjunct Venus on the 12th, bringing an important focus onto your love life and especially if you were born early in July. You may make a key commitment to someone at this time that could alter your status.

CAREER

Chiron at the zenith of your chart may bring out your vulnerabilities, and rather than allowing this to make you feel inferior in any way, consider learning from developments in your career as you'll gain strength as a result this month. A favourable aspect between Mars, Uranus and Pluto could truly catapult your work life into fresh terrain, so be prepared to take the initiative.

HOME LIFE

Mars in your fourth house of home, family and property will motivate you to be more proactive in these areas of your life. You may be drawn to making changes that at any other time would seem out of the ordinary or unexpected. Mid-August will be particularly conducive to spending time and energy on your home life. If, though, you decide to visit someone else's home or enjoy a holiday, this is likely to be just as motivational.

September

WEEK 1: 28 AUGUST–3 SEPTEMBER

You're likely to gain ground with certain goals and plans you wish to act on and achieve. However, initially you may discover some communications or developments are either unexpected or will require more from you than you had initially hoped. Rest assured your hard work and diligence will pay off. You may enjoy a lovely reunion or boost at work.

WEEK 2: 4–10 SEPTEMBER

The Pisces total lunar eclipse on 7 September will shine a light on your career, status and general direction in life. If you feel that you have lost direction you're likely to regain it this week even if in unexpected ways. A domestic development will spotlight your true feelings. Someone you feel you have a fated connection with will be significant and could open doors for you.

WEEK 3: 11–17 SEPTEMBER

Key decisions or commitments can be made this week that will determine your path for some time to come concerning either your career, home life, family or a property. You may in the process enjoy a financial or personal boost. Be proactive and positive. However, certain conversations will merit tact and diplomacy to avoid giving or taking offence.

WEEK 4: 18–24 SEPTEMBER / WEEK 5: 25 SEPTEMBER–1 OCTOBER

WEEK 4: this weekend's solar eclipse brings into being a fresh chapter in your home life or with family or a property. You may need to enter into a serious agreement or make a commitment. You're heading into fresh territory with regard to shared resources and, for some, at work. This promises to be an exciting phase, so avoid being daunted by challenges. **WEEK 5:** where do you see yourself moving forward? It's important to be clear about this now, as you have a wonderful opportunity to move things in the direction you want to be moving towards and especially career-wise and at home. Just be sure that you're being realistic and looking at things from a fair and equal perspective, as Jupiter in Cancer currently could mean you underestimate the reality of circumstances.

FINANCES

September brings the opportunity to make considerable changes in your life, not only financially but also at home, in your career, the areas of your life you share and at work. Your finances will inevitably need focus as you're likely to be making some serious commitments and/or financial transactions. Be sure to seek financial advice if you're unclear about your options as you may otherwise be liable to make ill-informed choices or snap decisions.

HEALTH

In September you risk biting off more than you can chew energy-wise, which means it will be vital that you create the perfect environment in which to recharge your batteries when you do have some downtime. The days around the eclipse on 21 September and towards the 30th will spotlight important decisions that require a clear mind, so be sure to avoid being drawn into distractions or arguments that take your eye off the ball.

LOVE LIFE

While Jupiter in your sign can certainly bring a sense of joy your way you will also tend to see others in a larger than life perspective, so if you find yourself at odds with anyone just double-check that your perspective is balanced, as this process will help you avoid arguments and taking risks. The lunar eclipse on 7 September could bring in a fresh phase in your status; for example, from single to married or from married to single.

CAREER

If you've been looking for a promotion or new job be sure to circulate your resumé, as you are likely to strike gold and especially around the lunar eclipse on 7 September and the solar eclipse on the 21st. You'll be in a position to make important arrangements and agreements that could considerably alter your status and career. Just be sure to research your options carefully to avoid disappointment at a later date.

HOME LIFE

Domestic developments early in the month are best approached carefully and methodically so that negotiations are peaceful and productive, not frustrating or argumentative. The solar eclipse on 21 September indicates a fresh chapter is about to begin in your home or regarding a property or family, and that this can have a knock-on effect with broader developments. Be sure to consider the big picture at all times when making decisions to avoid mistakes.

October

WEEK 1: 2–8 OCTOBER

A change of atmosphere at home such as the presence of a visitor or a trip will cause a flurry of activity, but your efforts will be worthwhile. You'll enjoy a get-together. A meeting with a friend or organisation will be therapeutic, although you must be super careful with communications and remind yourself of all your many good qualities to boost self-confidence. Be careful with financial transactions to avoid making mistakes.

WEEK 2: 9–15 OCTOBER

A key decision will come down to practicalities. If you must focus on work, ensure you also give extra time to loved ones. If you make changes at home, consider how these may affect your status or career. You're likely to start to discover this week whether you have over- or underestimated someone and will as a result manage to get things back on track.

WEEK 3: 16–22 OCTOBER

Get ready for a fresh set of dynamics in your home life or family or regarding a property. This is a good time for home decorating and romance and for improving relationships with those at home, so be sure to take the initiative. Be sensitive to the feelings of other people, especially around 18 October, as otherwise feelings could be hurt and prospectively yours. Romance or a project could thrive early next week.

WEEK 4: 23–29 OCTOBER

This will be an excellent week to truly invest in yourself and it will be in the guise of backing your projects and believing in yourself. You may boost your status and direction in life and may be surprised by developments that are unusual or healing in nature as you step into a fresh, potentially abundant phase.

FINANCES

A tough aspect early in the month suggests that a financial review will be beneficial for you, especially if you're already in debt and have not yet found a way to stem spending. It will be a good time to research experts and advisers who could help you move forward financially. Jupiter in Cancer generally brings abundance but it does make some tough aspects between 17 and 21 October, so be sure to avoid gambling and overspending then.

HEALTH

Your usual daily routine and activities are likely to undergo considerable change in October, so as you configure a fresh schedule be sure to factor in space and time for health and well-being as otherwise you may be inclined to focus on changes at work and in your status and at home. Developments from the 20th onwards will encourage you to infuse your daily routine and health schedule with more passion and activities you love.

LOVE LIFE

The second week in October is potentially a romantic time for you. If you've been considering making a commitment to someone, this is it! However, you must be sure that what you perceive is true as you may otherwise experience disappointments in your love life that come down to differences in values or a financial disagreement. The conjunction between Mercury and Mars on the 20th before the new moon could be perfect for a romantic get-together.

CAREER

You'll gain the opportunity to make a commitment to a particular career path. You may discover new interests that encourage you to consider fresh territory that entails doing more of what you love. The second half of the month especially could see increased opportunities, so be sure to keep an eye out. If you don't work, the commitment will stem from your domestic obligations and have an impact on your big-picture status.

HOME LIFE

The first week of October and mid-month are excellent times to invest energy in your home, property or domestic relationships, as your efforts are likely to succeed. A reunion or return to an old haunt will be inspiring and may motivate you to make further domestic changes. If you need help at home, rest assured you'll find the manpower. If you've been considering a move, this would be a good month to undertake it.

November

WEEK 1: 30 OCTOBER–5 NOVEMBER

You may be surprised by developments this week, as unexpected news comes your way. The supermoon on 5 November will highlight strong emotions, as you re-evaluate certain friendships, loyalties and activities. You have every opportunity to boost your career, finances and status but must be discerning about who you spend your invaluable time and efforts with. Avoid financial and emotional gambling.

WEEK 2: 6–12 NOVEMBER

Abundant Jupiter turns retrograde, bringing a change of focus in your personal life, finances and general direction. If you have key decisions to make, try to get your plans on the table before 9 November to avoid delays further down the line. This weekend will bring romance and people you admire into your sphere, so plan an event if possible. Just avoid arguments for the best results.

WEEK 3: 13–19 NOVEMBER

Positive developments could take you into new territory. There may nevertheless be a sense of déjà vu or, at the very least, familiarity with your circumstances. It's certainly a good week to take the initiative with your various projects both at work and in your personal life, with the proviso that you exercise patience as some developments will move quickly while others are liable to do the opposite.

WEEK 4: 20–26 NOVEMBER / WEEK 5: 27 NOVEMBER–3 DECEMBER

WEEK 4: be prepared to turn a corner at work or in your personal life, depending on your birth date. You may receive unexpected news from the past or from a friend, group or organisation that has a bearing on a new chapter that unfolds. Some Cancerians will be prepared to approach your health from a fresh perspective, in the big picture enabling you to gain strength, purpose and self-esteem.
WEEK 5: a chance meeting or the opportunity to catch up with someone who always has a refreshing take on life will motivate you to do something different this week. A focus on boosting your career and finances will be rewarding. This is a lovely week for romance, music and creativity, so be sure to invest in your favourite activities and reach out to those whose company you love.

FINANCES

A lovely aspect between Saturn and Jupiter provides the opportunity to boost finances early in November. You may be surprised by developments at work that enable you to take optimistic steps, for some in fresh territory. If you have a tendency to gamble this is unlikely to work out for you, especially around the supermoon on 5 November. If some financial development seem slow, the end of November and December will bring a smoother cash flow.

HEALTH

There is the chance of bumps, knocks and minor accidents early in November, so be sure to take your time and avoid rushing, especially around the 4th. Mercury turns retrograde in your sixth house of health on the 9th, which will enable you to review and replan your health schedules in your own time during the rest of November. However, you may feel slightly lacking in energy so ensure you avoid fatigue by pacing yourself and improving your diet.

LOVE LIFE

Your social life is likely to come full circle, so if you've been very sociable you're likely to wish to seek your own company more and vice versa. Singles may feel particularly drawn to socialising around the supermoon on 5 November and couples may experience stronger emotions than usual. You're naturally intuitive, and your intuition will prove invaluable if you hit speed bumps. You'll regain a sense of flow at the end of November and further into December.

CAREER

Positive astrological aspects early in the month point to a wonderful opportunity to improve your career and status. You're likely to feel motivated at the very least to enter fresh territory work-wise. Be sure to make the most of this proactive phase. You may be surprised by developments before the full moon supermoon on 5 November. If you're considering making new legal agreements, try to get paperwork on the table before the 8th to avoid delays.

HOME LIFE

Ask yourself where you derive your feelings of belonging the most. It's a feeling that you can expect from your home, and if it's lacking you'll feel increasingly motivated this month to establish a sense of belonging. A return to an old haunt or visit from someone close will remind you how important a happy home is. You have wonderful opportunities to improve many of your circumstances, so be sure to factor your home life into your considerations.

December

WEEK 1: 4–10 DECEMBER

You'll enjoy a get-together or event that may be therapeutic. A situation will benefit from expert advice. You may begin a fresh work or financial contract or must look at new ways to boost health. Trust your instincts. A career or personal commitment will be long lasting. Be prepared to negotiate and listen to expert advice, and avoid getting stuck in details that may no longer be greatly relevant.

WEEK 2: 11–17 DECEMBER

While there is a go-ahead atmosphere at work and the opportunity to boost health, if you have important decisions to make bear in mind that it's virtually impossible to make choices if key facts are missing. Ensure you do your research. The entry of Mars in your opposite sign of Capricorn will bring focus to your love life over the coming weeks but may initially spotlight differences of opinion.

WEEK 3: 18–24 DECEMBER

The new moon on 20 December will kick-start a fresh chapter for you in your daily routine that will include work and health. You'll appreciate the opportunity to indulge in your favourite activities with your favourite people, which will feel therapeutic and especially around the 18th. At the solstice, however, it will be in your interest to be careful with communications to avoid misunderstandings.

WEEK 4: 25–31 DECEMBER

A change of routine or location may be appealing and revitalising, but you must be prepared to adjust to new circumstances. You'll appreciate the social aspect of the week and will find certain meetings particularly therapeutic. This is a good week to attend to your health and well-being, and if someone asks for your help it will of course be available and vice versa.

FINANCES

A development regarding your career or status could also boost your finances. A fresh chapter is about to begin in a work context or in your usual daily routine, which will automatically impact your finances. Developments around 18 December are likely to be positive. However, if you haven't budgeted carefully you may find the pre-Christmas week a little taxing financially, so it will be in your interest to put in place a careful contingency plan for the month.

HEALTH

This is a good month to invest in your health and well-being, as your efforts are likely to be productive. A group, friend or organisation may be particularly constructive where health is concerned. You'll enjoy team sports and activities that develop a sense of creativity and spirituality, so investing in your mental health will also be productive. The Christmas week will be enjoyable as you'll love the social atmosphere, but you must avoid difficult communications towards New Year's Eve.

LOVE LIFE

Mars in your seventh house of partnerships from 15 December will revitalise your love life, and you'll appreciate experiencing more earthy and sensual aspects of your existing relationship. Singles may discover you seem more attractive to others during the festive season and will enjoy the attention. In the final week of the month you'll appreciate an increasing sense of togetherness in an existing relationship, especially if you devote extra attention to good verbal and non-verbal communication skills.

CAREER

The supermoon on 4 December will kick-start a fresh phase at work, and for some Cancerians a new agreement or arrangement will be made with a group or organisation. The first two weeks are excellent for moving ahead career-wise and you may experience an unexpected development that could take you into different territory. It's certainly a good month to trust your intuition when making considerable changes in your work life. You'll feel enthusiastic about renewed direction.

HOME LIFE

Mid-month important decisions – for many to do with work and your general direction – will also have an impact on where you feel you belong. Your home is your principal seat of belonging, but if you're unsure about how to best navigate moving ahead then do your research and gather information to avoid having to make uninformed decisions that will have a long-term impact on your home.

January

WEEK 1: 1–8 JANUARY

Working Leos will be busy, and if you're organising events with family, at home or with a partner your efforts will be worthwhile. Just avoid being easily distracted and ensure you're clear if you're making long-range agreements to avoid mix-ups. Romance could flourish, but you must check you're not seeing the world through rose-coloured glasses. Someone may wish to make a commitment to you.

WEEK 2: 9–15 JANUARY

Music, dance and romance will all appeal to you this week, but you may need to keep an eye on fatigue, health and well-being and especially if you're back at work and need to curb some of your holiday activities. That said, a change of environment or pace will be enjoyable. A work, personal or shared circumstance will require more tact and a sensitive approach to someone who can be fiery.

WEEK 3: 16–22 JANUARY

A change of routine will boost your mood, but you must be well prepared, have a plan of action and be ready to adapt to a new environment. A financial or work boost could be on the way and, at the very least, a work or health matter will draw your focus. A change of routine or health matter may bring out strong emotions. Someone close may have surprising news mid-week.

WEEK 4: 23–29 JANUARY

The Aquarian new moon on 29 January points to a fresh start in a close relationship if you were born in July, and a fresh daily or health routine if you were born in August. You may be surprised by developments, and a different approach to someone may be necessary. Lateral thinking will help. If you've been stuck in conflict, aim to move ahead with cleverly chosen words and intentions. Avoid taking the emotional turmoil of other people personally.

FINANCES

Crucial matters to do with shared ventures such as joint financial responsibilities and shared domestic expenses will require an original approach. Otherwise, those you share financial arrangements with may see you as unreliable when perhaps you see them this way. Returning to work in January will put your expenses and duties in a new light, and you may see that some duties are best shared and therefore mutually agreeable arrangements must be made.

HEALTH

There is no better time than the start of the year to put your New Year's resolutions to good use to boost your health. A fun activity or group venture will help you in this endeavour. You may discover that a particular relationship proves to be therapeutic on many more levels than purely romantic. However, with Mars retrograde in your sign until early February, avoid feeling you are doing something wrong health-wise if your energy levels are below par. Simply pace yourself.

LOVE LIFE

You'll be feeling adventurous and open minded about your love life in January, which will create a fun, outgoing mindset for singles. You're likely to meet someone who seems perfect but you must double-check you're actually on the same page. Couples will be drawn to new adventures such as travel, broadening your knowledge of each other or your relationship and generally improving your love life or relationship in fresh ways. The Aquarian new moon on 29 January will signal a fresh agreement, especially for July-born Leos.

CAREER

There will be several reasons including looking after your health and well-being to alter the course of your career in 2025. You may realise, for example, that your health is your most important asset and will alter your career duties accordingly, or will be drawn to working in the health sector. The full moon mid-month offers you the chance to continue as you are or begin something new. Be open to moving into fresh areas or collaborating with different people as opportunity will knock!

HOME LIFE

You're far too busy having adventures in January to pay attention to your home because there are people to visit and potentially countries or states to travel to, yet those you love such as family and friends would love to spend some downtime with you in your territory. A risk in January is that you're caught in a spiral due to overwork or overplay and will then need your home for rest rather than relaxation.

February

WEEK 1: 30 JANUARY—5 FEBRUARY

A favourite activity or person will make your heart soar this week, and romance will be alive. You may be ready to turn a corner in your personal or professional life as a fresh circle or group will appeal. Take your time to plan for lovely creative, upbeat activities. You'll enjoy getting together with like-minded people, and someone may need your help. Avoid knee-jerk reactions and research your options carefully to avoid making mistakes.

WEEK 2: 6—12 FEBRUARY

The Leo full moon on 12 February signals the chance to turn an important corner in your finances. Some Leos will be drawn to expressing a fresh intention in your personal life, with key talks being a hallmark of the need to make changes. You'll also be drawn to the arts, study, spiritual development or travel: anything that broadens your mind and frees your spirit. Just be sure to focus on work if you're not on holiday!

WEEK 3: 13—19 FEBRUARY

A trip, visit or conversation could lead to a fresh understanding of someone who may at times seem mysterious or elusive. It's a great week to plan a trip somewhere beautiful or embellish your surroundings at home and work. It's also a good time to improve your relationships. Adapting to fresh dynamics may take extra patience, so aim to usher more luxury into your daily life and enjoy a little sumptuousness in the process.

WEEK 4: 20—26 FEBRUARY

Keep communications clear as you may be prone to misunderstandings or will discover your expectations far exceed the realities of circumstances. If a trip or important health matter must be attended to, ensure you're clear and plan ahead to avoid delays. Someone has key news, and it could be what you've been waiting for to make a binding agreement. If you're unsure, get the facts you need.

FINANCES

Your chickens come home to roost now, so if you've been prudent financially until now you could make wonderful headway as your investments pay off. However, if debt has been accruing it's likely to snowball, so it'll be important to head this trend off. The new moon on the 28th will be beneficial for putting a fresh financial plan in place. The help of an organisation will be useful.

HEALTH

Pluto in your health zone all year brings to mind how important this aspect of your life is. For Leos born between 24 and 26 July Pluto will bring most change to your personal life, but for most it will impact your health and well-being and encourage you to make the necessary changes to ensure you're healthy in mind, body and spirit. If you don't make the necessary changes yourself Pluto has the habit of making you, so it's far better to take the initiative and then your efforts will pay off.

LOVE LIFE

This will be an excellent month to kick-start fresh plans in your personal life, and if you feel change has been on the way for some time but hasn't yet materialised this month's full moon on 12 February could jettison you into fresh circumstances. If you're looking for love be sure to look for someone compatible, with the 1st, 9th and 25th being particularly promising. Couples may receive unexpected news that has an impact on your relationship. A fresh way to share important assets or duties will unfold this month.

CAREER

As a new approach to your career and status takes hold you'll be drawn to planning ahead carefully and realistically. The full moon on 12 February will spotlight certain elements of your career that are unpredictable or frustrating, which will enable you to consider how best to plan ahead for your long-term well-being in your chosen field. Some may, however, discover that a particular relationship is on shaky ground and as a result discover that your career offers you security.

HOME LIFE

While you're busy transforming aspects of your work and personal relationships in February your home takes a poor second place, yet it will be important to figure your home and property into some of your decisions and especially those that concern shared assets or responsibilities. It would otherwise be a pitfall to see shared duties purely in an idealistic light as opposed to the way in which changing some of your arrangements will affect your home life or family.

March

WEEK 1: 27 FEBRUARY—5 MARCH

You're likely to enter fresh territory with someone close or a partnership. Be ready to make mutually beneficial agreements and don't be afraid to ask for clarity where there is uncertainty, especially regarding shared duties, but you must be sure to avoid arguments. Be tactful and prepared to look for innovative solutions should issues arise. A trip or exciting project will be enlivening.

WEEK 2: 6—12 MARCH

You can make headway at work and financially. However, you may be prone to making snap decisions or assumptions, so ensure you maintain perspective. You'll enjoy connecting with someone who means a lot to you even if some aspects of your get-together are challenging. An exciting project, trip or work agreement could ring in long-term changes. A legal agreement must be adequately researched.

WEEK 3: 13—19 MARCH

The lunar eclipse on 14 March will spotlight where you might be more practical, especially financially and in your interpersonal relationships and business. You may receive key news. A trip or the need to plan travel will arise. You'll gain insight into your feelings and those of someone close. You may experience an unexpected boost at work or in your social life, but if you feel let down take steps to build a more solid foundation that can succeed.

WEEK 4: 20—26 MARCH / WEEK 5: 27 MARCH—2 APRIL

WEEK 4: this week's sun–Neptune conjunction spells indulgence in your favourite activities and pastimes. You may enjoy travel or contact with someone who is wildly idealistic or romantic. Neptune is known to mislead and misdirect, so be sure if you're making considerable financial changes that you research facts adequately. Work could be particularly productive. **WEEK 5:** a new arrangement or contract may be appealing, but you must check it aligns with your big-picture values. It's a good week to consider opportunities to improve work and health. A lovely place will be attractive. Someone special such as an expert, adviser or friend will help you with key decisions. Seek advice if you're considering big investments.

FINANCES

Revealing information and a surprising boost at work could improve your finances, so be bold if you're asked to step into a more senior role but ensure you are adequately paid. The lunar eclipse on 14 March could bring a fortunate new financial cycle, so be sure to be open to opportunities. Try to get agreements on the table before mid-March if possible and avoid overspending towards the end of the month. The saying 'Neither a borrower nor lender be' applies this month.

HEALTH

Pluto in your health sector continues to bring the opportunity to transform your health. You may be particularly drawn to investigating new ideas and treatments that complement existing therapies, such as a diet or fitness regime that supports your constitution. A favourable aspect around the time of the lunar eclipse suggests you could find a teacher or another professional who will help you boost your health.

LOVE LIFE

You'll be inspired, enthused and motivated to enjoy this aspect of your life this month, so plan ahead! a key meeting or news early in the month will fire up your imagination as you gain an unexpected opportunity to invest more time in your love life and in someone special. Couples will appreciate being more imaginative and inventive to boost your love life, and if you're single you may wish to commit to someone special.

CAREER

An unexpected or unusual opportunity to boost your career and status is not to be missed. This month's lunar eclipse on 14 March could bring a fresh agreement or collaboration that takes your career into a positive direction but you may need to undergo a course correction in the process. The enthusiasm of a friend or organisation will boost your confidence regarding new pathways. Be prepared to step into something new but be practical with financial considerations.

HOME LIFE

Your imagination and inventiveness are peaking and you'll be looking for activities and pastimes that really strike a chord. For now, many of these will not directly involve your home life because you'll be drawn to travelling and deepening certain relationships, and to learning new skill sets and broadening your horizons. It is likely then that your home life becomes a place for rest, yet all the more precious because of it.

April

WEEK 1: 3–9 APRIL

You could manage to secure a commitment from someone. However, a project or investment may require a little more attention if you prefer your activities to proceed on an even keel. A change of circumstance or an impromptu visit will cast a fresh light on your ideas. Be open to new notions and receptive to the viewpoints of other people as they may be illuminating.

WEEK 2: 10–16 APRIL

You may be drawn to making a personal or financial commitment to a person or venture that promises to be successful. You may be pleasantly surprised by an offer that could considerably alter your status and direction in life. The full moon on 13 April spotlights developments at home for some Leos, and for others the chance to take an exciting trip and improve your communications device or vehicle.

WEEK 3: 17–23 APRIL

Developments will be decisive, and you may need to dig deep to demonstrate a great sense of responsibility and duty. Romantic Leos may be prepared to make a considerable commitment to someone special or break an agreement. Working Leos could make great progress at work, but you must avoid rushing into projects without forethought.

WEEK 4: 24–30 APRIL

You're likely to make a considerable financial or personal decision or commitment this week. It will be long-standing, so it's important the decision is correct. If you're unsure, get expert advice. You may be drawn to travelling, studying and creative expression, which will prove to be fulfilling. You may experience an unexpected boost at work or in your status.

FINANCES

This is an optimal week for financial decision-making, especially choices in connection with a long-term investment, travel or joint duties and responsibilities. Some aspects of your financial situation may be inevitable or anticipated, and you'll find that your status or career direction can improve in unexpected ways as a result. Just be sure around the full moon on 13 April and the new moon on the 27th that you don't undertake risky financial behaviour such as gambling.

HEALTH

Your actions in April will determine how you feel, so be sure to choose ventures and projects that bring you a sense of achievement and progress as you otherwise risk feeling stuck. There is the opportunity in April to move on from circumstances that no longer suit you, so it's in your interest to consider options in genuine terms and take appropriate action to synchronise your head and heart as this is the path to true good health.

LOVE LIFE

If your focus has been on love, developments this month will be transformational. Someone close may have important news that affects aspects of the life you share, such as joint finances and duties. Even if some of their actions are not initially to your liking, some developments this month will have unexpectedly good if not enjoyable outcomes. If you're single and wish to find a companion, this is your month! It's a good month to make a commitment.

CAREER

You may experience unexpected developments that will revolve around a fresh agreement or arrangement, either in your personal life or at work, that puts you on a slightly different career trajectory. You may be surprised by the opportunities that arise. The Taurus new moon on 27 April points to the possibility of a more stable phase in your career, so be prepared to commit to a secure course of action.

HOME LIFE

The full moon on 13 April falls in your home sector, suggesting you gain the chance to alter aspects of your home life that could create an increased sense of peace, harmony and balance at home. This may come about through a change at work or in the situation of someone who is close to you. You're moving towards a fresh understanding of yourself and your priorities, which will be reflected in developments at home and/or with family.

May

WEEK 1: 1–7 MAY

This is a romantic week, so if you have nothing planned yet arrange a treat! However, if you're making career plans it's important you are super clear to avoid making mistakes. Avoid idealism; be realistic now regarding your work and projects as you could otherwise make mistakes. That said, a change of routine such as a holiday or break will be wonderful.

WEEK 2: 8–14 MAY

This week's Scorpio full moon will shine a light on domestic developments. Take the time to process developments as emotions may run high, either your feelings or those of someone close. A situation at work or a change in status may be unexpected, although positive communications are likely to produce a successful outcome.

WEEK 3: 15–21 MAY

Mars in your sign will add to the sense of adventure or at the very least a feeling of restlessness and wishing to be more active in life. You'll enjoy taking steps to bring more delights into your life such as planning a trip or fun event or being more adventurous in your private life and at work. You're communicating well, so be sure to enjoy being gregarious: within reason!

WEEK 4: 22–28 MAY

Get set for more variety and a faster pace over the coming days because the new moon on 27 May will reinvigorate your work and interactions and could open new doors, as a fresh agreement or work opportunity is in the air. You will be drawn to socialising more and spending time with like-minded people. You may unexpectedly bump into an old friend.

FINANCES

Pluto retrograde in your work zone could slow the pace at work in early May, which could decrease income if you're self-employed. However, there is a wonderful opportunity towards the end of the month to improve your financial circumstances as a work or personal development improves your self-esteem and ability to generate income. You may need to discuss new options with a friend or organisation, so be open to options but avoid taking uncalculated risks.

HEALTH

If you're drawn to a short break or planning a holiday your activities are likely to raise morale and boost well-being. A favourite activity or romance will certainly buoy your mood. Pluto retrograde in your work and health zone from 4 May could slow the pace at work, which could work in your favour if you utilise the additional energy you gain from working less to boost your health. Be sure to maximise the use of your free time to improve stamina.

LOVE LIFE

You'll appreciate the chance in May to demonstrate your adventurousness and sense of fun, especially towards the second half of the month. You will be drawn to expressing yourself more vividly and may find as a result you socialise and network more, enjoying travel and diverse interests. In the process you'll be meeting new people if you're single, and if you're a couple you'll enjoy bringing more of a sense of fun and light-heartedness to your relationship.

CAREER

The Venus–Neptune conjunction at the start of May will inspire you to engage in activities that really inspire you. You could land an ideal contract or circumstance, but if you're unsure about whether to make changes in your career be sure to research the situation and avoid making assumptions. A change of pace in early May will add a sense of purpose to your career, even if the pace seems slow. A positive opportunity at the end of May will also arise.

HOME LIFE

The Scorpio full moon on 12 May will highlight strong feelings domestically that may lead to a fresh understanding of how invested you are in a particular place or a person. You may need to make changes at home due to unexpected developments that are outside your control. A change of environment is likely to be conducive to growth and improved relationships, so avoid feeling stuck and find ways to breathe fresh air into your home life. A trip may appeal.

June

WEEK 1: 29 MAY–4 JUNE

A carefully laid plan will produce the best results, so if events demand that you make a decision based on a hunch or on little other than your preferences, ensure you do your research first to avoid misunderstandings and making mistakes. You'll obtain news from a group, friend or organisation and will enjoy socialising.

WEEK 2: 5–11 JUNE

You'll appreciate a therapeutic development this week, although you may be surprised by some news. There are certain people and events you are enveloped in, and you might call these fated. Now, developments will shine a light on where you must focus. For some this will be on family and those close to you and for others on your social life and the organisations you interrelate with.

WEEK 3: 12–18 JUNE

You're in the position to make solid progress with your career or in connection with an organisation, so if you have important progress you'd like to make this is your week to be proactive. However, you may encounter some surprises and the need to adjust some of your expectations in the process. It may simply come down to differences in values.

WEEK 4: 19–25 JUNE / WEEK 5: 26 JUNE–2 JULY

WEEK 4: be ready to implement the positive changes you'd like to see at work or with your favourite ventures. A new friendship or your relationship with an organisation could signal a refreshing way ahead, so take the initiative with your ventures. An interest or favourite activity may require a new approach, especially if you discover that your expectations are not met. **WEEK 5:** Mercury in your sign will improve your communication abilities, and you'll appreciate the opportunity to spend time with some of your favourite people doing some of your favourite activities. However, if you've recently experienced some friction with anyone in particular or even in an organisation it would be wise to be careful with communications this weekend and at the start of next week, as intense talks are likely.

FINANCES

Mars in Leo will bring out your generosity and tendency towards being a big spender when the mood takes you. However, tough astrological aspects early in the month will reveal whether you'll need to rein in your spending. If not, you'll enjoy spending money on activities such as holidays, study and self-development. Some Leos will experience a considerable financial boost if you have been working towards a bonus.

HEALTH

Mars in your sign makes a fortunate aspect with Chiron, known as the 'wounded healer' in Greek mythology. This astrological aspect between Mars and Chiron is an excellent opportunity to truly boost your health. However, for some Leos this aspect could magnify already-existing health issues, pointing to the need to visit a medical expert or adviser. Be sure to do the latter if your health has been underperforming, as you're likely to experience good healing.

LOVE LIFE

June will be a good month to focus on those you love and find ways to interrelate better to bring a closer feeling. The full moon on the 11th will encourage you to turn a corner with someone close and create a therapeutic yet fun atmosphere in your relationship. However, if you sense that your aims and goals are completely different, June may be the month when you finally go your separate ways.

CAREER

Chiron at the apex of your chart suggests you'll be undertaking new projects in your career and general direction. In some ways you may feel that you have not attained the goals you previously set yourself, yet there is a powerfully therapeutic aspect to the month that will enable you to recharge batteries and overcome feelings of inadequacy. A fortunate aspect on 10 June will encourage you to be proactive, but you must avoid overstating your case.

HOME LIFE

A great deal of focus will revolve around your status, and for many this points to preoccupation with your career. However, if your status comes from your home life, family or property you'll gain traction in June that could transform your home life. The key to success domestically relies on understanding your vulnerabilities while working proactively towards strengthening your position. You may benefit from the help of an expert if you're making considerable changes at home.

July

WEEK 1: 3–9 JULY

Activities may take you outside your usual territory or will demand you be more adaptable, especially socially. You may receive unexpected news and will be busy or in demand. Look at the bigger picture to ascertain where life could perhaps provide you with more fulfilment. If you find you're constantly at loggerheads with someone, look for ways to defuse the tension as otherwise arguments could escalate.

WEEK 2: 10–16 JULY

If you're looking for more security at work or in your personal life without losing a sense of fun and spontaneity, this is the ideal week to do just that. The Capricorn full moon on 10 July will spotlight ways to create more stability in your work and health. You may hear unexpectedly good news from a group or organisation, so be prepared to take the initiative.

WEEK 3: 17–23 JULY

You'll feel revitalised next week as the sun enters your sign, but beforehand a tough aspect involving Venus suggests you may have a difficult decision or experience conflicting feelings about someone so some decisions this week are best taken with expert advice and research. Try to get important decisions clear in your mind by Friday, as otherwise some arrangements will need to be rethought at a later date.

WEEK 4: 24–30 JULY

The Leo new moon on 24 July points to a fresh chapter in your personal life, especially if it's your birthday on Thursday. If you were born on or after 25 July a fresh chapter either at work or in your health schedule will arise that promises to bring exciting new ventures your way. Be prepared to negotiate with someone who can be intense.

FINANCES

You are known for being generous to those you love. This month you'll gain the opportunity to decide whether to lock in particular financial agreements or on the other hand to wait to see how certain relationships pan out. Your best approach is to research options so that you have a clear plan and try to do the heavy lifting in this regard by 18 July, when Mercury turns retrograde. Above all, avoid gambling.

HEALTH

A friend or organisation will be particularly helpful health-wise during the first and second weeks of the month, so take the initiative if you'd like to gain more information about your health. The third week of July will bring key news in the field of health and the new moon on 24 July will be an excellent time to configure a transformative health and well-being schedule that includes activities you enjoy.

LOVE LIFE

You'll enjoy a livelier social life and may be drawn to joining a new club or group of like-minded people. This will have the effect of improving your primary relationships and bring your focus more into your favourite interests, which will boost your mood. You may hear from someone from your past. Singles may meet someone who seems familiar yet you have never met, so keep an eye out towards 7, 12 and 24 July.

CAREER

This is a good month to be proactive and positive about creating a solid platform for yourself in your career. An outgoing, sociable and upbeat approach to your career and those you work with will be productive, especially in the first week of July. Certain connections you already have may be particularly productive. The new moon on the 24th may kick-start a fresh daily or work schedule, which could involve more projects and activities you enjoy.

HOME LIFE

You may need to decide where your loyalties lie in at least some aspects of your personal life in July, and the decisions you make are likely to affect your home life. As a sentimental character you prefer to be loyal to those you have known for a long time. However, you may need to rethink some of your commitments, especially around the new moon in your sign on the 24th.

August

WEEK 1: 31 JULY–6 AUGUST

The conjunction of the sun and Mercury in your sign on 1 August will bring key news in your personal life if you were born in July, and at work or regarding health if you were born in August. You'll feel motivated to move your projects forward or step into fresh territory. Ensure you plan well ahead to avoid mix-ups, delays and misunderstandings.

WEEK 2: 7–13 AUGUST

You're likely to receive key news either from your past or at work that will provide you with the necessary insight to make a decision that will affect your bigger-picture life moving forward. The full moon on 9 August will spotlight a significant business or personal relationship, making this a week of change. You could make great progress at work and health-wise, so be sure to be proactive.

WEEK 3: 14–20 AUGUST

Communications and interactions are likely to increase in volume and quality, both at home and at work. You'll enjoy a trip or visit. A financial or career matter is likely to improve. However, you may need to undergo talks or developments that bring out your vulnerability. If you show your best traits it could actually be a therapeutic development for you.

WEEK 4: 21–27 AUGUST

The new moon on 23 August will provide more clarity about how your life will progress, especially in terms of finances and your personal life. This is the ideal week for research, as your efforts to move ahead with clarity are likely to be well rewarded. A personal or health- or sports-related commitment can be made. A favourite activity, hobby, travel or interest will put you in a strong position. Just avoid impulsiveness.

FINANCES

The sun in your second house of finances continues to motivate you to be financially productive and meticulous. However, the first week of August may bring to light certain debts or arrangements that will need to be settled. Once Mars is in Libra from the 7th you're likely to gain a more even financial keel but you must avoid splurging, especially on your home, travel and socialising. You may receive unexpected work or financial news towards the 23rd.

HEALTH

As you are such a proactive and outgoing personality you prefer to be physically active. In August you're likely to discover new ways to boost your health and well-being, such as via a developing interest in spirituality, travel and therapeutic locations. For example, nature and the beach will appeal to you as healing options. You would certainly enjoy a trip or change of environment mid-month if not before.

LOVE LIFE

The full moon on 9 August will spotlight your love life and may highlight a quirky aspect of a partner or of the relationship. You're likely to wish to make a commitment to one specific course of action in your personal life. A strong connection with your past or a place will be significant towards the 12th. You may feel super nostalgic at this time, so avoid making decisions in your personal life based purely on sentimentality.

CAREER

The beginning of the month will be ideal for taking the initiative both financially and in your career, as you could make a great deal of progress and especially around 8 August. Just be a little careful with interactions with a group, friend or organisation to avoid unnecessary stress. It will take until the 25th for Mercury to regain its strength, so if you find some communications more difficult than usual until then be sure to be patient.

HOME LIFE

With so much focus on your activities and projects, investment in your home life may take a poor second place. However, as Mars continues through Libra you may discover later in the month an increasing interest in feathering your nest. Certain aspects of your home life may no longer resonate with the person you're becoming, and you'll find in September that you may be ready to make changes in the way you share some aspects of your home or a property.

September

WEEK 1: 28 AUGUST–3 SEPTEMBER

This will be a lovely week to reconnect with someone you feel a strong link with and/or to re-engage with a hobby you love. However, some communications and interactions may be more complex or conflicting than you may initially have liked, so it will be in your interest to be careful with negotiations and especially to do with finances.

WEEK 2: 4–10 SEPTEMBER

There is a great sense of freedom and enjoyment in life, so if you have nothing planned yet this week ensure you take advantage of a positive, dreamy time astrologically and breathe fresh air into your activities in your spare time. The total lunar eclipse on 7 September signals a great deal of romance and excitement in your life, but if you're making financial decisions ensure you have all the facts.

WEEK 3: 11–17 SEPTEMBER

Important financial or personal decisions and commitments will need to be made. You have reliable experts and loyal friends you can consult, but ultimately the correct decisions are best made based on facts as opposed to hunches or feeling under pressure from others. You will enjoy hearing from someone close and may experience a financial or ego boost.

WEEK 4: 18–24 SEPTEMBER / WEEK 5: 25 SEPTEMBER–1 OCTOBER

WEEK 4: this weekend's solar eclipse will help you configure a solid structure for a project and for your finances. If you tend to look at your ventures idealistically you'll see the basics and realities of your circumstances more clearly, enabling you to fill the gap if need be and especially financially. You'll make a commitment to a particular person or plan and gain a boost in self-esteem as a result. **WEEK 5:** the effects of last week's solar eclipse and the major aspect between the sun, Uranus and Pluto continue this week, bringing the opportunity to shift your work, projects and ventures into positive territory. You may consider a fresh communications device or vehicle as a way to improve relationships, transportation and general ease in life. Just avoid going deeply into debt if you're already in debt.

FINANCES

The total lunar eclipse on 7 September will spotlight how you prefer to invest your money in your spare time. Holidays, money, savings, joint finances and even debt will come into the frame early in September, offering you the chance to put in place a process that allows you not only to earn well but also to spend well. You may be inclined to overspend, especially at the start and at the end of the month, so be sure to maintain perspective, especially if you are already in debt.

HEALTH

A trusted medical professional could truly boost your health early in the month, so if you've been experiencing any ongoing health worries then this will be a good time to double-check you're on track health-wise. Someone either at work or at home, or prospectively you, must be careful to avoid minor accidents, bumps and scrapes mid-month. Your help may be needed at that time, and if you need help health-wise it will be available.

LOVE LIFE

The way you share your responsibilities, duties, space at home and potentially love will change in September. You'll have every opportunity to find inspired ways to make an existing relationship more rewarding, and if you're single to meet someone you wish to spend more time with. However, it will be equally important to place attention on the practicalities of your relationship. While this may not be termed technically as romantic, it does show care for one another.

CAREER

This month's eclipses are across your money zone and suggest there will be changes in your earning and/or career path. You'll gain the opportunity to step into fresh territory in both these areas, so be prepared to make changes in your usual work routine. The stars are aligning for you towards the solar eclipse on 21 September and on the 24th, enabling you to create a work environment or daily routine that suits you better.

HOME LIFE

The opposition between Mars and Chiron on 16 September may bring to mind certain areas of your home that deserve a little more attention. If you need expert advice it will be available, so reach out. Proactive Mars enters your fourth house of home on the 23rd, bringing the opportunity to invest energy into this important part of your life. Just be sure to avoid impulsive decisions around the 24th, but if an ideal opportunity arises then grab it!

October

WEEK 1: 2–8 OCTOBER

A trip or change of routine will bring fresh logistics to your week, and your efforts to problem solve will be successful. Consider a fresh attitude to persistent issues, both at work and at home. However, you'll need to decide where your priorities lie for now and be super tactful with communications. Some Leos may experience a financial or ego boost this weekend. Romance could thrive.

WEEK 2: 9–15 OCTOBER

A meeting or trip will provide you with food for thought this weekend, as a reunion or the prospect of beginning a fresh chapter will prove enticing. It's vital to get a key personal or financial decision right, as this is a catalytic week where who and what you invest in will determine your path for some time to come.

WEEK 3: 16–22 OCTOBER

The new moon on 21 October signals you'll be turning a page either in your home life or with family or regarding a property. Some Leos will be completing a cycle in your career or status, making this week another important one decision-wise. Avoid sticking with past preconceptions and aim to move forward in a constructive and adventurous way for the best results. A trip or visitor will be welcome.

WEEK 4: 23–29 OCTOBER

You'll appreciate the opportunity to get ahead with your various projects. If you need collaboration, teamwork and help will be productive so be sure to reach out. If you initially experience a challenge or tension at home or regarding family and property, rest assured your hard work will pay off and you may even be surprised by news mid next week.

FINANCES

You may need to consider a financial situation carefully at the start of October. If you've been putting off making financial decisions for some time you'll no longer have the option to do so, as pressures, duties or commitments mean you must now face certain realities. If some circumstances are beyond your understanding be sure to enlist the help of an expert or adviser, who will be particularly informative.

HEALTH

Pluto, the dwarf planet associated with transformation, ends its months-long retrograde phase this week, and as it sits in your health zone you're likely to experience an improvement in energy levels or focus regarding health mid-month. The last two weeks of October will be particularly beneficial for you to focus on transforming your health schedule so it better suits your circumstances such as your current career and status.

LOVE LIFE

The conjunction between Venus and the moon's south node on 4 October will be ideal for investing time and effort in romance and your relationship with someone special. If you're single you may meet someone with a karmic or predestined link, although you must also take into account whether travel or communication differences could be an issue if you wish a relationship to progress. You're communicating relatively well this month, which is ideal for discussing your options.

CAREER

The start of the month is particularly conducive for making progress in your career and work life, especially if you're prepared to step into fresh territory. Once Pluto ends its retrograde phase in mid-October developments are likely to speed up, leading to the potential to gain true traction in your work circumstances between now and early next year. You may receive unexpected work news towards the 29th or will gain the chance to experience something new.

HOME LIFE

Mars in your domestic sector brings a sense of purpose and passion to your home life that is excellent for completing chores and investing in your property, but you could also experience more frequent arguments or strife so bear this in mind and especially around 5, 17 and 24 October. The 21st will be particularly conducive to creating a welcoming and nurturing vibe at home. If you have been considering a move, this month you'll gain the motivation to take action.

November

WEEK 1: 30 OCTOBER–5 NOVEMBER

You could make great progress in your career and general direction in life. Take the initiative, but if you're unsure of yourself seek the insight of an expert. Decisions are likely to concern your home life, so the bigger picture must be taken into account. The supermoon on 5 November will spotlight relationships both at home and work and will provide insight into your best path forward.

WEEK 2: 6–12 NOVEMBER

Both Mercury and Jupiter turn retrograde this week, drawing attention to the past and old haunts. You may be drawn to travelling or reconnecting with someone you love and welcoming them into your home. If you have important discussions to undertake, try to float ideas before 8 November to avoid possible delays or misunderstandings this weekend and/or later this month.

WEEK 3: 13–19 NOVEMBER

Good communication and collaboration skills are the keys to success this week, as various ventures will take you into territory where being able to review, analyse and critically evaluate circumstances will put you in a strong position. Be prepared to demonstrate your courage and avoid falling prey to believing you are less then you are and accepting less than you deserve.

WEEK 4: 20–26 NOVEMBER / WEEK 5: 27 NOVEMBER–3 DECEMBER

WEEK 4: a fresh chapter is about to begin in your personal life, home or with a creative or sporty and adventurous project. You may find that a relationship deepens or that you discover something about a friend or organisation that leads you either to invest more in them or unexpectedly part ways. A trip or change of environment will be pleasing. **WEEK 5:** unexpected news from a friend or organisation may take you by surprise. It will, however, be an opportunity to break out of a tired routine. If you're looking for a new job, opportunity will knock. If, on the other hand, you're looking for inspiration at home or in a personal context then fresh opportunities will also come, so keep an eye out and take action accordingly.

FINANCES

Your finances are tied into your principles, loyalties and values, and this month you're going to re-evaluate your priorities and especially those financial decisions you've based on previous values. Ask yourself whether some of your priorities are changing as you progress through life? As a result, your financial patterns will change. The supermoon on 5 November and the new moon on the 20th will spotlight this process and reveal where your money must go.

HEALTH

Find time to maintain a positive outlook and high self-esteem for the best results. Your health focus this month revolves more around self-esteem and your ability to demonstrate self-confidence as opposed to the focus being on physical health. Nevertheless, sporty and athletic Leos will need to demonstrate your physical strength in your sport activities. However, it's your mental strength that underpins your success, not only in the sports arena but also in your personal life and at work.

LOVE LIFE

Someone is likely to surprise you or will have an unexpected impact on your life just before the supermoon on 5 November and then again towards the end of the month. You may hear unexpected news from a group or organisation you associate with, but for some Leos there will be an unexpected development in your love life at this time. You'll gain insight into where your focus is best to go, especially concerning your long-term decisions.

CAREER

Important decisions are on the table and the supermoon on 5 November will spotlight where your priorities and loyalties lie, so keep an eye on developments then. The third week of the month will bring a busy time when you could truly forge ahead in your career. However, you may need to review or revise some of the steps you've already taken up until now. Avoid allowing some delays to distract you from your bigger-picture goals.

HOME LIFE

Venus will continue to put the spotlight on your home life during the first week of the month and particularly in respect to the people you love and whether your existing arrangements still support your big-picture hopes and wishes. You may need to make a tough call, so the more information you gather the better. Avoid making rash decisions. If you're making changes at home be sure to be super clear towards 8 November to avoid arguments and misunderstandings.

December

WEEK 1: 4–10 DECEMBER

This is a good week to zhuzh up your home. Enlist help, as someone will be available. Keep an eye on communications as there may be some mix-ups. The supermoon on 4 December points to a fresh phase with a friend or organisation and for some Leos in your career, status or general direction. A fresh work contract or interest could take off, and things may progress quickly so avoid impulsiveness and stubbornness.

WEEK 2: 11–17 DECEMBER

This is a week when miscommunications and all manner of errors can arise, so ensure you're careful in your transactions and especially at work and with the people you love. As long as you're super clear with communications, especially those that involve travel arrangements, work, any form of self-development and study you can still make great progress with your projects. You may experience a therapeutic development.

WEEK 3: 18–24 DECEMBER

The combination of the new moon and the solstice points to a busy week with creativity, music and romance in your life and also a sense that you're making tracks with your various projects such as your career. It's certainly a good time to kick-start the holiday season if you haven't already. However, you must plan ahead both with travel and family matters to avoid confusion and delays.

WEEK 4: 25–31 DECEMBER

Changes in your usual daily routine will be uplifting, especially if you can see the positive reasons for altering your schedule. A difference of opinion needn't push you into a corner: be inspired by a change of environment and the chance to do something different. The overall influence will be therapeutic, so find ways to deepen existing relationships both at home or if you're on holiday or at work.

FINANCES

This is an excellent month for an appraisal of your finances this year. If you're happy with the outcome there's every reason to stay on the same track. However, the supermoon may spotlight some aspects you'd prefer to alter and you'll gain the opportunity to do so. You are known for being a generous person and especially when you're enjoying life, which is likely during the festive season, so you must avoid overspending during the pre-Christmas week.

HEALTH

It's a good month, especially early in the first week of December, to engage in activities you love and that you know will boost both your mood and vitality. You may be drawn to joining a gym or health club. The sun, Venus and Mercury will bring out your gregarious, adventurous and romantic outlook. For this reason it will be important to plan a clever budget, especially during the Christmas week, as you may be prone to overspend then.

LOVE LIFE

The supermoon in early December will spotlight where you see yourself going with your partner. It will be a good time to discuss domestic and shared responsibilities as you're likely to reach agreements. The new moon on the 20th indicates the chance if you're single to meet someone upbeat. Couples will enjoy spicing up your love life around Christmas, and music, dance and film will be therapeutic. Exercise good communication skills to avoid arguments in the final week of the year.

CAREER

The supermoon on 4 December will spotlight new avenues, especially if you were born after 3 August, and you will gain insight into the best way forward and especially with activities that provide a sense of purpose and fulfilment as opposed to work that simply pays the bills. You'll gain the opportunity mid-month to improve some of your circumstances, so be sure to initiate conversations with groups and organisations you'd like to work with. You may be surprised by the outcome.

HOME LIFE

Early December is an excellent time to discuss options to do with your home and family and to take constructive measures to see plans through. From mid-December onwards you'll gain a sense of progress with your domestic projects and developments. If you've been contemplating a trip or are receiving visitors your efforts are likely to be successful, although you must be careful during the second week of the month to avoid miscommunications and complexities.

January

WEEK 1: 1–8 JANUARY

This is a good weekend to make agreements and plans with those you love. If finances or duties need a fresh approach, do it now! If you're making long-term decisions ensure you base them on facts, not assumptions. It's a good week to get down to the nitty-gritty with your agreements and shared concerns both at home and work. Always have the facts at your fingertips.

WEEK 2: 9–15 JANUARY

Developments in your personal life will require a little adjustment. If you're travelling you'll appreciate the change of environment but you must be patient, as some delays may arise. Someone may need your help either with a domestic or personal matter. If you need help it will be available. Romance could flourish, so be sure to put some time aside for love.

WEEK 3: 16–22 JANUARY

As an earth sign you like to take your time to make careful choices and adapt to circumstances, yet this weekend you may need to think on your feet and be spontaneous. A close friend or family member may be on your mind, and the more you can indulge someone a little the better for you. You must, however, avoid allowing intense emotions to dictate your actions.

WEEK 4: 23–29 JANUARY

Opportunity may come knocking at your door if it hasn't already recently, so keep your eyes peeled! Be prepared to take the initiative when making changes in your direction, career or projects as your efforts are likely to be successful. The new moon on 29 January will mark a turning point in your personal life or family and in connection with someone special. Intense emotions may arise, so be prepared to retain perspective.

FINANCES

You may feel that it's two steps forward and three steps back financially in January, yet if you can anchor your budget in a particular pattern you'll make headway by the month's end. Find the time to work in practical terms with accumulated debt rather than simply adding to it in the hope it will disappear. Be realistic, and you'll manage to make solid progress.

HEALTH

Venus in your health sector will encourage you to invest time, money and effort in your appearance, fitness and diet. Be prepared to look outside the box at options such as a fresh look, haircut or diet and avoid fad diets or fitness crazes that have unproven results. Concentrate instead on tried and trusted methods that underlie new ideas.

LOVE LIFE

The Mars–Pluto opposition on 3 January could bring fiery passion. Someone and perhaps you will experience strong emotions, so make sure these are of the passionate kind and steer clear of arguments. The conjunction of the moon's north node and Neptune in your seventh house towards the end of the month and early February brings the opportunity to deepen love and romance in your life. If you're single and you wish to find someone truly compatible this is the time to look.

CAREER

Uranus brings variety and spice to your career, which you'll appreciate and especially if some projects or aspects of your career have seemed stuck. You may need to choose between your career and domestic or personal commitments early in the month, but this will be a case of time management rather than a choice of one over the other. Jupiter retrograde in your career sector will ask that you reconsider some aspects of your career in this light.

HOME LIFE

Mercury travelling through your domestic sector will bring visitors, and you're likely to wish to visit other people's homes during the first 10 days of the month. The rest of January will be good to make changes at home such as a little gardening, DIY projects or adding touches to your home that add a taste of freedom such as allowing the air to circulate, opening windows or furnishings that breathe fresh air into your environment.

February

WEEK 1: 30 JANUARY–5 FEBRUARY

This is one of the most romantic weeks of the year, so if you're looking for someone special be sure to take the initiative and go and find them! At the least you'll appreciate the chance to get together with like-minded people. You may enjoy a group event but must choose your company carefully to avoid disappointment. You can boost your work and personal status, so be proactive.

WEEK 2: 6–12 FEBRUARY

This is a good week to configure a fresh daily timetable that will encourage a healthier outlook. Make plans to move forward even if events occur in unusual or unexpected ways. Developments may require you to change your routine or be adaptable to new circumstances. Romance could blossom. You'll appreciate the opportunity to bring more creativity, music and art into your life. Just avoid misunderstandings.

WEEK 3: 13–19 FEBRUARY

If your expectations have been unrealistic you may get a reality check this week if you didn't already recently, but for most Virgos this could be a productive time when your generous and kind heart receives many rewards for being optimistic and industrious at work. You'll enjoy adding a little romance or luxury to your week: it is St Valentine's week after all! Arty Virgos will enjoy being creative.

WEEK 4: 20–26 FEBRUARY

You may need to adapt your schedule due to a change of routine, but if you're practical you'll progress well this week. Keep an eye on work communications and financial transactions to avoid making mistakes. You'll be happy to go ahead with an agreement, especially if this has taken time to plan. However, if you need someone to commit they may require more assurances or vice versa.

FINANCES

The idea that the harder you work the more money you make comes under scrutiny in February; the axiom 'Work smarter, not harder' comes to mind. You'll feel inspired by people and ideas in February that could set you down a fresh path in your career, and as long as you don't adopt unrealistic expectations and are subsequently disappointed you could indeed work smarter to make as much money as you do now, if not more.

HEALTH

February offers the unique option to improve your appearance and well-being. In addition you'll gain an opportunity for spiritual and personal self-development, so February is an excellent month to search for health modalities that will help you maintain or peak your fitness and potentially in new ways. Meditation, yoga, beauty treats and a fresh hairstyle, for example, will all boost your feel-good factor.

LOVE LIFE

The conjunction of Venus, Neptune and the moon's north node is rare and falls on the 1st of the month. This is perfect if you'd like to meet someone new or wish to ramp up the romance in your existing relationship. The Mercury–Saturn conjunction on 25 February could bring a commitment your way; just ensure it's not too restrictive. If you've been in a committed relationship for some time, this conjunction will bring key talks that require serious consideration.

CAREER

Be discriminating about the work you choose, as you could pick a fresh, inspiring path that will bring more money your way. To ensure you choose the right path, avoid rushing into the first agreement that comes your way if you're looking for something new. That said, if it's as good as it looks grab it with both hands, as you could make truly remarkable progress at work and especially towards the end of the month. A commitment could be made towards 25 February.

HOME LIFE

The new moon on 29 January brought the chance to revitalise aspects of your domestic or family life, and this month is ideal to continue the trend. You're likely to be drawn to altering important aspects of your domestic arrangements, even if at first you look purely at the research involved to ensure you make the right choices. If you've been considering travel or moving, some of your plans will begin to take off this month.

March

WEEK 1: 27 FEBRUARY–5 MARCH

A fresh business or personal partnership arrangement or agreement is on the way, especially if you were born in early September. All Virgos will relish the chance to revitalise a relationship, move into a fresh work phase or boost health and well-being. You may discover something new about someone close and must avoid taking circumstances personally, especially at work.

WEEK 2: 6–12 MARCH

Take the initiative as you'll feel motivated and perhaps even a little restless. If it's the latter you'll feel more productive if you channel your energy into favourite ventures rather than feel under pressure. Unless you harness this upbeat energy you may feel directionless. Your personal life will be undergoing considerable change. Music, dance and socialising will appeal. This will be a good week to make a commitment.

WEEK 3: 13–19 MARCH

Friday's lunar eclipse will be in Virgo and signals a fresh phase in your personal life. If you were born after mid-September you may receive key news at work or regarding health. Talks and meetings are pivotal, and important news from a personal or business associate may arrive. This is a good week to bring important discussions to the table. You may be pleasantly surprised by some results but must avoid pushing an agenda if it's unclear.

WEEK 4: 20–26 MARCH / WEEK 5: 27 MARCH–2 APRIL

WEEK 4: you'll be drawn to enjoying life, such as taking a lovely break or trip to the sea. It's a great week to indulge a little, so a health or beauty treat might appeal. Romance is on the cards, especially this weekend, so plan a special treat to revitalise your love life. You may be prone to overspend and overindulge, which you'll regret. **WEEK 5:** be prepared to look at a relationship from a fresh perspective. Think laterally about how you share duties and workloads. Ensure you avoid arguments and conflict, as these could flare as though from nowhere. You'll enjoy a reunion with someone special. You may need to make a tough decision on behalf of someone else or at work, so if necessary obtain expert advice.

FINANCES

Early in the month an agreement you make could be very grounding and stabilising financially, so be sure to seek solutions if financial issues arise. During the latter half of the month you'll need to rein in spending as you'll be drawn to enjoying some of the luxuries and indulgences in life. If someone close needs money think twice about lending it to them, as you may come to regret this decision unless you can put an agreement in writing.

HEALTH

The new moon on 28 February plus the total lunar eclipse on 14 March mean this is an excellent month to reconfigure your health and daily routine. As you tend to live on your nerves it will be vital to find peaceful and calm ways so you don't overstretch your nervous system. It's a good month to work collaboratively with someone to build a stronger picture of health.

LOVE LIFE

This is a month of new arrangements and agreements, and for some these may be unexpected or unprecedented. During the second week of the month serious talks may result in a commitment. The total lunar eclipse on 14 March will be in your sign and signifies a brand-new cycle in your personal life if you were born before mid-September, and at work or a change of daily routine if you were born afterwards.

CAREER

You may be drawn to making a work commitment or at least an agreement that could take you further up the career ladder, so be sure to take the initiative with collaborations and discussions. Jupiter will be helping you communicate better, so be confident with your interactions. Communications are likely to improve exponentially throughout the month, so avoid being deterred if at first some of your interactions fall flat.

HOME LIFE

Ask yourself how you would most benefit from altering any arrangements or agreements that affect your home life. This will be a good month to bring fresh arrangements into being that can improve your quality of life at home. You may receive important or unexpected news from someone close that affects your status at home. If you've been trying for a family, this will be a productive time and may bring surprising results.

April

WEEK 1: 3–9 APRIL

This is an excellent time to make progress in your career and work. You may be ready to make a commitment to someone in your personal life, and this is likely to proceed well. You may receive good news but, if not, take the initiative towards your goals. Someone close may reveal a vulnerability or ask for help. Be sure to be tactful to avoid misunderstandings.

WEEK 2: 10–16 APRIL

This is a good week for socialising and meeting new people. You may be drawn to a fresh place via a short break or holiday. You'll enjoy doing something different and may be surprised by some of the activities you partake in. The full moon on 13 April will kick-start a fresh focus on health and well-being, either your own or that of someone close.

WEEK 3: 17–23 APRIL

This is a wonderful week to make a romantic commitment to someone you love, and for working Virgos to make a commitment to a group, friend or organisation. You may enjoy a particularly romantic or sociable weekend. Towards Sunday and Monday it will be in your interest to maintain perspective regarding a shared duty or collaboration to avoid arguments.

WEEK 4: 24–30 APRIL

You'll appreciate the opportunity to get together with someone you love. You'll enjoy a sociable time, but you must avoid making assumptions that cannot carry the weight of reality as otherwise you risk experiencing strong emotions that override your better sense. If it's your birthday between 18 and 20 September you may experience the need to commit to someone or to a job. A fresh agreement with someone could be constructive.

FINANCES

It's likely you'll be making a significant commitment to someone you love or a group or organisation, so it will be in your interest to ensure you have done adequate research into the financial implications of the agreement. There are various ways to approach negotiations diplomatically so research ways to be tactful to avoid potential arguments about shared assets and interests, especially around 21 April.

HEALTH

Considerable focus on your health or that of someone else may arise towards the full moon on 13 April. You may then gain insight into both their or your own strengths and weaknesses health-wise. It's certainly a good month to enlist the help of experts and advisers who can help you build a strong health and well-being routine, so be sure to reach out.

LOVE LIFE

This could be a big month for you in your love life. It's a wonderful time to meet new people, and also for reunions. If you're single you're likely to feel more proactive about meeting new people and prospectively to enter fresh territory in your relationship status. Couples will find this a very productive time to find deeper ways to connect spiritually, creatively and artistically.

CAREER

Jupiter, the planet of abundance and expansion, will grow in influence throughout the month and this spells two things: on the one hand a busy month career-wise, and on the other the chance to expand your skill sets and experience. This points to an abundant time in your career, but you must avoid taking on too much responsibility at this time as you'll feel optimistic about the groundswell of activity during April but risk tiring yourself out.

HOME LIFE

This is a good month to run with your ideas, whether they directly impact your home life or not, as you'll find that where you place your attention will determine future domestic changes to come. For example, if a work matter takes your full focus then rest assured the progress you make will eventually contribute to a happier home. In the meantime, if your attention is elsewhere such as on travel or work then your home will provide a place of security.

May

WEEK 1: 1–7 MAY

You may enjoy a particularly ideal week, especially if you have romance planned. The conjunction of Venus and Neptune will certainly amp up the love in your life. Family get-togethers are also likely to go well. However, for some Virgos developments may be annoying due to unexpected developments, so be sure to maintain perspective. Financial transactions will deserve careful attention. You may receive an unexpected gain.

WEEK 2: 8–14 MAY

This week's Scorpio full moon will spotlight a fresh agreement. You may realise you have strong feelings about a person or place as someone's news arrives. This is a good time to consider a change of environment such as a holiday or updating a communication device or vehicle, as your efforts to improve your relationships in these ways will be fruitful.

WEEK 3: 15–21 MAY

A surprise development at work or a change in or revelation about your status will add clarity to your life and general direction this weekend. You may become clearer regarding your feelings about someone or an issue, and this will be enlightening. News or a favourite activity will prove to be therapeutic and at the least fun. A little extra focus on communications will oil the wheels.

WEEK 4: 22–28 MAY

This will be a good week to kick-start a fresh chapter either in your career or a favourite project or interest. You may be drawn to travelling or broadening your horizons in another way such as, for example, investing in your skill sets through study. You may receive positive news from someone close and romance could flourish, so be sure to organise a date!

FINANCES

The conjunction of Venus and Neptune at the start of the month suggests that a focus on either love or money during the first week of May will be productive. Financial transactions are likely to go well unless you haven't done adequate research or are careless, so if you have considerable financial commitments ensure you pay attention to the details and especially at the start of May.

HEALTH

May will be a good month to consider how you spend your spare time such as your holidays and weekends. During a usual working week, do you set time aside for your favourite hobbies such as sport or fitness? If not, mid-month will be ideal for scheduling in some of your favourite activities. Just be sure to keep those who depend on you in the loop so they understand your aims and goals.

LOVE LIFE

This is a good month to make a key commitment with someone important. You may prefer to renegotiate some of your existing agreements. You may be surprised by news that comes your way mid-month but must be wary of giving or receiving mixed messages. Careful discussions will lead to a positive outcome towards 22 May. The end of the month is ideal for romance and socialising, which you'll enjoy.

CAREER

Consider where you put your main focus, as it's important this month to consider a revamp of your career trajectory. There's so much potential for your career in May that it's important you're up to date with your various aims and projects. Take a moment to consider your true priorities at work so you can make the most of the Gemini new moon on 27 May, which could help you turn a corner.

HOME LIFE

You have a wonderful opportunity in May to improve and truly relish your closest relationships such as your family connections, yet much of your focus may be elsewhere this month. Make the choice in May to adjust your perspective a little so that key decision-making regarding your personal life, home and big-picture direction includes domestic and family considerations, as you may otherwise miss out on invaluable time spent with those you love.

June

WEEK 1: 29 MAY–4 JUNE

Key decisions or agreements can be made, so ensure you seek direction or advice and especially regarding your work and direction in general. Avoid restricting your options; be practical, and as a result you're likely to see progress. Study, research and self-development will progress well, so take the initiative. If you're in an advisory role you're likely to be busy this week.

WEEK 2: 5–11 JUNE

If you're single this will be a good weekend to socialise, as you're likely to meet like-minded people. For many Virgos the full moon on 11 June will highlight the end of a productive phase either at home or in your career. For some it's time for a change of scenery, and a trip or visit will appeal. Couples will enjoy spending time in a mutually enjoyable activity that will boost your relationship.

WEEK 3: 12–18 JUNE

As Mars enters your sign you'll gain improved energy levels but you may also be prone to appear a little feisty to others, so if you experience a push back to an everyday suggestion you know why! Before, though, you'll enjoy socialising and the chance to indulge in a favourite activity or pastime. Just avoid contentious topics and impulsiveness, which will backfire.

WEEK 4: 19–25 JUNE / WEEK 5: 26 JUNE–2 JULY

WEEK 4: your profile or direction is about to change; you may even see your status step up a level at work or in your personal life or both. A decision is best made with the long term in mind. Be sure to keep those who are affected by your decisions in the loop to avoid misunderstandings or disappointment further down the line. **WEEK 5:** proactive and upbeat Mars in your sign is bringing some of your best qualities to the surface, and you'll find that communications and socialising may feel more straightforward and easy. However, certain collaborations will still merit careful attention to detail to avoid misunderstandings. A get-together or development in your personal life at the weekend may be intense, so if you prefer to avoid intense situations be careful!

FINANCES

You'll manage to meet your financial obligations in June. However, you will need to undertake research and, if necessary, secure the insight, help or support of an expert, especially if you find yourself in debt or in a challenging situation regarding a shared financial situation. You'll also benefit from sharpening your negotiation skills with regard to shared finances, especially just before the full moon on the 11th and towards the end of June.

HEALTH

Mars enters your sign on 17 June, which will help boost your self-confidence. You may be drawn to updating your look or creating a fresh impression on those you care about. Beforehand, if you're lacking in vitality take the cue and rest up. This is particularly relevant as you risk exhausting yourself and at the end of the month could find certain interactions exhausting, which often leads to low morale.

LOVE LIFE

This is a good month to find ways to improve your usually reliable communication skills in your love life, especially if you find towards the new moon on 25 June that there's a misunderstanding or the need to renegotiate some of your arrangements and agreements with that special someone in your life. Singles may find that a connection with your past is therapeutic in relation to your love life, especially around the 10th, but you must avoid making rash decisions.

CAREER

The second week of the month will be perfect for socialising and networking so that you're able better to interact with those you work with, including colleagues and employers. You'll find that being dynamic yet sensitive to other people's feelings and collaborating well with others could produce a therapeutic atmosphere at work. Just avoid in mid-June making rash decisions and speaking before you think things through, which you may come to regret.

HOME LIFE

The full moon on 11 June will spotlight a key development. For some this will revolve around a domestic or family-related circumstance, and for others around the need to adapt domestically to circumstances that impact your home such as your career or a relationship. You'll gain insight and the key to resolving any emerging differences with others by evaluating whether your goals and principles have changed in line with changing circumstances, and that therefore you must renegotiate some agreements.

July

WEEK 1: 3–9 JULY

A change of activities or a surprise could be ideal, but you'll need to adjust to circumstances. You'll enjoy a new look or a health treat. A fresh phase in your personal or domestic life will add a sense of adventure. You'll enjoy the opportunity to deepen your relationship with someone and make a commitment to new arrangements.

WEEK 2: 10–16 JULY

The full moon on 10 July will spotlight your personal life and commitments to those you love such as your family. Someone special has important news for you, and you may be surprised by their feelings or developments. You'll gain the opportunity this week to do something different such as take a trip or engage in fresh activities, and to enjoy the company of a new social circle.

WEEK 3: 17–23 JULY

It's likely that you re-evaluate, in the back of your mind at least, what you value in your work life and who you prioritise in your personal life. You're likely to prefer sticking with what and who you know, yet an aspect of you may wish to change aspects of your work or personal life. The next few weeks will provide the opportunity to quietly consider your options.

WEEK 4: 24–30 JULY

You'll turn a corner in some relationships, especially in a social or networking circle. You may find you become closer to a particular group, colleague or friend or that you're more in demand. You may be surprised by developments so be prepared to be practical, as you could truly excel this week by focusing on your goals.

FINANCES

You're likely to experience unexpected developments at work or regarding joint finances, so be sure to seek expert advice and help and especially if an investment seems to be practical yet entails more research. Just ensure that the financial agreements you make are super clear or you may need to review them at a later date. Try to get key paperwork on the table by 18 July, when Mercury turns retrograde and may delay matters afterwards.

HEALTH

Mars in Virgo will motivate you to be busy, and unless you monitor your energy levels you could assume that you have limitless energy at your disposal. The result would be that you inadvertently revert to bad habits in your health practices that will potentially create a deficit of energy, especially around 19 and 20 July and during the last week of the month. To avoid this ensure your health comes first, and as a result you'll build stamina.

LOVE LIFE

You'll be drawn to being more outgoing, and wishing to travel and learn more about yourself and other people. Your love life will either accommodate these wishes or may at worst cramp your style. In the lead-up to the new moon on 24 July you may be restless or wish to make considerable changes in your love life. However, Mercury retrograde from the 18th suggests you take your time before making hasty decisions and mistakes.

CAREER

You may hear unexpected news at work or regarding your career trajectory early in July, which will encourage you to look at fresh avenues and/or find ways to boost your circumstances, which you could do this month. Some Virgos will experience a change in status such as through retirement or marriage, and will look at new ways to structure your shared responsibilities. The new moon on the 24th will help you devise a fresh daily schedule.

HOME LIFE

Uranus will bring changes to your status, career and/or activities and you may feel a little restless. At the least you'll be prepared to try new things in your life. All of this will add to a feeling of busyness and for some Virgos there will be a draw to adventure, so there will be all the more reason to find time to relax at home and cocoon, be this in your own home or while on holiday.

August

WEEK 1: 31 JULY–6 AUGUST

You'll enjoy a reunion or news from a group or organisation. Trust your intuition and be sure to be guided by your values and a sense of fair play, especially at work, as this will provide understanding if differences of opinion arise. If you discover you're at odds with someone in your personal life the same applies: be sure to look for fair play and common ground.

WEEK 2: 7–13 AUGUST

This is an excellent week to kick-start something new in your usual daily routine, either at work or in your health and fitness schedule. You're likely to experience a surprise or something different in your status and career and could also boost your finances. However, some shared finances will require careful analysis to avoid making mistakes. You'll enjoy a sociable or fulfilling week.

WEEK 3: 14–20 AUGUST

A connection with your past is likely to be upbeat and rewarding. Financially, a debt may be repaid or you may enjoy a financial boost. However, you may also be inclined to overspend, so check your bank balance first before using your credit card! Romance could flourish this weekend, so be sure to organise a date. Singles may meet someone significant and romance could be born.

WEEK 4: 21–27 AUGUST

This is a good week to invest in your health and well-being by adding healthy treats to your usual daily routine. Ask yourself how much attention you actually place on your physical, emotional, mental and spiritual health and make changes accordingly. You may be surprised by news regarding work or your status. You'll enjoy socialising and romance could blossom, so be sure to organise a date or two.

FINANCES

Mars in your second house of finances from 7 August onwards will feel motivational and you will be drawn to investing more heavily in your favourite activities and people. You may, however, tend to splurge on life's luxuries, so remember to maintain your sense of perspective financially and especially if you're already in debt. The full moon on the 9th will spotlight the need to more closely consider your shared financial responsibilities in particular, such as joint duties including taxes.

HEALTH

The full moon on 9 August will spotlight the need to bring something new into your health routine to create more vitality in your life. It's certainly a good month to consider fresh health practices more in line with your current personal circumstances. You may enjoy upbeat and group or team efforts that engage you in a social yet healthy activity, such as dance or a ball game. Mid-August will be particularly conducive to finding ways to boost your health.

LOVE LIFE

The month begins on a sociable note, which you'll enjoy. You may also appreciate a return to an old haunt. Some Virgos may be particularly keen to be in touch with an ex or will need to provide support to a partner. If you require extra help be sure to ask for it, because it will be available. A difference of opinion early in the month needn't set the tone for the entire month.

CAREER

This is an excellent month to try something new in your career, as the stars will support your efforts and especially around 8 August. You may experience a financial or ego boost as a result. Be sure to consider fresh options and ways to incorporate more activities and projects that you enjoy in your daily life. Mid-August may bring a breakthrough in a collaboration or project that provides motivation.

HOME LIFE

This month includes the first of two consecutive Virgo new moons, which will breathe fresh air into many corners of your life. You're in the process of re-evaluating how to create more peace and harmony in your life, and your home life will invariably come under the microscope as well. However, as this is a sociable month it's likely much of your energy goes into ensuring the people you love are happy and creating new memories, be these at home or elsewhere.

September

WEEK 1: 28 AUGUST–3 SEPTEMBER

The upcoming lunar eclipse on 7 September will be in your opposite sign of Pisces and your relationships, especially your love life, are likely to already be in the spotlight this week. You'll have certain agreements to make such as financial or work arrangements that will require patience and diligence. You'll enjoy getting together with someone whose company you truly admire.

WEEK 2: 4–10 SEPTEMBER

This week's total lunar eclipse puts a spotlight on romance. Singles may meet someone special so be sure to organise a date, but if you were born after 7 September this week's eclipse will underline the fact that you're ready for a new phase at work or in your health and fitness routine. It's time to be inspired by the people and events that represent growth and excitement to you.

WEEK 3: 11–17 SEPTEMBER

You'll enjoy socialising and being with people you love. Singles may meet someone familiar yet whom you've never actually met before, so ensure you organise a date on Friday or Saturday. There are therapeutic aspects to the week both on health and personal levels. Ensure when making agreements that you avoid jumping in without adequate research.

WEEK 4: 18–24 SEPTEMBER / WEEK 5: 25 SEPTEMBER–1 OCTOBER

WEEK 4: get set to make a financial or personal commitment. If you have a great idea you'd like to pursue, research your plans as you may find that you're ahead. If not, you must make up time. The good news is that a lovely surprise will boost your fortunes in the shape of support, finances or love. It's the week to go for your goals with full confidence you can succeed. **WEEK 5:** you'll find out this week whether you've over- or underestimated someone's involvement in your life. You're likely to experience the excitement of moving into fresh territory in your personal or professional life. Ensuring you have your feet on the ground is the key to solid progress. You must also be sure to keep communications clear and especially mid next week, as otherwise misunderstandings could arise.

FINANCES

Mars in your second house of finances until 23 September suggests you will have several outgoings and payments that need to be made and can no longer wait. It will be in your interest for this reason to avoid overspending. You may need to review your financial circumstances, especially mid-month. The solar eclipse on the 21st will spotlight the potential for success with a financial arrangement, so be sure to research clever options then.

HEALTH

You'll be drawn to updating your appearance through, for example, a new hairstyle or outfit and will be drawn to zhuzhing up your daily or health routine. This is likely to be beneficial for you but you'll need to stick to a particular schedule for it to be effective. If you have had niggling health worries and were born after 7 September this will be a good month to consider a fresh treatment plan or diet.

LOVE LIFE

The total lunar eclipse in your opposite sign Pisces on 7 September and the solar eclipse in Virgo on the 21st put the focus on love. The key to turning a page in your partnership will come down to good communication skills and the willingness to experience new aspects of your relationship through re-establishing common ground, such as pastimes you both enjoy doing together. Singles may meet someone strangely familiar, especially between the 7th and 12th, so be sure to socialise and reach out.

CAREER

Be prepared to forge fresh agreements in your existing work environment or turn a corner and begin something new with a different organisation. Your negotiation and communication skills will be put to the test, especially early in the month and towards 30 September, but with care and attention to details you could devise a fortunate new arrangement. The astrological alignment on the 24th could bring exciting projects your way and will at least bring diversity to your work.

HOME LIFE

You have the co-operation you need early in the month, so if you have repairs or changes that must be done at home reach out for the help you need earlier rather than later. As this month involves considerable change in your personal life you'll lean more heavily on the importance of your home life, so you must be careful to avoid being super critical about aspects that are not perfect as you may otherwise make impulsive choices.

October

WEEK 1: 2–8 OCTOBER

If you're making long-term financial decisions ensure you obtain expert advice and avoid impulse buys, which you may come to regret. A change of location or fresh circumstance will ask that you're super focused. A very strong and loyal link with an old friend or family member will prove its weight in gold, so be sure to connect with someone you love. Romance could blossom.

WEEK 2: 9–15 OCTOBER

A choice concerning finances or a close relationship will merit careful consideration, as you're about to begin a fresh chapter in these areas or at work. Consider upbeat plans and solutions and be sure to research financial fine print if you're drawn to making a large investment or commitment to someone that would affect your finances. Romance is likely to flourish towards mid next week, so organise a date!

WEEK 3: 16–22 OCTOBER

You're generally a good communicator, but even you can fall prey to misunderstandings and misinformation. This week it's very important to carefully analyse any agreements or financial interactions you undertake that put you in fresh territory, as it's possible you'll make mistakes or that others will do so. You may be drawn to booking travel or purchasing a fresh communications device or vehicle.

WEEK 4: 23–29 OCTOBER

This will be an excellent week to make progress in your personal life and enjoy a little socialising. You may be drawn to taking a short break and would enjoy a change of environment. If you've been considering making a change in your career or at home, look out for news or developments mid next week as these will provide insight into and direction for your options.

FINANCES

The first week of the month will merit careful focus and attention to your finances, especially if you'll be undertaking large transactions or making long-term financial commitments. Be sure to engage the help of an expert if necessary, not only at the start of the month but also mid-month and towards the new moon on 21 October, when key financial developments will require an objective viewpoint. Avoid allowing emotions to affect financial choices.

HEALTH

A beauty boost will do wonders for your self-esteem and you may be drawn to remedying a health situation already early in the month. The more practical you are with your health and that of someone you care for the better for everyone concerned. Your health may come under the microscope towards 18 and 21 October, when it's best to avoid minor bumps and scrapes and erratic drivers for the best results.

LOVE LIFE

This is a romantic month, as Venus remains in Virgo until 13 October and makes an important link with the moon's south node on the 3rd. You may be drawn to reuniting with an ex, and if you're single you may meet someone who is mysteriously familiar. Couples may discover a vulnerable aspect in each other and will find ways to connect more deeply through good communication skills. Mid-month is particularly romantic, so be sure to organise a treat then.

CAREER

Uranus at the zenith of your chart continues to bring a degree of restlessness your way regarding the correct path in your career, yet you'll also gain the opportunity to retrace your steps in ways that could magnify your appreciation of the best qualities of your current career choice. There is no rush to make changes unless pressures dictate otherwise. You'll gain the chance in 2026 to make radical change if necessary.

HOME LIFE

The full moon on 7 October will shine a light on shared duties and relationships that impact your home life, property or family, so be discerning about the arrangements and agreements you make to ensure you're happy. The new moon on the 21st and the few days preceding this may produce a flurry of activity at home. You may be inspired to bring elements you've enjoyed while on holiday, such as a little luxury, into your home.

November

WEEK 1: 30 OCTOBER–5 NOVEMBER

A realistic and practical approach to your work and a partnership or collaboration will put you in a strong position. Avoid limiting your vision; be bold and courageous and trust your intuition, principles and values. The full moon and supermoon on 5 November will spotlight your favourite activities, interests and pastimes. Be sure to provide yourself with adequate opportunity to enjoy life.

WEEK 2: 6–12 NOVEMBER

Your sign's ruler Mercury turns retrograde this weekend. You may receive news regarding your home, family or a property. It's a good week for domestic repairs and to redecorate and receive visitors or visit someone else's home. Try to get changes at home done by the weekend to avoid delays later this month. You'll enjoy a reunion, and singles may meet someone strangely familiar.

WEEK 3: 13–19 NOVEMBER

This will be an excellent week for socialising and reuniting with like-minded people. You may be drawn to travelling somewhere familiar and reuniting with family. Working Virgos are in a position to make positive agreements with a group or organisation that could be advantageous to both parties. Domestic developments are likely to move ahead even if some matters are still caught up in red tape or delayed.

WEEK 4: 20–26 NOVEMBER / WEEK 5: 27 NOVEMBER–3 DECEMBER

WEEK 4: a fresh phase is about to begin at home with family or a property. You may discover key information that can lead to a deeper understanding of someone or of yourself. A change at home is likely to be pleasant. Unexpected news regarding work or from a friend or organisation will have a bearing on the new chapter, and gaining collaboration from those close to you will move mountains. **WEEK 5:** an event will take you outside your usual routine; you may enjoy a trip or welcome an impromptu visitor. Some Virgos will be surprised by developments at work and others by robust changes at home. Making your week a pleasant one revolves around positive aspects in your relationships. You're likely to enjoy reunions and socialising although you must watch for and avoid tactlessness.

FINANCES

Finances will gain considerable focus early in the month, and if you need the help of an expert or adviser their information could prove invaluable and especially if a group or organisation requires you to make a rapid decision. It's far better to make agreements based on reality and fact rather than expectations or assumptions. You may need to review some of your arrangements regarding shared finances and are likely to make a breakthrough later in the month if not before.

HEALTH

Your sign's ruler Mercury, which also rules health, will turn retrograde on 9 November. This may contribute to a slight lack of energy or motivation, so it will be in your interest for the remainder of the month to pace yourself and find ways to replenish energy levels should you feel fatigue set in. This will be a good month to find ways to connect more with your intuition. You may experience stronger dreams.

LOVE LIFE

This will be a sociable and upbeat month for you and singles will enjoy meeting all circles of people, both socially and through work opportunities. If you're travelling you may be surprised by some of the unexpected developments and the ways in which they can enhance your relationships. Singles are likely to meet someone familiar or likeable on the weekend of 8 November, so be sure to make a date then.

CAREER

Uranus makes a tough aspect with Mars at the start of the month, which could bring unexpected developments your way. If you've been considering making changes in your career you may gain the motivation and impetus to see your plans through. Networking and being prepared to step into fresh territory will certainly help your endeavours. Try to get some of your plans and ideas floated before 8 November to avoid possible delays later in the month.

HOME LIFE

It's a good month for repairs and redecoration at home, not only cosmetically but also regarding relationships and interpersonal family dynamics. Avoid arguments, especially between 5 and 8 November, as these are likely to escalate quickly. You may receive key news at home around the weekend of the 8th. Retrograde Mercury may delay some of your plans regarding your home, but nevertheless this will be an excellent time to deepen and improve domestic or family relationships and especially around the 17th.

December

WEEK 1: 4–10 DECEMBER

Discussions will produce a refreshing new chapter, especially if you're flexible with people in your environment or plan to enjoy a change of scenery either at work or home. Some talks will require tact, especially towards Monday. Be practical, lay strong foundations and avoid swift, impulsive moves. You'll enjoy a trip or visitors.

WEEK 2: 11–17 DECEMBER

Family or personal developments may require you to deal with them carefully to avoid making mistakes. While you like to be realistic and practical in life in general, events may point out where you've been idealistic with your plans. Avoid subscribing to a negative outlook now; take things one step at a time and avoid arguments. Romance could thrive, especially on 11 December.

WEEK 3: 18–24 DECEMBER

The new moon on 20 December falls in your home and property sector and points to a fresh chapter in this area. You may experience a therapeutic development. If you've been considering entering fresh territory, for example by moving or remodelling your home, this will be a good week to do so but you must be sure you're super clear about your plans with everyone involved.

WEEK 4: 25–31 DECEMBER

You'll appreciate the feeling of togetherness and potentially healing that occurs in your home life or a particular relationship. The key to success this Christmas week lies in good planning and the willingness to change your outlook, especially regarding someone special and your home life. A change of environment may cause some disgruntlement, so be sure to be patient.

FINANCES

A considerable amount of focus on your home life, environment and for some lucky Virgos the option to travel will require expenditure. If you have budgeted well for your adventures in December then your finances will cover expenses, but you may discover towards mid-month that some expenses are far more than you'd hoped so be sure to plan ahead. For the sake of clarity it will be important to spell out domestic or shared financial arrangements to avoid complications down the line.

HEALTH

A change of pace or place in December is sure to raise morale, which will have an automatically positive effect on your mental and physical health. However, some interactions in mid-December will merit careful focus to avoid arguments and making mistakes, both of which would add to stress levels. Some lucky Virgos will gain the opportunity to take a break that will certainly be replenishing.

LOVE LIFE

There is a constructive and stabilising influence around your love life in December, and the key to making the most of this lies in good communication skills, especially during the first week of December and around the solstice. There is a therapeutic influence around a particular domestic circumstance; perhaps you receive help in this area that enables you to spend more time with someone special. Singles may enjoy the company of someone who has a therapeutic influence. Just avoid making assumptions.

CAREER

Consider what is working for you and what no longer appeals. The supermoon on 4 December will spotlight your career and especially whether your current circumstances still resonate on a deeper level. You'll gain the opportunity to discuss and negotiate new options and may be surprised by some developments mid-month, and the more flexible you are about which of your options to choose the better for you.

HOME LIFE

You'll feel motivated to make changes in your immediate environment at home. You may prepare for visitors at Christmas or to visit someone else's home. Luckily, it's an ideal period to invest time and energy in your home and immediate environment, especially in the first week of December and towards the new moon on the 20th. The way you share duties and space at home will change in the final week of December.

♎︎

LIBRA

22 September – 23 October

January

WEEK 1: 1–8 JANUARY

This is an excellent weekend for improving your domestic circumstances and family dynamics. A change of routine could be ideal. If you're venturing into new territory ensure you research details for the best results. You'll appreciate a health or beauty boost, so be sure to organise something special. A friend or someone close may surprise you with a spontaneous invitation or offer.

WEEK 2: 9–15 JANUARY

The Cancer full moon on 13 January will spotlight your career, status and/or general direction, and some decisions may be necessary to obtain the sense of security you wish for. Someone may need to be handled with kid gloves, either due to their health or sensitivity. If you're unsure of your true feelings or choices, listen to your instincts. You'll enjoy an unexpected boost in your personal or domestic life.

WEEK 3: 16–22 JANUARY

A change of circumstance could impact your home or certain relationships, so choose your actions carefully. You may be surprised by someone's reactions to events; avoid being swayed by their inconsistencies. A change in your domestic circumstance or family will benefit from care and attention. Avoid allowing strong feelings to boil over: instead, find a safety valve and especially mid next week if need be.

WEEK 4: 23–29 JANUARY

You'll appreciate a change of pace or place this week and the spontaneity to enjoy your time. A trip or change at home will breathe fresh air into your environment. However, a fresh chapter at home with family or an emotional person in your midst will require delicate handling for the best results. This is a good time for some DIY projects, a little home improvement or planning a move.

FINANCES

You will be drawn to making improvements across the board in your life and this is certainly a good time to invest in yourself, especially in your general direction, status, career and home life. The nexus that enables you to make changes rests in financial matters, especially shared finances with people such as partners and arrangements such as investments and debt. There's no better time than the present to figure out clever strategies. Above all, you must avoid gambling.

HEALTH

You'll gain the chance in January to truly focus on your health and well-being, especially circumstances that you may feel are outside your control such as existing health issues. The focus will then turn to what you do have control over in your health and well-being, and much of the power you possess rests in your ability to be positive, take affirmative action and research and gain the information you need to live the healthiest life possible.

LOVE LIFE

You'll be focusing a great deal on your love life all year and specifically in connection with either your own health or that of someone close. This focus may well be on one or several of the following health areas: mental, physical, spiritual and emotional. It will therefore be in your interest already now at the start of the year to find ways to discuss any of these areas that you know would benefit from attention so you are able to experience a fulfilling love life.

CAREER

The presence of Mars retrograde in your career sector suggests your career may not progress as quickly as you would prefer. January's events will spotlight how intensely you feel about the impact your chosen career has on your home life and vice versa, which will enable you to make important choices about exactly where you wish to place your attention in 2025. The full moon on the 13th will highlight this choice, especially in relation to someone close or health matters.

HOME LIFE

Pluto in your personal life counsels fresh direction, and this draw to the new and something different will most definitely impact your home and/or family life. Developments already right at the start of January will spotlight where certain aspects of your home life are simply there to support your well-being and health, but also other aspects that will need to change. The new moon on the 29th will provide added insight into your best path forward.

February

WEEK 1: 30 JANUARY—5 FEBRUARY

You may receive an ideal offer of work or an activity that resonates with you. Romantic Librans born at the end of September may meet someone new who plays a key role in your life. It's a good week to consider a different look, hairstyle or wardrobe. A work matter is best approached carefully, and if a collaboration is difficult look for ways to mend bridges if possible or agree to disagree.

WEEK 2: 6—12 FEBRUARY

It's a good week for romance and to bring a therapeutic aspect alive in a close relationship. A change of circumstance may come as a surprise and bring up intense feelings. A partner may surprise you. The full moon on 12 February will encourage you to be more productive at work, home and in your personal life. You may also be drawn to a fresh social group or organisation.

WEEK 3: 13—19 FEBRUARY

You may be inclined to be led by your hopes and ideals rather than practicalities and realities, yet your optimism is likely to be rewarded: at least to some degree. You may find that a health, well-being, work or domestic matter blossoms. A change of environment will feel refreshing even if it's a little stressful at first. You'll enjoy being with the people you love.

WEEK 4: 20—26 FEBRUARY

Be practical and resourceful this week and your good intentions and plans will come together, but you must avoid distractions and circumnavigate unreliable people. An agreement can be made where you require co-operation and transparency in relationships or at work, so ensure you research circumstances so you feel you're working at your best capacity.

FINANCES

Financially it's in your interest to work out how to budget, given the changes and opportunities surrounding your work and/or home life. If you're making key work and health decisions be sure to be realistic while also taking advantage of potentially ideal options to progress. If you're drawn to investing in yourself in February be sure to invest in your health and well-being first, and everything else will fall into place.

HEALTH

The rare alignment between Venus, Neptune and the moon's north node in your health zone will bring your attention to what must be done to improve your well-being. You may initially be drawn to enhancing your appearance and even wardrobe as a pick-me-up or confidence booster. Be sure that you're clear about health matters, especially at the start of the month and if you feel fatigued then. Avoid being too idealistic and seek an expert if you need some health advice.

LOVE LIFE

Deep feelings are likely to emerge this month, so be sure to take things one step at a time. The full moon on 12 February suggests a change in status, and for some Librans this will mean a change from single to married! However, if you've been in a difficult place with a partner for some time this full moon could mean you decide to go your separate ways. Nevertheless, St Valentine's Day and the 25th will offer a chance to establish some stability in your love life.

CAREER

You may receive ideal news early in February that could potentially change the face of your daily work routine. The Mars–Saturn aspect on 9 February will highlight opportunities in your career that could take you places. For some this will literally be to a new environment, or a distant place may become a drawcard. The Pisces new moon on the 28th further suggests fresh options at work or the chance to modify your personal life to accommodate new opportunities.

HOME LIFE

This will be a good month to build stability and security in your home life in whatever ways you find the best, as Pluto continues to bring change to your home and domestic lives. February's full moon on the 12th will highlight news that concerns your home or family that could alter how you share some of your domestic duties such as joint responsibilities or space at home. Binding commitments could be made towards the 25th.

March

WEEK 1: 27 FEBRUARY–5 MARCH

A fresh daily routine may appeal. Ensure you're being realistic with some work and domestic plans. A new health or beauty treat will suit you or someone close. A partner's changing circumstances may have a strong influence over your usual daily life now, so be prepared to plan ahead confidently in ways that enrich your life.

WEEK 2: 6–12 MARCH

A strong link with your past or a feeling of destiny and inevitability could create considerable change at work or in your general everyday routine. For some, developments will be due to health and the wish to boost your energy levels. A decision, trip or commitment could signal long-term change. Someone close or in authority may have a key influence. You'll enjoy an impromptu reunion.

WEEK 3: 13–19 MARCH

This week brings the opportunity to turn a corner at work or in your daily routine. A partner or family member may have key news. This is a good time to consider in more detail a fresh and revitalising health routine. Events may take you to a past occurrence or reunion with someone who has important information for you. Events will be best approached in a factual way; avoid speculation.

WEEK 4: 20–26 MARCH / WEEK 5: 27 MARCH–2 APRIL

WEEK 4: this is a changeable time. Health-wise, ensure you rest up or give yourself or someone you love a fitness or health treat. Avoid forgetfulness, mix-ups and being misled, especially at work. You may need to go over old ground with a business or personal agreement. You'll enjoy or appreciate an uplifting development regarding someone close or a property. **WEEK 5:** the Aries solar eclipse on 29 March will kick-start a fresh work or health schedule if you were born in October, and a new phase in a business or personal relationship if you were born in September. A work or health development may involve a different set of rules or fresh agreement. You may receive good news in relation to a past work or health matter.

FINANCES

You'll appreciate the sense that your earning power and enthusiasm for work return, and therefore that you can bring home the bacon. However, the power of the eclipses this month cannot be underestimated, so it's always important to have a kitty for a rainy day should unexpected developments arise at work due to changes beyond your control. A slush fund would be worthwhile starting now if you don't already have one.

HEALTH

You may need to resume a health routine or will receive particular news that indicates it will be in your interest to put in place a stable health schedule that enables you to move forward. You may be pleasantly surprised by particular news that comes around the eclipse on 14 March. The conjunction of Venus and Neptune on the 27th will be ideal for a beauty or a health treat; just be clear about exactly what you want.

LOVE LIFE

Venus retrograde will contribute to a retrospective phase as you go over old ground in your love life. While this could be super romantic, because you'll gain the chance to revisit an old haunt or resume a romantic phase in a relationship, you do risk being idealistic about your love life now. This is an eclipse season that suggests a brand-new cycle will begin in your love life, especially if you were born at the end of September.

CAREER

Be prepared to pursue fresh options in your career and interests. You could make a significant commitment to a work or career prospect early in March. The total lunar eclipse on 14 March will kick-start a fresh phase in your usual daily routine, and for some this will be due to changes in your career while for others changes in your status or personal life will mean that you begin to look at your daily work schedule in a new light.

HOME LIFE

You're in the process of expanding your horizons in many different ways, especially at work and in your personal life, and this will inevitably alter your home life. This month will have an impact on your home life and it will be in your interest to obtain expert advice if necessary. Travel and escapism will appeal to you. The more information you can gather the better.

April

WEEK 1: 3–9 APRIL

Mars at the zenith of your chart will provide you with the motivation and energy to get things done so be sure to take the initiative, especially at work and with family and your personal and creative projects. You could gain a degree of stability in any or all of these areas of your life, so maintain a clear view of your aims. Someone close may reveal their deeper thoughts, and a diplomatic approach will suit.

WEEK 2: 10–16 APRIL

The full moon on 13 April will be in your sign and indicates an ideal time to turn a corner in your personal life. If you were born after mid-October you may find your work and health are the areas that take the focus now. Key news either at work or from someone close signals a fresh chapter. Be brave as you step into new territory.

WEEK 3: 17–23 APRIL

Be bold about changes and developments at work, as these could not only be inspiring but will also take you into fresh territory. For some Librans the focus will be on your health and you'll be able to commit to health practices that will enable you to build strength and stamina. A business or personal partner has news that is best approached tactfully. Avoid making snap decisions.

WEEK 4: 24–30 APRIL

This is a good week to make a commitment at work or regarding your health and well-being. You may be drawn to a particular health or cosmetic procedure, and as long as you've researched your options and obtained adequate expert help it is likely to succeed. Likewise, a work contract or arrangement could be lucrative but it will keep you busy.

FINANCES

Your finances will gain attention, principally as a result of either work or health developments that mean you must configure a fresh budget to embrace your new daily work or health routine. The last two weeks of April will be ideal for reorganising some of your investments or commitments so you're on top of developments, as you're likely to achieve a sense of perspective and the help of someone who can see things from a fresh perspective.

HEALTH

Key developments regarding your health and well-being will bring a fresh perspective to this important aspect of your life. An expert or adviser will spotlight ways in which you can work most productively towards a positive picture. The full moon in your sign on 13 April points to coming full circle with a personal or health matter, and this will demand that you adopt a fresh approach either to your health-care schedule or someone close.

LOVE LIFE

The Libra full moon on 13 April combined with the new moon on the 27th points to considerable changes in your love life. It will be in your interest to consider patient and productive ways to navigate a partner's feelings or circumstances. If you're single you may be reminded that rash decisions are rarely rewarded, so be sure to take things one step at a time this month and especially towards the 27th, when couples are best to avoid conflict.

CAREER

You'll gain the opportunity to make a fresh agreement at work and perhaps the chance also to move forward in unexpected ways or into new territory. Someone with whom you share duties and responsibilities will be helpful or cooperative, suggesting that collaborations are a key to progress for you now. However, the full moon mid-month and the new moon at the end of the month will spotlight shared duties that must be attended to carefully.

HOME LIFE

The full moon in Libra on 13 April points to a fresh phase in your personal life that is likely to impact your home. Key decisions or developments concerning a personal partner or business connection will merit careful scrutiny to avoid a power play and battle of egos. However, if you plan your daily duties well you may experience an unexpected breakthrough that enables you to gain a sense of freedom and discovery.

May

WEEK 1: 1–7 MAY

You'll find out whether you've overestimated work schedules and the time you have left for everything else. The good news is you'll get the chance to put things right. You'll appreciate a health or beauty treat and the opportunity to improve your usual daily and health routine so they better suit you. A domestic or personal situation may require additional tact for it to flourish.

WEEK 2: 8–14 MAY

You may be ready to turn a corner in a key financial agreement, which could also feather your nest: not only at home, but also in your daily routine or work life. Take the opportunity while change is in the air to direct your life in the direction you wish it to go in. Focus a little more on communications to avoid intense emotions and conflict.

WEEK 3: 15–21 MAY

A friend or partner is likely to have unexpected news for you and you'll enjoy being a little spontaneous. A visit somewhere lovely or a get-together is likely to be enriching. A change of pace or place will be therapeutic this weekend if not before, so be sure to organise activities you enjoy. The key to making the most of your spare time lies in keeping those who depend on you in the loop.

WEEK 4: 22–28 MAY

Your desires and abilities will be centre stage this week as a key decision in your love life, home life or family will come down to practicalities and good communication skills. A trip could be the deciding factor. Luckily the excellent aspect between Mars and Venus will encourage you to socialise and network and gather information so that decisions you make now are well informed.

FINANCES

This will be a good month to kick-start fresh financial arrangements and agreements with the people you share duties and responsibilities with, both at home and work. Developments that could improve your work or health circumstances early in the month will predicate the kinds of allowances and budget you put in place. Avoid feeling that you must stick with a tried and trusted financial arrangement if it no longer suits your circumstances.

HEALTH

Early May is ideal for a beauty or health improvement, so take the initiative to formulate a revitalised health or beauty schedule. Your endeavours are likely to be successful. You'll gain the opportunity in May to find ways to breathe fresh air into your fitness routine, and the new moon on the 27th will inspire you to take a trip somewhere refreshing and alter a stale daily health routine if necessary.

LOVE LIFE

A partner has key news for you early in the month that may be related to health and well-being and considerations you both need to take into account. The key to working things out together lies in careful research. A holiday or trip somewhere lovely will certainly boost your relationship, perhaps in unexpected ways. Singles may be inclined in May to leave your comfort zone and be explorative and adventurous, which you're likely to enjoy.

CAREER

The beginning of the month will be ideal for reconfiguring your usual daily work routine so you are on top of rapid developments. Ensure your work commitments synchronise with your domestic or personal circumstances so that all areas can flourish, particularly at the start and end of the month. Be prepared to negotiate mid-month so you create a schedule or timetable you're happy with.

HOME LIFE

Emotions are likely to be strong, especially mid-month around 12 May due to the powerful Scorpio full moon. Take time to process news from a partner or at work before responding impulsively, as you may regret hasty words. Careful negotiations will produce far better results. The aspect between Mercury and Pluto towards the new moon on the 27th could kick-start a fresh phase at home that enables you to see the benefits of a flexible approach.

June

WEEK 1: 29 MAY–4 JUNE

You'll find out over the next few days whether you've underestimated a situation or someone, perhaps even yourself. You may learn a key lesson. Be realistic with investments, debts and spending to avoid making mistakes, especially those you share with someone. The advice of a group or expert will be invaluable. A trip or visit will be educational, if not enjoyable.

WEEK 2: 5–11 JUNE

The full moon on 11 June will spotlight communications, a decision, study or travel-related matters. You'll gain the opportunity to consider the best way forward regarding personal and work matters that involve certain negotiations. This weekend is a good time for discussions regarding joint responsibilities and collaborations, as your efforts are likely to succeed. A trip or meeting could involve romance or will be therapeutic, so take the initiative.

WEEK 3: 12–18 JUNE

Romance, music and the arts will thrive now. Keen talks over logistics or activities could take you a long way towards a better understanding of someone close. A dynamic approach to solving mysteries and riddles will work well and improve work collaborations. Consider bright and proactive ways to understand someone who may behave unpredictably or seems at cross purposes to you.

WEEK 4: 19–25 JUNE / WEEK 5: 26 JUNE–2 JULY

WEEK 4: current stars will bring out your inner nurturer, adventurer and dreamer and lead you to all kinds of activities you'll enjoy. Be sure to choose carefully and keep those you love in the loop. Romance should blossom over the next few days but then so, too, could unexpected disagreements. For that reason, be sure to keep communications very clear both at work and home. **WEEK 5:** Mercury will put your communication skills in the spotlight. You may be in demand at work and will be required to shine. Rest assured you will make a positive impression. You may be surprised by news from a collaborator or colleague at work or a partner. Be careful with discussions early next week as these could be intense.

FINANCES

Key discussions regarding finances in relation to work will require patience, understanding and good negotiation skills. There are likely to be developments regarding your work, status or health, and the better you're able to put in place sound financial management practices the better for you in the long term. Consider how your domestic life impacts your finances, as you may find you can make some savings there.

HEALTH

If you've been trying to research and understand your health and well-being you may find the first half of the month is particularly revealing, even if you must initially undertake some difficult communications or activities. Be prepared to find ways to boost your energy levels, because this is likely to be a busy or challenging month as several activities take you in various different directions. By the end of the month you'll gain a sense of structure in your health routine.

LOVE LIFE

The second week of June will be perfect for discussions as long as you have an open mind about how best to move forward as you organise your daily health and work schedules. Romance could blossom between 5 and 7 June, and if you need to overcome past disagreements this is the week to approach important discussions with an optimistic outlook. However, you must avoid contentious topics that involve power plays.

CAREER

Key discussions and changes regarding your career and daily work schedule are best taken with a patient approach to ensure the new circumstances you agree to and put in place are to your liking. Towards the end of June you may discover an anomaly regarding some of your work activities and will need to clarify your duties with those they concern. Be sure to rely on the facts when making fresh agreements and arrangements career-wise.

HOME LIFE

This is a good time to consider ways to feather your nest and bring more comfort into your home life. Certain relationships will require more patience than usual. Above all, avoid a battle of egos in mid-June. The new moon on the 25th will spotlight how key big-picture decisions will impact your home life, and it will be important at this time to remember that your home life and those in it such as children are a constantly evolving scenario.

July

WEEK 1: 3—9 JULY

You'll enjoy a fun event, something new or a fresh interest. You may be ready to commit to someone or step into different territory in a relationship. A development that could broaden your horizons, whether through travel or simply a new pastime or hobby, will provide a fresh perspective. Logistics may require patience and clarity and the ability to commit to change at home or to changed circumstances.

WEEK 2: 10—16 JULY

You'll gain a sense of purpose and direction this week and may enjoy a lucky break such as a trip somewhere different, fun activity or financial improvement. The full moon on 10 July will spotlight your domestic life or family, and for some Librans there will be an opportunity to improve communications by updating your communications device or investing in a new vehicle.

WEEK 3: 17—23 JULY

You'll appreciate the opportunity to find time for your favourite activities and people. Key news regarding work or health, either your own or that of someone close, will merit careful attention. Decide where your priorities lie, especially regarding those you love. Someone close may surprise you. You may need to make a tough call regarding your long-term plans or shared responsibilities.

WEEK 4: 24—30 JULY

A fresh commitment or job offer or the chance to devote more time to your favourite activities will appeal as the new moon on 24 July kick-starts an upbeat phase in your career or status. You can get ahead at work, financially and in your general ventures by organising your day and duties well and realistically. Avoid intense interactions towards Friday.

FINANCES

This will be a good month to renegotiate some joint financial arrangements such as those you share with someone in your house or family or with organisations such as debt providers. You will gain the opportunity to step into new territory in the area of shared finances. Some Librans will also gain the chance to step into something different at work and potentially to improve your income in the process.

HEALTH

July will be an excellent month to retrace your steps regarding your health practices so you're able to maximise your health in ways that draw on your previous experiences with treatments that worked well. The first week will be particularly constructive in this regard and then you'll gain the opportunity over the coming months to gather your strength in constructive and productive ways.

LOVE LIFE

Developments this month will focus your mind on your true priorities. Your family and those you love will come first, but you'll need to find ways to agree with your partner to ensure that fair play can take place. Either you or your partner's vulnerabilities are likely to surface towards 19 July. Luckily, you have the gift of the gab in July and will find ways to discuss sensitive topics so they could ultimately be liberating.

CAREER

You may be surprised by developments that will improve your daily work schedule; for example, a colleague or employer puts in a good word for you. You'll certainly gain the opportunity to spotlight your skill sets. The new moon on 24 July will kick-start an upbeat and exciting phase that could lead to a fresh and dynamic daily schedule, so ensure you're open to new opportunities. You may need to reconfigure some domestic duties to suit.

HOME LIFE

Developments in areas you share with someone close such as your partner or family will take much of your focus in July as your home life becomes the centre of change in this regard. You must be prepared to be adventurous and outgoing and take existing arrangements or agreements into new territory. You may discover in the second half of the month that the key to moving forward lies in good communication skills that circumnavigate conflict.

August

WEEK 1: 31 JULY–6 AUGUST

You'll appreciate a reunion or meeting on Friday and may receive key news from a friend, group or organisation. Financial and work matters are best handled carefully to ensure you're on track with your big-picture plans. An upcoming trip or change at home is likely to be fruitful, but you must plan ahead to avoid delays or difficult conversations.

WEEK 2: 7–13 AUGUST

You'll enjoy a breath of fresh air entering your life this week. Be prepared to take steps into new territory, especially in the areas of work and your home life. Someone you rely on or collaborate with may surprise you with their smart ideas and ingenuity. Be sure to apply the full facts to a key work or health decision and avoid making impulsive choices.

WEEK 3: 14–20 AUGUST

It's an excellent week for socialising and networking. If you're a businessperson or growing your career an agreement could be just what you're looking for, but you must be sure to avoid rushing into arrangements. A therapeutic or healing connection with someone who boosts your feel-good factor will raise morale. This is a good week to make a commitment in your personal life or at work.

WEEK 4: 21–27 AUGUST

This will be an intriguing and sociable week. There is a watershed quality as you discover an arrangement at work could be altered and that you can seek more of a sense of purpose and fulfilment as you reorganise some of your commitments. A delicate matter is best kept on the table to ensure all avenues are researched, but you must avoid being pressured into making decisions.

FINANCES

It's possible to transform your finances in August through sheer hard work; however, it would be far better to follow the maxim of it being better to work smarter, not harder, as you otherwise risk burning yourself out. For some a development at home or with family will spell changes financially. Work or options to improve your health and well-being that will boost your productivity could advance your finances in mid-August, so be sure to keep an eye out then for options.

HEALTH

Saturn and Neptune make a tough aspect to your sign's ruler Venus at the start of the month, which suggests it's best to take your work and projects one step at a time to avoid overtiring yourself in August. If you can do this you'll find your month so much more productive. You will nevertheless be tempted to go full steam ahead with your various projects but would be much better advised to pace yourself.

LOVE LIFE

Mars in Libra from 7 August is going to ramp up romance but first, during the first week of the month, Mars may contribute to you feeling vulnerable or sensitive about yourself or regarding a partner. A partner may also feel sensitive, which is likely to come to a head in mid-August. You'll be able to overcome challenges through a healing and nurturing approach. Singles may meet someone appealing in mid-August, so be sure to make dates then.

CAREER

This is likely to be a busy month career-wise, especially once Mars has entered your sign on 7 August. You'll gain a sense that your projects really produce their own momentum, so if you're happy with the direction you're heading in it will be a successful month. However, if you feel that some aspects of your career are no longer to your liking it's an equally productive month to make changes.

HOME LIFE

This is an excellent month to make long-overdue changes in your domestic life and suggest something new to your family or housemates. The start of the month is already conducive to making changes you've been considering for some time. You may be surprised by some developments that will have an impact on your home life or family, especially around the full moon on 9 August and towards the end of the month.

September

WEEK 1: 28 AUGUST–3 SEPTEMBER

This is an excellent week to retrace your steps health-wise to ensure your daily schedule supports your current needs. You could make a great deal of progress either at work or with a personal venture, so be sure to take the initiative. This will also be a good week to take communications, research and work practices one step at a time and avoid difficult conversations that may arise unexpectedly.

WEEK 2: 4–10 SEPTEMBER

Be prepared to turn a corner in your work, daily and health routines. For some October-born Librans a personal, family or creative venture may be due for change. Take the time now to find out how you could achieve your dreams in practical terms, as the Jupiter alignment with the lunar eclipse on 7 September will be empowering. Someone special will prove particularly helpful.

WEEK 3: 11–17 SEPTEMBER

News from your past or a reunion will be significant this week. If you've been looking for ways to boost your status, career or social life this is an excellent week to take the initiative, as your efforts are likely to succeed. You may experience a therapeutic breakthrough if a relationship has been difficult, but you must be tactful.

WEEK 4: 18–24 SEPTEMBER / WEEK 5: 25 SEPTEMBER–1 OCTOBER

WEEK 4: health and work are key areas that will catch your attention, and a get-together or news from a friend or organisation could be pivotal in your understanding of health and fitness: your own or someone else's. A lovely reunion could raise your mood even if you feel under pressure. Someone you love will surprise you, and a mystery may be revealed. **WEEK 5:** this is a good week to get ahead with your projects and ventures as they're likely to succeed. Just be careful with financial agreements, as you may have a blind spot. It's better to seek expert financial advice if necessary rather than make a mistake. Romance may well flourish now, so be sure to take the initiative but avoid misunderstandings by being super clear.

FINANCES

September's eclipses bring a sense of reckoning with them so, financially, if you've overspent in the past or mismanaged your savings or investments this month you're likely to have to deal with the consequences and especially towards mid-month and 30 September. However, you have the opportunity to improve your finances at the same time, so this is in fact an excellent month to get ahead financially as your efforts to improve your career are likely to work.

HEALTH

Saturn in your health sector takes a step back into the introspective sign of Pisces, enabling you to retrace your steps in your health schedule to ensure you're on top of your current health needs. You may be drawn towards spiritual or mental health practices that enable you to visualise your future clearly, and therefore help you structure your daily activities more accurately. You may discover a particular health expert is especially informative.

LOVE LIFE

September is going to be a month of change and this will play out in your personal life. If you're single, consider looking at fresh, inspired ways to meet someone or join a group of like-minded people to add a sense of camaraderie into your life if it is lacking. It's a good month for romantic Librans to consider making a commitment to someone special. Just avoid difficult conversations towards 16 and 30 September.

CAREER

Jupiter, the planet of abundance, is at the zenith of your chart and could bring fresh horizons to you in your career, especially around 3 September, the lunar eclipse on the 7th and towards the end of the month. However, there will also be some difficult conversations to undertake, especially earlier in the month. Luckily, you have support either in the workplace or through family that helps you make solid progress.

HOME LIFE

This will be an excellent month to make changes at home or with a property or family, as your efforts are likely to show long-term results: if not immediately then by early next year. If you've been considering changing how you share common ground, duties and responsibilities both the beginning and the end of the month will be particularly conducive to doing so, as will the week beginning 22 September.

October

WEEK 1: 2–8 OCTOBER

The Mercury–Chiron opposition may heighten your sensitivity to people, so ensure you maintain perspective. You may be surprised by someone's news this week, and the key to moving ahead should someone disappoint you lies in great communication skills and not taking other people's issues personally. You can get well ahead in work and with health issues through good advice and best practice.

WEEK 2: 9–15 OCTOBER

Key decisions or agreements can be made so ensure you seek guidance or information, especially if much of your decision-making depends on good financial and work decisions. The entry of Venus in Libra and the wonderful aspect between Venus, Uranus and Pluto also point to positive change at home and with shared assets and/or responsibilities. This would be an ideal time for a move, redecoration or new start at work.

WEEK 3: 16–22 OCTOBER

The Libra new moon on 21 October signals a fresh chapter for you. It may involve difficult talks or intense decisions in association with someone special, your work or status. Help is at hand so be prepared to discuss ideas, and if you need expert advice or help rest assured it will be available. Some Librans will experience a financial or ego boost.

WEEK 4: 23–29 OCTOBER

The stars are aligning this week to bring you optimum opportunities to improve your career, daily routine and finances, so be sure to keep an open mind and a view on the horizon for new ventures. You may already experience something exciting mid next week that could bring a surprising financial outcome. If you experience some challenging communications, be diligent: you're sure to overcome them.

FINANCES

A practical approach to finances will be beneficial. It's possible that a business or personal partner's situation affects you financially, so it's important to discuss circumstances. The Venus opposition to Saturn on 11 October points to increased focus on finances, and also around the entry of Venus in Libra on the 13th. Commitments are likely to be long term. You may experience a financial improvement towards the 19th and 25th but you must also avoid overspending at this time.

HEALTH

If health has been a worry it's important to keep an eye on niggling health concerns. The first week of October will be a good time for health and beauty appointments. Be sure to communicate clearly what you need to discuss, as misunderstandings could arise early in the month. The new moon on the 21st may spotlight a health situation, either of your own or that of someone very close. Rest assured you will find the expert advice you need.

LOVE LIFE

You will be drawn to nostalgia and perhaps even an ex at the start of October. If you do consider a reunion, ask yourself whether this is due to love or sentimentality. The entry of Venus in Libra on the 13th points to an increased focus on your love life and a particular commitment. Is it time to alter some parameters of this commitment or make a fresh commitment to someone new if you're single? It would be a good month to do so if you've been considering this already.

CAREER

Jupiter in your 10th house of career will spur you on to make great progress in this area of your life, especially towards the end of October. However, the key to success at the start of the month revolves around good communication skills and teamwork, as without these it will be difficult to make progress. Important decisions will merit careful analysis towards the new moon on the 21st, and you could experience a positive career or morale boost around this time.

HOME LIFE

Consider what must be done in your home, property or family that will lead to happiness. If you feel stuck or that some things are too difficult to consider you'll see early next year a great shift in your home life if you do not already, making this a good time to prepare. The mid-month developments point to a wonderful opportunity to improve or enhance your home life, whether through better relationships, redecoration or, for some, a move.

November

WEEK 1: 30 OCTOBER–5 NOVEMBER

Financial and personal decisions merit detailed analysis. Avoid taking risks or making large investments without researching options. If you're unsure of someone, ask where you stand. You may need to put yourself out on a limb emotionally but you'll at least get the low down, either at work or home. The supermoon on 5 November spotlights shared assets and duties, enabling you to plan ahead.

WEEK 2: 6–12 NOVEMBER

As your sign's ruler Venus steps into Scorpio your deeper thoughts and feelings are likely to surface. It's a good week for get-togethers and reunions with those you love, and also to re-evaluate where you place your loyalties in your personal life and at work. You may be surprised by some news, but it will help you gain perspective. Be sure to avoid arguments, especially this weekend.

WEEK 3: 13–19 NOVEMBER

The stars are aligning, bringing the opportunity to make some advantageous arrangements in your daily life, career and finances. You may feel nevertheless that every two steps forward are followed by three steps back, so you'll need to be patient with negotiations. Be prepared to look at your finances from a big-picture perspective. Health will merit attention to detail so you can put in place a workable plan.

WEEK 4: 20–26 NOVEMBER / WEEK 5: 27 NOVEMBER–3 DECEMBER

WEEK 4: a fresh chapter is about to begin in the way you interact with someone close such as a personal or business partner. This could be a particularly therapeutic time, as meetings and get-togethers are likely to please you. However, you may also receive unexpected news or must adjust to a change of environment or outside circumstances that takes you by surprise. **WEEK 5:** your interests will guide you to enjoyable activities this weekend. You may delight in a change of environment that will bring into your circle not only those you love but also refreshing people. Working Librans may be busy. As Mercury ends its recent retrograde phase you may receive key news financially or at work that could be a surprise or change of circumstance.

FINANCES

You will be drawn to making considerable changes financially in November. The more research and information you can gather the more likely your decisions will be the right ones. The entry of Venus in your money zone in the second week of the month will help you be more focused on establishing a balanced budget. However, simultaneously you may be inclined to overspend, so watch your expenditure.

HEALTH

November will be a productive month health-wise as you'll gain the motivation to take practical and adventurous steps to improve your well-being. The start of the month will be particularly conducive to this. For the sake of your own peace of mind it will be in your interest to avoid arguments early in the month, as these are likely to escalate quickly. Try to find less stressful ways to discuss differences of opinion.

LOVE LIFE

Your ruler Venus is under considerable stress astrologically early in the month, and you may find as a result that your love life suffers unless you make a concerted effort to create a relaxed space and plenty of time for those you love. A partner may express their vulnerability or deliver unexpected news. It will be in your interest to contemplate or design a workable plan that suits both of you.

CAREER

Early in November you'll gain the opportunity to improve your daily routine and work circumstances, although you may need to negotiate or work hard to get the status and outcome you desire, so be prepared to play a long game. Jupiter in your career zone will turn retrograde on the 11th, which will bring certain conversations to do with your big-picture career direction under review. By the end of the month you may gain an increased sense of direction.

HOME LIFE

Both the very start and end of November will be particularly conducive to making adventurous decisions and changes in your domestic life. Your home life will be the nexus of important decisions even if more immediate ones such as finances seem to demand your primary attention. Be sure around the 8th to avoid arguments, as these could spiral quickly.

December

WEEK 1: 4—10 DECEMBER

Discussions will be fruitful and could provide solutions to problems, so be sure to initiate talks and especially at work and financially. A trip, project or exciting venture will catch your eye. For some the supermoon on 4 December will bring the desire to study, settle legal matters or a change of location. For others, areas of your life you share such as duties, space at home and finances will be a focus.

WEEK 2: 11—17 DECEMBER

You'll appreciate the opportunity to spend time with people you love and doing activities you enjoy. You'll also appreciate the effects of a therapeutic place or relationship. However, you may need to pay attention to details to avoid making mistakes and absentmindedness, especially in connection with travel and work. If health has been an issue, ensure you obtain all the necessary information so you can move ahead most productively.

WEEK 3: 18—24 DECEMBER

The new moon on 20 December will kick-start a fresh phase in a key relationship. For some lucky Librans this will revolve around travel or a return to an old haunt, while for others it will be due to a lovely visit of someone special. If you were born after mid-October you're likely to venture into a fresh financial phase that could feel therapeutic but will involve courage.

WEEK 4: 25—31 DECEMBER

You're constantly on the lookout for harmony in life, and this week the arrival of visitors or the opportunity to take a trip will help. Be sure to plan ahead with travel to avoid delays but also remain open to being adaptable, as you risk missing the magic of spontaneity if you focus too hard on planning. A change of routine will be therapeutic.

FINANCES

Finances will flow early in December and you may be in line for a financial improvement. However, you may also be inclined to overspend, so you must avoid impulse buys and gambling. If you encounter a surprise that impacts your finances around 10 December you'll gain the opportunity to put in place an arrangement that enables you to proceed on a more even footing. If you were born after mid-October you'll gain the opportunity to turn a corner around 20 December.

HEALTH

You'll enjoy lovely opportunities early in December and towards the solstice to boost your health. Some Librans are likely to enjoy the positive influence of a partner or expert on your health and morale. It's certainly a good month to invest in yourself, especially your health, through enjoying favourite activities and relaxation. Travel and at the least day trips to somewhere beautiful or adventurous will be uplifting, as a varied and inspiring daily routine will be revitalising.

LOVE LIFE

Someone close will have a therapeutic effect on you during the first week of December and around the solstice. As long as you avoid discussions that you know lead nowhere fast the beginning of December and towards the 20th could be a romantic time. Consider organising activities you love such as a short break and fun outings. The final week of the month includes a healing quality as long as you maintain a realistic outlook and focus on good communication skills.

CAREER

Jupiter at the zenith of your chart continues its retrograde phase, and this may contribute to a sense of stagnancy in your career but nevertheless you'll gain a sense of flow during December. You must, however, avoid difficult or tense topics, especially towards the end of the month. If there are various negotiations that are unavoidable, the more sensitive to others you can be the better for you.

HOME LIFE

You'll gain the opportunity to engage a proactive plan concerning your home and one that is also practical and realistic. The second half of the month will be particularly productive for getting things done at home. Visitors or a holiday will impact your immediate environment, and the presence of someone whose company you find therapeutic will certainly be uplifting. Events around the solstice will require you to lean into your peacemaking and negotiation skills to avoid arguments and mistakes.

January

WEEK 1: 1–8 JANUARY

Creative and artistic Scorpios may be particularly inspired at the moment. All Scorpios will enjoy music, dance and romance but must avoid overspending. Someone from your past may need your help or advice, even if they don't ask for it outright. Rest assured that help is available if you need it. There's also a therapeutic quality to the week. Romance could flourish, so organise a treat with someone special.

WEEK 2: 9–15 JANUARY

A health or fitness matter will require focus, as someone close or a work routine will keep you on your toes. The Cancerian full moon on 13 January will provide you with the opportunity to boost your career and/or status by being more involved in projects you like. You may need to travel or alter some of your communications to benefit from work opportunities. Romance, good food, wine and music will appeal, so enjoy those.

WEEK 3: 16–22 JANUARY

The chance to do something different will add excitement to your week. However, a change of environment may be tiring or require extra focus, so be sure to plan ahead if you're travelling. You'll enjoy a trip to your past or resuming a favourite hobby. An event or get-together will bring like-minded people together. A talk or news mid-week will bring focus to the need to be innovative.

WEEK 4: 23–29 JANUARY

You'll enjoy the company of like-minded people this week, so consider organising an upbeat event. It's a good time to consider planning a trip or a longer-term change of pace. A new approach to communications will offer you the chance to break into fresh territory. For some this may relate to travel and for others to work. It may be time to invest in technology that will boost your efficiency.

FINANCES

Beware of going into debt in January as you risk being one of the last big spenders! You may have a large outlay or important aspects of your life you must invest in such as your family and also enjoyment. A holiday or fresh environment may add to the outlay. You're likely to gain a more realistic approach to finances after the 9th, but unless you're careful you may get a reality check mid-month. Above all, you must avoid gambling.

HEALTH

It's a variable picture in January, but you'll at the very least gain a sense of what is and isn't viable health-wise this month. For some this will concern your health and well-being and for others the health of someone else. The start of the year will already illuminate how to improve health and fitness, and it's important you maintain health resolutions throughout the year to avoid resuming bad habits.

LOVE LIFE

The arrival of Venus in Pisces will shine a light on your love life, and romance and all the aspects of life you love will draw your attention. While you're likely to enjoy the good things in life at least for a while in January, you must beware of one pitfall: that you become super idealistic about what your love life should look like. If you succumb to this pitfall you risk seeing everything and everyone through rose-coloured glasses, and mistakes could be made.

CAREER

Certain aspects of your life are inescapable, such as the need for money. The opposition of Mars and Pluto will put this in perspective, and even if you enjoy a lovely holiday or have done so recently you'll know in January that certain projects cannot be delayed. While this may get in the way of your enjoyment of life you gain the chance now to create a more beneficial daily life, and this includes being able to configure your work hours and location to suit you better in 2025.

HOME LIFE

You'll appreciate the opportunity to enhance your environment either by investing in your home or going somewhere else such as on holiday. Venus and Saturn will help you attain a foothold in a more secure home life and add a little of what you love in life, such as a sense of progress. However, if you're planning long-range changes in this important area of your life be sure to plan well and remain grounded and practical to avoid disappointment.

February

WEEK 1: 30 JANUARY–5 FEBRUARY

This is one of the most creative, fun and romantic weeks of the year, so it's a great time to include more activities you love in your life. Domestic matters could thrive, and you'll enjoy bonding over a favourite pastime. If study appeals to you, you may meet an influential teacher. However, you must be careful to keep an eye on work chores, otherwise you could fall foul of a housemate or family member. Keep an eye on your health to avoid fatigue.

WEEK 2: 6–12 FEBRUARY

You may be surprised by the intensity of some conversations. A trip may represent a turning point in a family or personal circumstance. Look for ways now to ring in the changes, as a new phase is about to begin in your work, general direction and interests. Avoid making assumptions. A domestic matter will benefit from careful discussion. You must avoid financial and emotional gambling.

WEEK 3: 13–19 FEBRUARY

Hope and enjoyment are the themes for the week. You'll enjoy your favourite pastimes and adding weight to your predilection for romance, love and creativity. If you discover that your expectations have been unrealistic you'll appreciate the chance to adjust these. This is a good week for home improvements, including not only décor but also family or domestic relationships.

WEEK 4: 20–26 FEBRUARY

You'll feel motivated to get ahead with your bright ideas and plans in a practical and down-to-earth way. Avoid communication mix-ups, especially at home or with someone special. You'll avoid travel delays by planning ahead and being careful. It's a good time to make plans to do with your home and travel, and you may be inspired by an upbeat person.

FINANCES

This will be a progressive and changeable month if you run your own business, full of potential and opportunities to kick-start fresh incentives and ideas. If you're employed or don't work you'll gain the chance to discuss your plans and make solid progress in both areas, so be sure to consider early on in February how you'd like your finances to shape up as you'll gain every opportunity to improve them. Just avoid gambling early in the month.

HEALTH

You are a powerhouse of energy and can tend to take on too much at once. Keep an eye on energy levels at the start of the month and towards 10 and 20 February. Events around these dates will point to areas in which you may be overtiring yourself and could find ways to avoid depleting your energy levels. There is a lot going on for you, and with your ruler Mars retrograde until the 24th it's important this month to look after yourself.

LOVE LIFE

Ever the passionate lover, you risk throwing caution to the wind in February as your lust for life and love for someone could consume the rest of your life if you're not careful. The conjunction of Neptune and the moon's north node at the start of the month points to a predestined love connection that will be hard to ignore. Couples will enjoy a truly romantic time, so be sure to plan a wonderful event.

CAREER

The Leo full moon on 12 February will spotlight important considerations in your career and general direction, especially from the perspective of how these will affect your home life and personal life. There is room to be adventurous but not fool-hardy in your career and with long-term goals. Be sure to discuss your options with those they concern such as your family, partner and colleagues or employer to avoid hasty actions.

HOME LIFE

Considerable changes at home are likely. If you've been considering a move or improving your environment in and around your home for some time you'll enjoy taking on work that brings more beauty to your surroundings. If well planned to avoid disappointment, a move is likely to take you somewhere better. The Pisces new moon on 28 February will make your priorities and path clearer.

March

WEEK 1: 27 FEBRUARY–5 MARCH

The Pisces new moon on 28 February will kick-start a fresh phase in your personal life. Singles may meet a romantic character. Creative or spiritual Scorpios could deepen your interests. A fresh work schedule or healthier phase will appeal; however, you must be tactful and keep those with whom you share responsibilities in the loop to avoid difficult conversations. A refreshing and upbeat mood will infuse some of your relationships, which you'll enjoy.

WEEK 2: 6–12 MARCH

You may need to go over old ground or review commitments to make progress in your personal life. A health matter, domestic situation or relationship will require a careful approach. Discussions may be more serious than you'd hoped. Avoid extravagance and making promises you can't keep.

WEEK 3: 13–19 MARCH

You may make a key commitment; for some this will be at work and for others at home. You may be prepared to discuss matters that have been on your mind and find practical ways to move forward. Whether you find this week's news challenging or therapeutic, uplifting or disappointing, the upshot is you'll be clearer by the end of the week about your options and especially regarding someone close or a friend or organisation.

WEEK 4: 20–26 MARCH / WEEK 5: 27 MARCH–2 APRIL

WEEK 4: you're known for being passionate and romantic, and this week's stars certainly favour indulgence in your favourite activities including romance, music, dance and film. You'll enjoy treating your family and friends. You'll be prone to overindulgence and overspending, so be sure to avoid this pitfall. A trip or get-together with someone special will make your heart soar. **WEEK 5:** talks with family and those close to you will be productive, ensuring everyone feels on track. It's a good week to kindle love and romance. A fresh start is waiting in the wings domestically or with family and, for some, with financial arrangements. It's a good week for domestic improvements.

FINANCES

As a passionate person you prefer to live life spontaneously, and as you have a lust for life you can also tend to spend money like water and on a whim. This month's eclipse season could see you being drawn to gambling, and if you're already a gambler you'll know the odds are stacked against you. It will be in your interest to avoid gambling, as this month could precipitate a loss. It's far better to bank on a certainty.

HEALTH

This will be a good month to review your health plan or that of someone close so you're clear about your options moving forward and can plan your daily life and activities all the better. You may receive key news regarding the long-term prognosis for someone's health and well-being. Key dates for boosting health matters are 11, 15, 26 and 29 March.

LOVE LIFE

There will be a particularly romantic and passionate time that you'll enjoy but you must beware of overindulgence, which you'll be prone to now. The eclipses on 14 and 29 March signal a fresh phase in your love life. If you're a couple this will be an excellent time to indulge in aspects of life you both love. If you're single you'll enjoy a fun, uplifting end of the month as long as you remain realistic and practical.

CAREER

The lunar eclipse on 14 March will spotlight your status, and for many Scorpios this will involve focus on your career and general direction in life. A new chapter is beginning that will have an impact on your home life and/or family. You may be pleasantly surprised by some of the welcome upshots of changes, but you must take into account the importance of considering the practicalities of sharing duties and responsibilities in a different way.

HOME LIFE

Be prepared to look at your home life with a new perspective, as developments bring a completely fresh chapter in this important area of your life. You may feel somewhat nostalgic as situations change but you're due to feel a boost in morale and energy by the month's end, if not before. Key arrangements and agreements at home or concerning family will involve the need to be innovative.

April

WEEK 1: 3–9 APRIL

This is a good week to focus on your health and well-being. Someone close has a surprise for you. It's a good week to work towards building a solid platform as domestic and personal circumstances change. The more you think things through the better will be the outcome. A commitment to a project or person promises to go well.

WEEK 2: 10–16 APRIL

You'll appreciate the opportunity to spend time with those you love such as family and friends and to engage in your favourite activities. A trip or lovely environment will truly boost your feel-good factor. You may be prepared to step into new territory in your personal or work life, which will benefit from a measured approach largely to avoid making mistakes.

WEEK 3: 17–23 APRIL

You'll be drawn to travelling and broadening your horizons and perhaps to throwing caution to the wind, but practicalities demand that you maintain a degree of groundedness and especially to a healthy daily fitness routine. If you're on holiday you'll enjoy the break. You are ready to make a romantic commitment to someone special or a project.

WEEK 4: 24–30 APRIL

This is a transformative time in your personal, family and domestic life, as key decisions must be made. If you're single you may meet someone significant and couples could make a further commitment to each other, but if the relationship has been rocky you may mutually decide to go your separate ways. The key to happiness lies in careful talks to avoid conflict.

FINANCES

You're in line to make financial decisions that could transform your personal life, and for this reason it's very important that you research circumstances in depth. It's likely that changes at home predicate financial investments, so if for example you're planning a move this could work out considerably well for you financially. However, you must avoid gambling, especially towards the last two weeks of the month, as you're likely to regret it.

HEALTH

The full moon on 13 April will spotlight a health situation and either in relation to work, someone close or to you. Developments will enable you to take constructive steps towards building a strong health profile, but you must avoid feeling this will happen super fast. You will need to build a rosy picture one step at a time. A professional or adviser will be particularly helpful at this time.

LOVE LIFE

The reality of your feelings for someone will no longer be easy to ignore and you'll take the steps to make a commitment to a particular course of action in this light. The behaviour of someone close to you may surprise you. There is a sense of the inevitable around one particular relationship that will take your attention. You may need to take into account the health and well-being of someone you love.

CAREER

There is a great deal of change afoot in your career and it will revolve around decisions you make regarding where you wish to place your focus. Your career may need to take second place if you decide your family or friends must come first, but you must avoid if possible sacrificing a strong career. If you decide your career comes before your family there will be considerable sacrifices to make, so be sure to choose wisely.

HOME LIFE

For many Scorpios the most change occurring this month will affect your home life and/or family, so it will be extremely important to follow good advice and your intuition and heart as much as possible. Commitments you make in mid- to late April could have a positive impact at home and on your general movements, but you must avoid power struggles as these could escalate rapidly. It will be best for all concerned to negotiate a positive outcome.

May

WEEK 1: 1–7 MAY

You'll enjoy catching up with someone special. Romance could sizzle, but you must avoid making assumptions that you're on the same page. Avoid emotional and financial gambling, as this would be a true pitfall you come to regret. A health or work matter will deserve careful analysis and your association with a friend or group will be an important focus.

WEEK 2: 8–14 MAY

The Scorpio full moon on 12 May will coincide with a Mercury–Pluto alignment that will bring your passions to the surface, so go easy as you may be liable to be a little impulsive: not only in your actions but also in your speech. If you channel your considerable energy into creating a secure platform for yourself and those you love you could build true stability now. You'll be surprised by someone's news.

WEEK 3: 15–21 MAY

You'll enjoy the sense that you're attaining fresh status, seeking new direction or turning a corner in your career. A personal decision could mark a different direction. You'll enjoy a little spontaneity now. The next two weeks are likely to be two of the most romantic this year, ideal for organising a treat such as a trip abroad or a visit to a music festival.

WEEK 4: 22–28 MAY

A fresh chapter is about to begin regarding the areas of your life you share such as your duties and love life. This could be a predominantly romantic week but you must avoid making assumptions about someone's feelings or hopes and wishes. You could make a great deal of progress with a venture or your career, and a trip will be exciting.

FINANCES

You may gain a financial boost in May but must be wary not to spend it all at once or borrow or lend money, as you may come to regret this unless you organise an iron-clad agreement. Shared finances will merit careful analysis to avoid disappointment in the future. You'll appreciate forking out a little extra cash for a therapeutic or health-based treat towards mid-May but must avoid spending money that leads to more debt.

HEALTH

Health and well-being will be focuses in the first week of the month. It will be a good time to consider whether your daily routine supports your health or whether there are aspects of your activities that could be healthier. A friend or organisation may figure in your challenge to improve health. A trip or change of routine at the month's end will most certainly be refreshing and exciting, so plan something special if possible.

LOVE LIFE

You may experience unexpectedly uplifting developments, and if you're single you may meet someone significant who you'd like to spend more time with, especially around the full moon on 12 May. The new moon on the 27th could point couples to a fresh arrangement regarding shared assets or space at home, as you find ways to continue to thrive through different mutually acceptable agreements. Be careful with communications as misunderstandings could arise.

CAREER

Mars in your career sector will encourage you to be enterprising and dynamic and you could make some true breakthroughs both early and at the end of the month, when your upbeat outlook and willingness to go outside your comfort zone could land you important new projects, arrangements or contracts in your career. Be sure to forge ahead with fresh ideas as you are ready to broaden your horizons career-wise.

HOME LIFE

At the start of May a key commitment in your home life could require renegotiation or a rearrangement of some of your shared duties and responsibilities to ensure you are all happy with commitments, duties and finances. The Scorpio full moon on 12 May will highlight your true feelings and have an impact on decisions to do with your home, which you're likely to enact towards the end of the month if not before.

June

WEEK 1: 29 MAY–4 JUNE

News from a personal or business source will be important. A choice concerning finances or a close relationship will merit careful analysis, as you could make a valid commitment or take a key financial step. Ensure you consider an optimistic plan in detail, especially regarding work. Health or beauty considerations will also merit careful attention.

WEEK 2: 5–11 JUNE

Get set for a fresh chapter in connection with finances, work or your health, or that of someone close. There are therapeutic aspects to the week, and this is a good time to reach out if you've been considering some health and wellness advice. This is the week to take the initiative to improve your career and finances, as discussions regarding shared concerns such as joint duties will be on the table.

WEEK 3: 12–18 JUNE

This is likely to be a week of many stops and starts and you may find that someone you have grown to depend on behaves erratically, which puts you on the back foot. Try to focus on what's working in your life this week as opposed to what isn't, as you may otherwise be easily distracted. A healing, therapeutic approach will work wonders.

WEEK 4: 19–25 JUNE / WEEK 5: 26 JUNE–2 JULY

WEEK 4: a fresh approach to a shared duty, joint finances or the space you share at home will bring inspiration your way. This is a good time to discuss your existing agreements both at work and home and to consider formulating new arrangements. However, you'll need to be tactful with those they concern. A fated or intense relationship will blossom. **WEEK 5:** this is again a week to be careful with communications, especially those regarding shared duties and finances with those they concern. However, you're likely to make considerable progress with enjoyable activities, leading to a sense of fun at the weekend. A partner or someone close is likely to pleasantly surprise you, but again you must be careful with communications or travel early next week.

FINANCES

The full moon in Sagittarius on 11 June will encourage you to consider your financial outlook from a fresh perspective. You may be drawn to taking risks, yet if you take a little time to investigate your circumstances you may find that risk taking is not necessary because favourable circumstances will boost your financial outlook in any case. Above all, avoid gambling in June as this is likely to set you back in the long term.

HEALTH

If you've been burning the candle at both ends you'll begin to feel the strain of your lifestyle, and if you're not inclined quite yet to make changes to your way of life you're likely to experience strains in relationships and potentially even at work. Developments around 24 and 25 June will encourage you to consider a fresh health routine that supports you better in mind, body and soul.

LOVE LIFE

You may be surprised by news from someone you have come to see as a steady and reliable person. While good communication skills will enable you to overcome any differences of opinion, the changes in some shared aspects of your life may nevertheless require patience and diligence. Consider looking at the relationship from a broader perspective: how to obtain peace of mind even while differences of opinion or priorities arise.

CAREER

This will be a good month to stride ahead with your career as you're likely to make great progress. If there are aspects of your career you'd like to improve your efforts will succeed. However, you must avoid pushing your agenda and find mutually agreeable ways to move ahead with colleagues and/or employers, otherwise you're likely to find yourself at odds with the people you must get along with.

HOME LIFE

Developments in June will spotlight an unavoidable domestic circumstance that can most certainly flourish given adequate attention. However, decisions will need to be made regarding how to share various areas of your life, some of which will have to be reorganised. It's likely that you'll need to undergo a degree of soul searching in order to find the correct and least-challenging path forward.

July

WEEK 1: 3–9 JULY

A love match will blossom unexpectedly or in unusual ways. You may be ready to begin a fresh business or personal relationship or to let one go. You're likely to hear unexpected news. If you're travelling you'll need to be open to understanding other people's ideas and values. It's a good week to make a personal commitment.

WEEK 2: 10–16 JULY

Communications can improve this week and the full moon on 10 July will shine a light on agreements, paperwork or other negotiations that will benefit from a serious and committed approach. It's also a romantic week, one in which you rediscover the romance in a relationship. If you're single you may meet someone attractive around the full moon or just after.

WEEK 3: 17–23 JULY

Aspects of your life that are unavoidable such as certain relationships or personal arrangements will come into the spotlight, and it's best to avoid conflict so that fresh arrangements if needed may be made. You'll enjoy a trip or get-together this weekend. Be sure to look after your health or that of someone close so you're best able to manage considerable changes in your life.

WEEK 4: 24–30 JULY

Key talks will illuminate who and what means the most to you and will help you determine your priorities regarding people and activities that are important to you. You may be drawn to studying, travelling or legal matters. You'll enjoy indulging in favourite pastimes. Over the next few weeks you'll find your customary joie de vivre will return, if it ever left you.

FINANCES

July is a good month to consider in your own time where you wish to invest your finances the most. You may discover that certain activities and people are truly where your interests lie, and the full moon on 10 July will highlight your priorities. You have the opportunity to invest more time and money in favourite activities such as travel, study and self-development, especially towards the end of the month.

HEALTH

Your health and well-being will come under the spotlight, especially from the perspective of how well or not you're looking after yourself or someone close. You'll gain the opportunity to find workable ways to boost your health or help someone close to improve theirs. Chiron in your sixth house of health makes some tough aspects in July, which indicates you'll gain true insight into health and especially on 1 and 19 July.

LOVE LIFE

You may be surprised by developments early in the month as a partner or someone close surprises you. The first two weeks of July are a good time to focus on romance and cultivating an exciting relationship, as the stars will support your efforts. Singles may meet someone who seems to have a strong connection with you, and it would be in your interest to explore further. The new moon on 24 July could kick-start a fresh arrangement.

CAREER

Communications maestro Mercury will be at the zenith of your chart this month and will certainly help with your career efforts. You're communicating well now and can make great strides ahead in your chosen career. A business associate or employer may surprise you earlier in the month. A career opportunity may clash with domestic responsibilities, so be sure to discuss this with those it concerns.

HOME LIFE

There are certain situations that are inescapable in your home life such as your relationships with parents or housemates. Aspects of these arrangements that you find difficult are likely to come to the boil in July and particularly during the third week, so take extra precautions then to avoid impulsiveness and arguments. The new moon on 24 July signals the opportunity to kick-start a fresh shared arrangement that could be productive.

August

WEEK 1: 31 JULY–6 AUGUST

A strong work ethic will get you places. You're likely to hear important news already early in August to do with your career. It will be a good time to weigh up your various obligations, both at work and in your personal life. Even if a change of circumstance appears to be challenging at times, you'll know in your heart what the right track is.

WEEK 2: 7–13 AUGUST

You'll enjoy a sociable week but must avoid overspending and overindulging, especially towards 12 August. A trip or shared project is likely to go well as you'll feel motivated to invest your energy in developments. This is a good week to make a decision regarding your personal life such as family or a creative project. Just avoid making rash decisions.

WEEK 3: 14–20 AUGUST

Take the time to get in touch with friends or a group or organisation to socialise and network, because you're likely to enjoy a get-together or at least a catch-up. News or a trip is likely to be upbeat. You'll also enjoy engaging in your favourite activities such as sports, spiritual development and the arts. Romance can certainly flourish this weekend, so be sure to organise a date.

WEEK 4: 21–27 AUGUST

A plethora of activities, interests and events this week could put you in a whirl. If you keep your feet on the ground you'll find this week therapeutic as well as enjoyable. The new moon on 23 August will usher in a fresh phase that could see your status and direction change a little as fresh considerations lead you to consider the relative value of home versus career. Choose carefully.

FINANCES

You love to splurge on favourite activities such as sports and music. August brings the opportunity to enjoy life, so financially you must be wary to avoid overspending and especially around 12 August. You appreciate the chance to spend time and effort on travel as this brings you closer to those you love, but again you'll need to keep an eye on expenditure. Some Scorpios will be drawn to investing in your home. You must avoid overincreasing debt.

HEALTH

You'll enjoy investing more time in your favourite activities and will experience a boost in morale, mental health and happiness as a result. Mid-August will be particularly conducive to broadening your horizons and enjoying upbeat activities. If you've been considering particular health and well-being modalities the 19th and the last week of the month will be positive times to begin something new or seek health and fitness advice.

LOVE LIFE

You will be drawn to making various changes in the way you share your duties and responsibilities, both at work and in your personal life such as your home, which will have an impact on your love life. Simmering disagreements are likely to arise early in the month, so if you don't wish these to turn into outright conflict be careful with communications then and also towards 24 August.

CAREER

A change of direction or news you receive early in August could present you with a productive and different path. Be prepared to negotiate with a group or organisation to ensure you don't put yourself in a vulnerable position. Positive, potentially even therapeutic developments in mid-August could also point to fresh ventures that you could invest either time or energy in. The new moon on the 23rd will bring a fresh chapter career-wise and negotiations may be necessary.

HOME LIFE

Developments surrounding the people you place in the heart of your home will determine domestic circumstances, and you may receive key news towards 12 August that provides you with the clarity you need at home. You'll gain the opportunity in mid-August to truly embellish and/or celebrate your home and domestic life and family, and financial investments in this area are likely to go well as long as you adequately research your options.

September

WEEK 1: 28 AUGUST–3 SEPTEMBER

You'll appreciate the chance to connect with someone you love. It's a good week to get on top of health and well-being schedules, either your own or those of someone you love. This will be a good week to consider how you can streamline your activities, work and projects so your schedule can accommodate both what is necessary and what you enjoy doing in your spare time.

WEEK 2: 4–10 SEPTEMBER

A fresh chapter is about to begin in your personal and/or domestic life. For some, considerable changes in your family or with children may take the focus. Be resolute as you enter new territory but also prepared to discuss the broader implications of your decisions and plans. For some, changes will come about due to developments in your career. You'll realise there are certain connections you cannot avoid.

WEEK 3: 11–17 SEPTEMBER

You'll enjoy a reunion or return to an old haunt. You may be drawn to travelling and at the least to spending time with your favourite people and pastimes. You could take several leaps forward at work as long as you avoid succumbing to pressure and find yourself feeling under the weather, aggravated and irritable. If you do, all the more reason to take breaks when you can.

WEEK 4: 18–24 SEPTEMBER / WEEK 5: 25 SEPTEMBER–1 OCTOBER

WEEK 4: prepare for an intriguing and romantic week in various ways. You may find that uncertainty lingers this week or that the behaviour of someone you love seems mysterious or garners attention. If you've been super sociable of late you may decide to be less so and vice versa. Some Scorpios will experience a brand-new chapter in your career and make financial agreements accordingly. **WEEK 5:** the effects of the solar eclipse and the sun, Uranus and Pluto alignment are still in effect this week and will bring the chance to meet a diverse group of people and also improve aspects of your personal and work lives. It's very much a busy, productive week, so be sure to maintain perspective. Keep communications clear, especially towards next Wednesday, to avoid arguments.

FINANCES

The finances you share with someone such as a personal or business partner could increase with careful management. The lunar eclipse on 7 September will spotlight how you could make not only your income but also your home work for you in ways you had perhaps not considered up until now. You may experience a lucky break or tax return or another financial boost, especially towards the 24th when you may get a career breakthrough.

HEALTH

The positive link between Mercury and Chiron in the first week of September is an excellent opportunity to find ways to boost your health and well-being or help someone you love do the same. You're likely to feel under pressure at the middle and end of the month, either at work or due to burning the candle at both ends, so it will be important to find ways to treat your mind, body and spirit well.

LOVE LIFE

A partner may surprise you early in the month and you'll gain the opportunity over the rest of the month to find ways to accommodate their ideas, plans or wishes. A change of location via a holiday or even a move is likely to be for the best but will take adjustment on your part. If you're single you'll be prepared to make fresh arrangements or a commitment to something or someone new towards the end of the month.

CAREER

Your career will be a key area of focus in September. The first week will offer the opportunity to find ways to bring the areas of your career you love into your everyday working life. There is a therapeutic quality to your career and activities, so be sure to take the initiative and look for ways to mend anything you feel is not to your liking. You may experience a breakthrough towards 24 September if not before.

HOME LIFE

The total lunar eclipse on 7 September will shine a light on your domestic life and especially in connection with your long-term aims in this important area. Some lucky Scorpios may find the opportunity to travel and explore new horizons in your domestic life, such as via a move. Others may be prepared to reconfigure how you share duties and responsibilities. The key to a happy home in September revolves around good communication and negotiation skills.

October

WEEK 1: 2–8 OCTOBER

A trip or change of routine is likely to put you in a positive frame of mind. However, a change of pace will require a little versatility and also tact on your part, as certain communications will be on a fresh platform. A career-related or personal event will put your heart on your sleeve as you gain the recognition you deserve. However, you must avoid bumps, scrapes and minor accidents.

WEEK 2: 9–15 OCTOBER

Developments include the chance to make a deeper commitment to someone or a group or family. You'll enjoy a change of routine such as a holiday or short trip, and socialising will be super exciting. If your focus is more on work and health this is a good time to work towards a positive outcome in these two areas, as your efforts are likely to succeed.

WEEK 3: 16–22 OCTOBER

The new moon on 21 October will spotlight the importance of being in tiptop condition. You may feel drawn to improving your fitness, appearance or diet. You'll enjoy an ego boost and financial improvement this week. Some Scorpios will kick-start a fresh chapter in your work schedule, while others will be ready to embrace a fresh chapter in your personal life.

WEEK 4: 23–29 OCTOBER

The sun in your sign for the next four weeks will certainly help boost your energy levels and motivation. This is an excellent week to invest in your favourite pastimes and extracurricular activities such as sports and creative and musical interests. It's also prospectively a romantic period, so this is an excellent time to organise a treat. Someone may surprise you.

FINANCES

You'll make progress in October through careful research and the willingness to commit to a project or person who could prospectively bring more stability and security your way. This is most definitely not the month to gamble financially as you'll find the risks you take will far outweigh the benefits, especially towards mid-month. It's far better to invest in your skill sets and abilities, which could bring positive financial progress your way through a rise in your productivity.

HEALTH

October will be an excellent time to invest in your health and well-being, so if you've had various health-related niggles this will be a good time to instigate ideas or research further into how you can improve your health. Health and well-being are cornerstones of your life, and the phase between 18 October and the new moon on the 21st will spotlight ways for you to kick-start a fresh health chapter in your life both from the perspective of physical fitness and mental well-being.

LOVE LIFE

This is a romantic month as your existing relationship can enter fresh territory, and if you're single you may meet someone whom you wish to commit to or someone who is a little different from your usual companions. The second half of the month is particularly romantic, so be sure to accept invitations or organise dates as you could certainly move into fresh territory. Both couples and singles will appreciate the opportunity to indulge more in romance, music and love.

CAREER

Developments in your daily routine will involve the opportunity to improve your career. There is a therapeutic quality to developments early in October, and even if you experience a disappointment at work rest assured the big picture will take you into better times ahead. Mid-month you'll have the opportunity to commit to a path that may be ideal. Be sure if you are signing new contracts or agreements that you're fully clear about the terms and conditions.

HOME LIFE

October is an excellent month to make some serious decisions regarding your home, especially if you were born in November. You may be ready to make a commitment that alters the face of your domestic life. Developments in your career may have a knock-on effect on your home and vice versa, especially mid-month. You'll appreciate the opportunity to infuse your home life with your trademark passion and motivation to make things work out for the best.

November

WEEK 1: 30 OCTOBER–5 NOVEMBER

You could take giant leaps forward with a clever and exciting plan that merits careful analysis, so take the initiative and put building blocks in place that can provide you with structure. For some this will be in your work life and for others in your personal or health schedule. The Taurus full moon and supermoon on 5 November points to a new chapter in a business or personal partnership.

WEEK 2: 6–12 NOVEMBER

Venus in your sign for the rest of the month will bring your focus to love and money. This week you'll enjoy some lovely get-togethers, and domestic dynamics or relationships with family could flourish. It's in your interest to avoid contentious topics as these are likely to spiral without notice. Try to get key financial and travel plans on the table before 9 November to avoid delays and misunderstandings.

WEEK 3: 13–19 NOVEMBER

This week in the lead-up to the Scorpio new moon on 20 November it will be in your interest to consider your longer-term plans, especially concerning your family, home life and work. You'll see an upswing in your abilities to negotiate and collaborate with important people in your life and especially those you care for. However, some negotiations do require time so patience will be of the essence.

WEEK 4: 20–26 NOVEMBER / WEEK 5: 27 NOVEMBER–3 DECEMBER

WEEK 4: a unique combination on the one hand of the need for change to take place and on the other slow developments will bring a stop-start atmosphere to your week. The Scorpio new moon on 20 November points to a fresh phase in your personal life and, for some, financially. You may be drawn to investing in a holiday and romance. Ensure you plan ahead well, as you'll enjoy get-togethers.
WEEK 5: some people have a habit of surprising you even if you already know they're full of surprises, so prepare for another wonder or revelation. You'll enjoy a change of pace or scenery this weekend. However, a development in a close relationship or an unexpected change of plan will merit a careful approach to avoid misunderstandings.

FINANCES

Unexpected news or developments early in November will encourage you to look at your finances in a new light. Mercury will turn retrograde in your money sector on the 8th, so it will be in your interest to at the very least float important financial decisions before then to avoid having to review your plans or experience financial misunderstandings later in the month. It's a good month to start a slush fund for fun activities.

HEALTH

Health and well-being are the cornerstones of a happy life, and key decisions and developments early in November will point the way to finding a healthier path ahead. You may need to reschedule some commitments to better take care of your health or that of someone else. Mid-month a mixture between fast-moving events and frustrating delays could tax your patience and energy levels, so be sure to find ways to release stress.

LOVE LIFE

The supermoon on 5 November points to the need to be practical regarding someone close to your heart. It's likely that you'll receive or must give unexpected news to your partner just before the supermoon and towards the 30th. The Scorpio new moon on the 20th points to the start of a brand-new phase in your love life. You may experience surprises, so be prepared to think on your toes but to also allow yourself time to think.

CAREER

If you have felt that your career has been flourishing of late you're likely to experience another busy time early in November. Jupiter in your 10th house will be turning retrograde on 11 November, which will enable you to catch your breath. The remainder of the month will then be ideal for reviewing and getting on top of projects so you're in a position to go full steam ahead in the first quarter of 2026.

HOME LIFE

The second week of the month will be ideal for reunions and improving domestic relationships. If you've been considering a move or home improvement this will also be a positive time to set those plans in motion. Mid-month you'll see there are positive opportunities to invest more in yourself personally and especially your family and home life, which will nevertheless require good negotiation and collaborative skills.

December

WEEK 1: 4–10 DECEMBER

Seasonal festivities begin early for you! Meetings and travel will be productive and fun, but you must aim for absolute clarity or you could make a mistake. You'll get the opportunity to make changes in some of your existing agreements. Be prepared to negotiate and you could make solid progress financially and in your personal life. A fresh chapter in a partnership could work, but you must be practical.

WEEK 2: 11–17 DECEMBER

This is a good week to look for inspiration and indulge in creativity, the arts and music but you must also keep an eye on practicalities as you otherwise risk seeing life through rose-coloured glasses, especially romantically and financially. You must avoid overspending and gambling as the seasonal festivities ramp up. If health has been an issue you're likely to receive news that is therapeutic.

WEEK 3: 18–24 DECEMBER

The new moon on 20 December falls in your finance sector and will bring focus to money. You'll be drawn to being generous and gregarious financially but must be practical as well, as no one has a bottomless well of money. Towards the solstice you must be careful with financial transactions to avoid errors. Similarly, conversations with those close to you must be super clear for the best results.

WEEK 4: 25–31 DECEMBER

If you have set ideas about what is fun in life you may need this week to adapt to circumstances that have their own momentum. When you do your mind will be expanded, and in the process you may find that life really does have more to offer than you'd expected. A therapeutic and uplifting change of pace or place will boost your morale. Avoid financial and emotional gambling.

FINANCES

December will kick-start a fresh chapter in your personal and joint finances. For some this will mean, for example, a change in the way you share domestic expenses and for others considerable changes in your personal life which, in turn, mean your expenses will either increase or decrease. Be prepared to initiate talks and find a solution if arguments arise. As this is the festive season avoid overspending, which you will regret and especially if you're already in debt.

HEALTH

The beginning of December is a positive time for a health check and to improve strength and vitality. You're likely to find the correct expert or doctor at that time, so look out for trusted advice. As the festivities are likely to begin early for you, keep an eye on consumption to avoid overindulgence. News will provide important insight into your health, if necessary, towards 14 December, and mid-December and the end of the month are good times to seek health advice.

LOVE LIFE

You may be surprised by news from a partner around 10 December, and the better your communication skills the better will be the outcome. If it seems that certain relationships no longer fulfil you it may come down to different expectations or the realisation you have very different life paths ahead of you, in which case there is little need for regret or recrimination. Singles will enjoy this festive season, which begins early with more fun than most could handle!

CAREER

It's a good time to appraise your journey this year and ask if you are where you want to be career-wise. If the answer is 'Yes' then you'll gain the motivation to work harder and smarter to attain your goals, but if the answer is 'No' you'll gain the opportunity this month and early in 2026 to configure a path that suits you better. The new moon on 20 December will help you reorganise your priorities.

HOME LIFE

You'll gain a sense of purpose through pursuing an ideal in your home life or regarding family, but the full moon and supermoon on 4 December will spotlight whether your expectations far exceed the realities of your circumstances. Nevertheless, you do have excellent stars for creating a domestic circumstance you're both happy and proud about. Just be sure not to overstretch yourself financially if you're making a fresh investment.

SAGITTARIUS

22 November – 21 December

January

WEEK 1: 1–8 JANUARY

A reunion or trip could be ideal. A surprising or unusual change of circumstance will merit focus. If you're unsure of your position and feel you need advice someone will prove to be super helpful, so be sure to reach out to an expert or adviser. If you're in a position to help someone, your support will be welcome. It's a good week to set plans in motion.

WEEK 2: 9–15 JANUARY

A reunion and the chance to indulge in the company of those you love will be revitalising. Romance could flourish under this week's stars. If you're looking to begin something new financially it's in your interest to research options, but you are well advised to avoid gambling. You'll enjoy sprucing up your home or improving domestic dynamics but you must avoid crossing swords with someone whose ideas differ from yours.

WEEK 3: 16–22 JANUARY

A change of pace or place will test your mettle. If some aspects of your circumstances, especially your finances, are unclear or require change be sure to do your research, as you'll be better able to negotiate and move forward. Mid next week you must be prepared to deal with a financial or personal matter and to carefully make decisions based on facts, not feelings.

WEEK 4: 23–29 JANUARY

This is an excellent time to resurrect elements from your past such as an interest at work or an old friendship. It's a good week to reconfigure your daily routine and chores so they suit your big-picture goals better. The new moon on 29 January will kick-start a fresh financial cycle that may involve some soul searching or the need to make a tough decision. A reunion should prove enjoyable.

FINANCES

You'll discover in January just where your attention must be financially, as past spending or a present budget may no longer suit your current needs. A clever mixture of realism and optimism, as opposed to pessimism, will help you build a strong foundation for yourself in 2025, but you must be careful to avoid unrealistic expectations. The full moon on 13 January will spotlight important and unavoidable domestic expenses that must come first.

HEALTH

Jupiter retrograde will add to an uncharacteristically sluggish feeling energetically, either in you or in someone close, so fair attention to buoying your physical and spiritual energy will be rewarded in January to avoid flagging energy levels. Mercury in Capricorn for much of the month will help you put together a practical and sensible plan that can help, so be sure to look at feasible fitness schedules and dietary demands.

LOVE LIFE

There are many ways to boost your love life in January, such as finding better ways to communicate romantically and new ways to connect emotionally, mentally and spiritually with your partner. Again, Jupiter retrograde is to blame if you or your partner experiences an uncharacteristic lack of interest in love and romance; avoid assuming that things will be the same forever. Your energy levels will pick up, so avoid making rash decisions.

CAREER

The start of the year is always a good time to look at your career from a fresh perspective and consider how you'd like it to play out better this year. The key for you now lies in deciding where your true interests lie and how to bring more of the qualities you want in your career into being. Consider your finances and values as well. By following your interests and principles you'll find your career choices become easier, not harder.

HOME LIFE

This is a good month for reconnecting with those you love and those in your home or family you have lost contact with. It may take a little soul searching or even difficult conversations, but you'll find a better path ahead if you approach difference or a lack of connection head on. It's also a good month for improving your domestic environment, either through addressing repairs and getting them done or making your home your health haven.

February

WEEK 1: 30 JANUARY–5 FEBRUARY

Someone special will help you with finances and/or your personal life so it resonates better with you. You may be drawn to travelling or meeting someone you admire. An expert, adviser or friend will be influential, and if you're asked for help you will be in a position to give it. A partner or someone close will wish to talk and you may make excellent agreements, but if you feel compromised it's important to re-establish boundaries.

WEEK 2: 6–12 FEBRUARY

Be prepared to be adaptable as there may be some adjustment necessary regarding a financial circumstance. Financial and domestic matters are best approached matter of factly. You'll enjoy a trip or visit that takes you into a beautiful environment or that brings someone beautiful into your sphere. A fresh phase will begin in a favourite interest or activity or regarding travel or a shared circumstance.

WEEK 3: 13–19 FEBRUARY

Key opportunities or developments will ask that you discuss your ideas more openly. You may be pleasantly surprised by the results, especially at home and/or financially. A change of scenery or environment at home will bring a new element into being, including more luxury and sumptuousness. Consider bringing a little more lavishness into your life by rekindling romance.

WEEK 4: 20–26 FEBRUARY

A trip or meeting will take you into fresh territory. Spend time planning and organising your week to avoid frustrating delays or mix-ups. Focus on your goals and you'll succeed. You could make a key decision but may first need to gain clarity about someone who you're unsure of. Matters should gain a more even keel, even if only because you gain extra insight into options.

FINANCES

This will be an excellent month to research new and proven ways to save, budget and invest your hard-earned cash. If you're looking for work, the start of the month will be particularly positive for looking for something suitable. The Mercury–Saturn conjunction and Pisces new moon towards the end of the month will be ideal for making considerable commitments and agreements, but you must avoid gambling at this time.

HEALTH

Uranus in your health sector all year will bring the need to look after your health due to unforeseen and unexpected circumstances. It also suggests that if health has been an issue a positive way forward is to look for tried and trusted methods to improve health, and complementary methods such as a good diet, fitness and skeletal and psychological health. Consider as well options to create more happiness in your life as a way to boost health.

LOVE LIFE

The Leo full moon on 12 February and Mars retrograde in Cancer both point to considerable developments with someone special. If you're single and looking for a partner or enjoy being single keep an eye out for someone new who may be ideal, especially early in the month and towards the 12th and 28th. If couples have been experiencing some tough conversations with your partner, look for fresh ways to communicate and avoid taking their actions personally.

CAREER

Uranus will also be shining a light on the unpredictable nature of your daily work life, suggesting you find ways to anchor ventures and projects you love into your career and establish a sense of stability where possible. Avoid feeling that Rome can be built in one day. Seeds that you plant now may take several months to grow, but rest assured that by the end of May at the least you'll see positive results for your hard work.

HOME LIFE

Considerable changes in your personal life are likely to affect your home life. The start of the month is ideal for looking for ways to bring more romance and luxury into your domestic life. If it has been chaotic, consider how to invest in your home to bring a more relaxing, therapeutic vibe into being. Saturn will help you anchor projects, so if you're drawn to improving your home life in any way this taskmaster will move your projects along.

March

WEEK 1: 27 FEBRUARY–5 MARCH

This is an excellent week to consider how you might beautify or even altogether change your environment. You'll enjoy a fun trip somewhere different. Spiritual Sagittarians may find this a truly inspiring and uplifting week. Investment in yourself and your environment will be enriching. However, one particular business or personal relationship will require more tact than usual to avoid arguments.

WEEK 2: 6–12 MARCH

This is an excellent week for socialising and short trips. A visit is likely to feel fulfilling. Working Archers could make great progress and may benefit from an unexpected opportunity. An adventurous approach will encourage you to set high goals, and there's no reason why you can't meet these. A commitment or financial matter may involve the need to view duties and financial arrangements more seriously.

WEEK 3: 13–19 MARCH

The total lunar eclipse on 14 March will spotlight your career, goals and status. A new interest or the wish to pursue your favourite activities more will propel you into new terrain. Travel and the chance to improve communications will appeal. Take the initiative and make appointments with experts and those you know who can help you make progress at work and home.

WEEK 4: 20–26 MARCH / WEEK 5: 27 MARCH–2 APRIL

WEEK 4: bringing a little luxury and sumptuousness into your home will help to boost morale. For some this will be in the shape of décor and flowers and for others music and light. A little romance will entice you, and a meeting could make your heart soar. It's a good week to indulge in your favourite activities, and you may experience a financial boost. **WEEK 5:** be prepared to let your inner hero out over the next few days as a fresh chapter in your personal life could bring out sensitivities. Meetings and communications may resonate deeply; you'll meet or hear from someone you have a predestined connection with. Key decisions at home or with family will kick-start a brand-new phase, so be brave.

FINANCES

This is not the month to wager bets, especially if you're already in debt. You or someone with whom you share finances may tend to overspend, so consider keeping a tab on expenditure as this will help avoid debt. A favourable aspect after 27 March could help boost your finances, and this may be in connection with a repaid debt or a project or venture you started many weeks ago.

HEALTH

You'll be thinking on your feet in March, so it will be in your interest to maintain a close eye on your energy levels. This is a good month to contemplate the benefits of spiritual development. A trip or communications with other seekers may open your eyes to the relationship between mind and body. Good communication skills are the key to increasing your self-esteem, which will add to your natural optimism.

LOVE LIFE

Be prepared to look outside the square at your options and collaborations, as you could work well together with others in March. That is, unless you allow other people's agendas or opinions to derail your usually upbeat outlook. As Jupiter begins to have a more positive effect on your love life over the coming weeks and months you'll feel more expansive and optimistic about your relationships. You may enjoy an impromptu and unexpected development mid-month that boosts morale.

CAREER

You're likely to experience considerable changes in your direction in March that will impact how you see your projects and ventures moving forward. This month will offer you the ideal opportunity to choose projects that align more deeply with your true interests. The people you meet and places you visit will have an important impact on the decisions you make. Be sure to look at the financial implications as well, or you risk being idealistic.

HOME LIFE

The solar eclipse on 29 March will shine a light on the importance of being proactive about your home life and taking steps to make it something you wish it to be. You'll gain the facility earlier this month to plan long term how you wish to see your home life develop, and to slowly and methodically place your focus on ways to make your plans happen in practical and realistic terms.

April

WEEK 1: 3–9 APRIL

Changes in your daily schedule may be unusual but you will progress well with adequate focus on collaborations and by making fresh arrangements. Avoid making assumptions. It's a good week to focus on health and well-being, which will help you feel revitalised. Someone from your past who you haven't heard from for a while is likely to pop up. A trip or chat may bring a lightbulb moment.

WEEK 2: 10–16 APRIL

Life is about to move fast towards something new if it hasn't already, and as one of life's adventurers you're likely to navigate this better than many zodiac signs. Be prepared to travel or enter new territory in other ways. You may need to alter the way you share some duties and responsibilities and receive unexpectedly good news, but you must avoid making rash decisions regarding your home or career.

WEEK 3: 17–23 APRIL

Shared areas of your life such as joint finances or space at home will be in the spotlight as you gain the opportunity to improve these areas. In the process you may reach fresh agreements and arrangements that will enable you to get on better with everyone concerned. To ensure a smooth process be sure to be tactful, especially on Sunday and Monday.

WEEK 4: 24–30 APRIL

Careful negotiations, talks and meetings this week could boost your circumstances, both at work and financially. Just avoid financial and emotional gambling, as this could truly set the cat among the pigeons and even precipitate loss. It's far better to work methodically towards a sustainable budget and steady yet potentially lucrative work ventures.

FINANCES

For many April will be a decisive month financially. The key to making positive decisions will revolve around paying attention to detail in your own financial circumstances and those of others you depend on or who depend on you. You're likely to experience an uplifting or unexpected development regarding your finances, especially if you were born in mid-December. However, you must avoid gambling.

HEALTH

A dedicated approach to your health will prove rewarding, and you may experience a surprise early in the month when a change of environment or pace lifts your mood and boosts energy levels. Be sure to pursue activities you love as you'll increase your feel-good factor in life, leading to better mental and spiritual health. Sports and a trip could broaden your horizons, bringing a sense of adventure and purpose to some of your fitness activities.

LOVE LIFE

The start of the month brings harmonious aspects in your love life that warm the heart, and as long as you avoid contentious topics with someone you love you can keep the romance alive in April. The full moon on the 13th will spotlight your career and status, suggesting you have something to prove this month, but you must avoid taking someone close for granted. A key decision will merit care and attention regarding shared assets such as finances and domestic matters.

CAREER

You are about to turn a corner in your career and general direction in life. However, you may need to choose very carefully between priorities, including domestic responsibilities or duties towards someone close. Consider carefully who and what has most significance in your life at the moment, and the values and organisational matters that will need to be implemented in order to excel at work and in your career without detracting from your home and personal lives.

HOME LIFE

Developments at home will benefit from a diplomatic approach, especially during the second half of the month. You'll gain the opportunity to turn a corner regarding a domestic situation towards the end of April as the new moon on the 27th provides the opportunity to put in place fresh arrangements and agreements. You may be drawn to investing considerably in your home life, so choose your investments carefully and avoid gambling. Someone close may require more care due to health considerations.

May

WEEK 1: 1–7 MAY

You'll appreciate the opportunity to improve your home décor, to take time out to add a splash of colour or comfort at home. A visit, trip or planned change at home may require a little patience, but if you're drawn to the ocean or a spiritually inspiring environment the effort will be worthwhile. You may receive a financial boost but you must nevertheless avoid overspending.

WEEK 2: 8–14 MAY

You're set to move on from a past circumstance, which may be as simple as adopting a fresh health routine or as complex as extricating yourself from a difficult work placement. However, you have the drive to make your ideas and plans a success so ensure you adopt an 'I can do it' approach and let your values and abilities do the talking. Just avoid crossed lines and gambling.

WEEK 3: 15–21 MAY

An unusual or unexpected change of routine may initially be frustrating, but you're likely to gain traction in your work or health routine as the week goes by. There is a therapeutic quality this weekend regarding your personal life or someone special. Perhaps someone will need your help, and if you need advice or expert help at home for example it will be available.

WEEK 4: 22–28 MAY

This week's new moon signals a fresh start in a relationship, especially if you were born at the end of November. For December-born Sagittarians it's time to turn a page in your work or health routine. Be sure to consider how you could improve your vitality, finances and home life, as all these areas are likely to move forward quickly now. Think big but check the details!

FINANCES

You'll be drawn to reconfiguring or reviewing your finances as Pluto turns retrograde. You may receive a financial boost early in May but it's best to obtain expert advice, especially regarding a domestic or personal investment. Be careful with financial arrangements around the full moon on 12 May to avoid mistakes. Gambling is to be avoided, especially mid-month. A fresh work or personal agreement could improve your finances towards the end of the month.

HEALTH

You'll appreciate a change of pace due to a break or holiday, or simply a visitor or change at home. You may be pleasantly surprised early in May and at the end of the month at how much a change of pace can boost health and morale. Mid-month someone may need your help, and if you discover you would benefit from expert health advice this will be available so ensure you seek information that could benefit you or someone close.

LOVE LIFE

It'll be important early in May to take into account your partner's opinions, especially regarding personal or domestic matters, as you may otherwise end up in a Mexican stand-off. The full moon on the 12th is likely to bring out strong emotions, either in you or someone close, so it's wise to avoid contentious topics at that time if possible. The new moon on the 27th will kick-start a fresh chapter in your love life, and romance could flourish.

CAREER

This month will be ideal for moving forward in your career, especially as you'll gain the motivation to make long-overdue changes. You may receive an unexpected offer mid-month or towards 27 May that will be worth considering. Just ensure you're clear about the financial side of arrangements so you're not disappointed further down the line. Be sure to take the initiative with developments at the end of the month, as you'll ably demonstrate your abilities.

HOME LIFE

You'll enjoy investing in your environment. For many this will include making changes at home such as improving your comfort levels and adding a few touches of luxury to your home. Repairs and general beautification of your home will appeal. Some may contemplate a bigger change, such as a move. There is a therapeutic aspect domestically in May that may include a change of environment, such as a holiday or the arrival of a visitor.

June

WEEK 1: 29 MAY—4 JUNE

Key decisions or agreements can be made with the understanding that they may produce new variables, especially with work and personal matters. Be adventurous but tactful, as you risk inadvertently putting someone offside. There are therapeutic aspects this week that could improve health and domestic happiness.

WEEK 2: 5—11 JUNE

The Sagittarian full moon on 11 June encourages you to turn a corner, especially in connection with your personal life and for some mid-December Sagittarians with health, work or your appearance and well-being. A key talk over the next few days will be significant regarding a personal or business agreement. Be sure to look for the most mutually agreeable arrangement to avoid conflict, especially at home or with someone close.

WEEK 3: 12—18 JUNE

You'll appreciate doing things differently and may enjoy a change of pace or a fresh project. You'll feel creative and wish to bring new activities into your schedule or at home and will appreciate creating a beautiful environment at home, as this will be therapeutic. It's a good week to boost health. You may be surprised by an unexpected development at work or health-wise, so be prepared to be spontaneous.

WEEK 4: 19—25 JUNE / WEEK 5: 26 JUNE—2 JULY

WEEK 4: expect a new chapter in a collaboration; for example, a business or personal partner may have news for you that will require some adjustment on your part and the ability to discuss options. To ensure this new chapter is satisfactory for everyone involved, fresh common ground will need to be sought. Be inspired, because being proactive and positive about your activities will certainly be infectious. **WEEK 5:** this will be a good week to consider getting your finances shipshape and mending any holes in the financial bucket. It's not a week to gamble financially or in your personal life, as gambling is likely to backfire. A careful approach to communications will certainly be rewarded. Key financial or personal news at the weekend or early next week will grab your attention.

FINANCES

Your values have a bearing on your finances, and by the end of the month you'll see how much your financial situation reflects your principles. Be prepared to look at your income and expenditure as a reflection of who you are. Consider how much you outlay for your domestic circumstance, home or children and consider whether a fresh agreement either at work or home could improve your financial outlook and mood.

HEALTH

You may receive unexpected news from someone regarding health or a change in their usual routine due to health considerations. If you have been feeling a little under the weather you'll appreciate the opportunity to put your feet up at home and create a nurturing and healing space for yourself or someone special, especially mid-June. You'll be drawn to investing time in favourite activities such as sports, which will boost energy levels.

LOVE LIFE

The Sagittarian full moon on 11 June will bring a sense of renewal in your personal life. For many this will be therapeutic in nature, but for some there will be the need to discuss sensitive topics and care must be taken to avoid causing a rift in the process. There is the chance that some discussions become a battle of egos and this is to be avoided, especially around the full moon, which will bring intense emotions to the surface.

CAREER

You'll be drawn to reviewing not only your personal commitments but also some aspects of your work life or daily schedule. Your ability to move into fresh turf career-wise may be in the spotlight at the full moon on 11 June, in particular in relation to your collaboration skills. A change of location or the necessity to brush up your skill sets may challenge the status quo, but nevertheless you'll be happy to be adventurous in this key aspect of your life.

HOME LIFE

This is a good month to evaluate your home life and find nurturing ways to enjoy your domestic life. This will entail the necessity to discuss your plans with those they concern, and unless everyone is realistic and practical it is possible that you fail to find common ground. However, communications do improve towards the end of June, when you may find an unexpected solution to any issues that arise earlier in the month.

July

WEEK 1: 3–9 JULY

You'll appreciate the chance to catch up with chores at work and at home and may be surprised by developments in either or both arenas. You may need to accommodate someone's wishes or untangle a conundrum. Your decisions and current developments will affect your home life and/or finances, so be sure of the exact facts. You may enjoy a change of routine.

WEEK 2: 10–16 JULY

You tend to prefer going through life full steam ahead and then attending to details as and when you have a moment, but this week's full moon suggests a little more focus on your finances and commitments will certainly benefit you. You'll enjoy hearing from or meeting someone you value or admire and romance can flourish this week too, so be sure to take the initiative.

WEEK 3: 17–23 JULY

During this week in the run-up to the Leo new moon on 24 July you'll notice certain agreements and arrangements such as joint duties and assets come under the microscope. As you're leading towards formulating new agreements it will be in your interest to manage conversations and discussions carefully to avoid disagreements and potential conflict.

WEEK 4: 24–30 JULY

You may hear unexpected news or will enjoy being spontaneous. The new moon on 24 July points to a good time to begin a fresh agreement concerning shared duties, space or joint finances. You can make some truly progressive decisions to do with your home, family or relationships but must be careful to avoid intense interactions, as they may escalate rapidly.

FINANCES

This is a productive time to consider ways to budget and manage your finances in the best possible way. Significant developments towards the new moon on 24 July may bring considerable change in your financial circumstances, especially in relation to those you share with others such as a partner or the tax department. You may decide to invest in property or, conversely, relieve yourself of a domestic responsibility.

HEALTH

You'll be entering fresh territory in your health and fitness regime in July, so there is no better time to devise a new schedule that suits you in all departments, including mentally and emotionally. You may be drawn to health practices that would previously have seemed out of character for you, yet you're currently in the throes of broadening your horizons and especially with regard to how you perceive yourself and others.

LOVE LIFE

If you focus more on your ability to nurture others you can truly make yourself and someone special happy. Some Sagittarians will be drawn to returning to an ex, but this option must be carefully appraised to avoid taking action based on sentimentality. Bad relationship habits are likely to resurface this month, so if you truly value your love life be sure to prevent allowing your negative traits to surface, especially in the third week of the month.

CAREER

Be prepared to step into new territory work-wise. If you have always considered doing something different, there's no time like the present. You may be surprised by developments already at the start of the month or by a changing daily routine or scenario that requires you to be more outgoing and communicative. The more you embrace your productive and optimistic attributes the better you will find your career progresses in July. Be brave, but not impulsive.

HOME LIFE

Both Saturn and Neptune will turn retrograde in your fourth house of home in July and encourage you to rethink some of your arrangements and decisions in this important area of your life over the coming months. Some Sagittarians will be travelling this month and experience a change of environment domestically. For this reason it will be in your interest to use best-practice communication skills to avoid causing difficult interactions.

August

WEEK 1: 31 JULY–6 AUGUST

Be practical and stick with the facts this week, as you may otherwise find yourself at odds with someone. A trip or conversation could be a catalyst to change. If relationships are strained, you may wonder whether your communication abilities are lacking or if someone else's are! Be prepared to look for common ground if arguments arise unless you know already some differences cannot be overcome.

WEEK 2: 7–13 AUGUST

Take the initiative with your career and extracurricular activities, as your efforts are going to take you into refreshing territory that raises your spirits. You may be prepared to make a commitment to a personal or business connection. The full moon on 9 August will spotlight a fresh financial chapter that may be unusual or different.

WEEK 3: 14–20 AUGUST

A dynamic and proactive week awaits, and you'll enjoy being with like-minded people in activities such as sports. This is a good week to invest time and energy in those you love in the shape of relaxing time at home or on holiday. Someone you hold dear has important news. A lovely get-together will boost your relationship, so be sure to organise something special this weekend.

WEEK 4: 21–27 AUGUST

You'll be in the spotlight at work, career-wise or with your favourite ventures. An engaging activity will put many of your values and projects in fresh perspective. You may enjoy a change of environment such as a holiday or the chance to begin a fresh study course or spend time with self-development. Avoid throwing caution to the wind. You'll enjoy a lovely get-together or news early next week.

FINANCES

Your finances will be stepping to a fresh level, and for many Sagittarians this will be due to a new business or personal arrangement. If you're unsure of the parameters of the agreements you make, be sure to enlist the help of an expert or adviser. Above all, don't make agreements you're unsure of. Shared financial options will be a focus, so be prepared to negotiate.

HEALTH

This is likely to be a busy month or one that takes you into a fresh environment. It's also likely to be an excellent month to be more active with undertakings you enjoy. You'll appreciate the opportunity to spend more time bringing fresh air into your health routine. An unusual development may involve a trip or the chance to do something different. Tuesday, 19 August will be a particularly healing or therapeutic day.

LOVE LIFE

Venus and Jupiter will spotlight the shared areas of your life. Ensuring that you're happy with a degree of play in your primary relationship will be the subtext of some of the discussions you undertake with someone special. Mid-August to the 20th will be the most romantic time, so be sure to organise special events then. Someone close may need more nurturance than usual, and the 19th is ideal for boosting health and well-being.

CAREER

Mars at the zenith of your chart is going to bring out your adventurousness. While this generally bodes well for career advancement, if you've found in the past that you can be super blunt when you're in intense situations you'll do well to maintain a professional hat, especially at the start of August. Your communication skills may be put to the test mid-month, but with an upbeat attitude you could truly improve your career.

HOME LIFE

Carefully contemplate a key decision regarding your home life or a change of environment. If you're travelling and therefore away from home be sure to adequately research your new environment to avoid disappointment. You may need to carefully negotiate certain shared areas of your home life around the new moon on 23 August. It's best to take into account other people's opinions to avoid arguments. When you do, progress can be made.

September

WEEK 1: 28 AUGUST–3 SEPTEMBER

A trip or fun get-together will be uplifting. However, you would do well to be prepared for delays or an abrupt change of schedule. Romance can flourish now and you'll enjoy spending time with someone you love. This will be an excellent week to review paperwork and agreements, as your efforts will be productive and you'll see constructive results.

WEEK 2: 4–10 SEPTEMBER

A new environment or the chance to catch up with friends and favourite activities will be ideal, but if a fresh circumstance feels disorienting take time to get your feet on the ground and especially around 7 September. You'll relish being immersed in a project or travel, and boosting energy levels in the process. You'll enjoy deepening a relationship, although for some this week's eclipse will mean distance.

WEEK 3: 11–17 SEPTEMBER

You'll enjoy trips and get-togethers this week. Any activities you really love are likely to go well. Romance could blossom, so be sure to take the initiative and organise a treat. Important conversations and agreements during next week are best handled carefully to avoid making impulse decisions you later come to regret. This is a good week for focusing on improving domestic dynamics and décor.

WEEK 4: 18–24 SEPTEMBER / WEEK 5: 25 SEPTEMBER–1 OCTOBER

WEEK 4: you'll be in the spotlight this week, and it's likely to be at work, career-wise or in your favourite activities. For some Sagittarians it's all about your status, as those you love begin to see you in a new or different light. An engaging activity this weekend will put many of your values and projects in perspective. A surprise or a little intrigue mid-week will inspire you. **WEEK 5:** this is a good week to push yourself forward and believe in yourself, as the stars have your back and especially regarding your work, favourite projects and ventures. You may experience a financial boost if you didn't already last week. The key to ensuring this is a smoothly running week lies in excellent communication skills, especially towards mid next week.

FINANCES

Financially, you're likely to gain a sense of true progress by the end of the month. This will largely come down to your communication and negotiation abilities. You'll gain the opportunity towards the solar eclipse on 21 September to make fresh arrangements or agreements either at work or within a personal or legal context. Developments around the 24th could see you truly boost your financial circumstances, so be sure to work towards a positive outcome.

HEALTH

You may be surprised by how powerful a change of routine can be health-wise. You'll gain an opportunity to review some of your fitness and dietary practices that will enable you to bring more varied and upbeat activities into your daily schedules. This will boost your happiness, and to ensure you continue on an upwards trend you must avoid resuming bad habits.

LOVE LIFE

A change of scenery such as a holiday or fun activity including sports will bring you closer to someone you love. If you're single you may meet someone new in unexpected or unusual circumstances. Couples will find this an excellent month to deepen your spiritual connection and relocate the joy in your relationship. Find time to explore new ways to connect or reconnect with an aspect of your relationship you let go by the wayside.

CAREER

Astrologically, you have as much of a positive opportunity to experience productive developments in your career as you do to experience difficult conversations or obstacles. It's therefore in your interest to be prepared for the likelihood of miscommunications, misunderstandings and even downright unco-operative people, because in this way you'll be one step ahead and able to make the most of positive career opportunities towards the end of the month.

HOME LIFE

This is a good month to make changes at home such as remodelling or redecorating and adding a touch of colour through soft furnishings. Some Sagittarians, however, will experience the therapeutic aspects of your home. If you're travelling you're likely to enjoy the healing influence of the fresh environment. Developments towards 21 September will remind you of the importance of a stable home life, as its effects have a healing and stabilising quality.

October

WEEK 1: 2–8 OCTOBER

This will be an excellent week to decide whether your priorities lie at work or at home, because otherwise you risk being torn between the two and will be unable to adequately complete duties in either realm. It will be a case where you may need to make a tough call. Your key to success this week lies 100 per cent in good communication skills and teamwork.

WEEK 2: 9–15 OCTOBER

You may be ready to commit to a course of action at home or work. Some Sagittarians will be ready to commit more time to your hobbies and the excitement of a trip or another investment such as study. You'll appreciate the opportunity to enjoy the company of someone you value or at least the chance to gain insight into a key relationship or venture.

WEEK 3: 16–22 OCTOBER

You'll be happy to meet new people and increasingly include your beliefs and goals in your daily activities. This weekend a get-together should be uplifting, but you must avoid a clash over a difference of values. The new moon on 21 October will encourage you to turn a corner in your career, status and general direction, but you must also take your home life, family or property circumstances into account.

WEEK 4: 23–29 OCTOBER

You'll appreciate the opportunity to get together with like-minded people to discuss your various projects and ideas. Your meetings are likely to be successful. If you have been drawn to travelling you're likely to enjoy your trip even if initial adjustment is necessary to a fresh environment. You may be surprised by news or a fresh schedule mid next week.

FINANCES

While there's every chance you can get ahead financially and at work, this month's stars suggest you may spend money as quickly as you earn it so keep an eye on your budget. Joint finances such as those you share with a partner or your housemates will require careful discussion early in the month to avoid arguments. Be sure to employ the advice of an expert if you find yourself in a financial difficulty, as they will be informative.

HEALTH

The positive aspect between the sun, Uranus and Pluto mid-month is an excellent opportunity to invest more in yourself and your favourite activities. You may be drawn to joining a fresh club or committing more to a hobby, which is likely to take you into fresh territory and certainly to zhuzh up your usual schedule, creating a sense of well-being and happiness. Travel will similarly be a drawcard, but you must avoid overspending as luxurious surroundings will certainly appeal.

LOVE LIFE

You'll gain the opportunity to set your sights on fresh ventures, especially in your social life and career. Bear in mind the circumstances or feelings of those close to you such as your partner and/or family, because otherwise you risk disagreements between 17 to 21 October. Singles will find the last two weeks of the month particularly conducive to romance and socialising, so be sure to organise dates then.

CAREER

The full moon on 7 October points to a fresh chapter either at work or home. As you turn a corner in one or both of these areas your status will change. You will be drawn to looking for more variety and excitement in your daily life so you must avoid an attitude of peace at all costs. Mid-month you'll gain the opportunity to enter fresh territory or negotiate new work options.

HOME LIFE

Both the full moon on 7 October and new moon on the 21st point to a fresh chapter in your home life. This may be the result of developments in your status or at work. You may need to make a tough call between work and home, and if your home life comes a poor second it's important to discuss this tactfully with those affected. You may need to help build the resilience of others to the pressures of life.

November

WEEK 1: 30 OCTOBER–5 NOVEMBER

As Mercury conjuncts Mars in your sign expect a busy or varied two weeks. You may be drawn to travelling and stepping into new territory, both at work and at play. If talks appear challenging, take the time to perfect your communication skills. Finances will merit extra focus, especially shared finances. The supermoon on 5 November will spotlight the importance of putting those you love and your own happiness first.

WEEK 2: 6–12 NOVEMBER

Mercury turns retrograde on 9 November, so it will be in your interest to get important personal and work matters up for discussion before then to avoid having to review or delay some of your plans later in the month. This will be a good week for meetings, although a financial or personal matter will require delicate handling. If you've planned a trip you'll enjoy a reunion.

WEEK 3: 13–19 NOVEMBER

If you have already noticed that certain communications and aspects of your life have been complex or delayed, be vigilant now to avoid adding stress to complex circumstances. Some Sagittarians will find this a super productive week at work and also socially. It's likely to be a fun or at the very least revealing time in your personal life. Avoid taking the bad behaviour of other people personally.

WEEK 4: 20–26 NOVEMBER / WEEK 5: 27 NOVEMBER–3 DECEMBER

WEEK 4: the new moon on 20 November will give you the chance to get up to date with your various chores and turn a corner at work and with your health schedule. A trip or change at home may be delightful and you'll catch up with people you miss. A get-together could be ideal. It's also a good week to reconfigure how you share important duties and, for some, financial obligations. **WEEK 5:** a surprise will usher in a fresh work or health routine that may ask that you be more practical and keep your feet on the ground. News from the past or regarding a change of schedule is best accommodated one step at a time, especially as you may feel more sensitive or vulnerable on occasion this week.

FINANCES

Jupiter retrograde suggests you take care and attention, especially from 11 November onwards. Developments towards the 21st will provide perfect opportunities to decide with more clarity which of your shared financial obligations require reimagining. You'll be in a strong position to negotiate but you must avoid allowing your emotions to dictate financial decisions, as you may be tempted to make rash decisions and especially towards the end of the month.

HEALTH

You may be surprised by developments in November, not only health-wise but in many other areas of your life including your work. There will be demanding qualities this month so it will be in your interest to find ways to be practical and grounded, especially as you tend to prefer to charge through life. November will involve the need to take careful and considered action with your health and well-being to remain mentally and physically strong.

LOVE LIFE

You'll gain the opportunity to discuss common ground with your partner and strengthen your relationship. It may on occasion seem that you're doing the opposite, as there is a retrospective or retroactive atmosphere this month that may contribute to a feeling that you're going backwards. Aim to maintain a strong sense of belonging within your relationship to overcome this. Singles are likely to enjoy meeting various different people, so socialising will appeal.

CAREER

It would be easy to say that you can make great progress at work in November, as on the one hand it's true but on the other your decisions are more complex, so the results will be variable. The subject of value comes into your decisions in November regarding your career. For example, how much is a particular role worth in monetary terms and the expenditure of your energy? Aim to work smarter, not necessarily harder.

HOME LIFE

As one of the most outgoing and adventurous zodiac signs your home can sometimes take second place to travel, socialising and your personal aims and goals. Early in November important decisions that may be more to do with your career and activities will impact your home life, so take this aspect of your life into account as you evaluate your various options. Your home could become a true haven at the end of November.

December

WEEK 1: 4–10 DECEMBER

You'll appreciate the chance to focus on improving your domestic circumstances. The supermoon will spotlight an important relationship if you were born before 5 December, and if you were born later a fresh work phase or daily routine. This is an excellent time to establish more stability and security domestically and avoid arguments. Be prepared to compromise and negotiate.

WEEK 2: 11–17 DECEMBER

Mars will leave your sign and enter your money zone, which may help curb spending. However, this week's events will nevertheless be motivational and stimulate your desire to get things done. Delays or an obstacle needn't colour your entire week. Be practical and you could accomplish a great deal. Just be sure to keep communications clear and plan travel in advance to avoid unnecessary delays.

WEEK 3: 18–24 DECEMBER

This week's new moon is in your sign and presents the opportunity to enter adventurous territory. You're likely to feel outgoing, and travel and fun festivities will appeal. You may be drawn to altering aspects around your home life for the festive season. If you're travelling you'll need to exercise patience, especially towards 21 December. Be sure to keep communications clear for the best results.

WEEK 4: 25–31 DECEMBER

Good planning will take you somewhere interesting this week, but if you feel that you're really all at sea about an important matter it's time to be practical and research options, especially financially and in your personal life. It's a good week to look at therapeutic and positive ways to zhuzh up your home life, including not only the décor but also interpersonal dynamics.

FINANCES

In the long term you have the opportunity to create something truly original financially. In the short term, however, you must be careful with expenditure to avoid blowing your budget. If you tend to be extravagant at this time of year you're likely to perpetuate this pattern, and while this will indicate fun times it could also put you back. If you're already in debt it will be important to monitor your expenditure.

HEALTH

You may receive unexpected news towards 10 December. If you must change your health routine you may at this time consider something new or different. If you were born after the 3rd this is a lovely month to begin a fresh health and well-being schedule, as it's likely to be productive and could potentially transform your health. You may be surprised by news that encourages you to improve your health mid-month.

LOVE LIFE

The supermoon on 4 December and new moon on the 21st spotlight a fresh arrangement or agreement in your love life. As the month progresses you're likely to feel increasingly adventurous. Be sure mid-month to be super clear with communications to avoid misunderstandings or arguments. If you're single you may meet someone who seems ideal. Just double-check that you're definitely on the same path, as the initial attraction may wain if your life expectations are very different.

CAREER

As one of the boldest signs of the zodiac, adventure, exploration, travel and fun activities will attract you in December and during the holidays. You may be reconsidering your career path now, especially if you've grown bored with some of the parameters of your work circumstances and particularly if you were born after 4 December. It's certainly a very good time early in December to discuss your options with those they may affect.

HOME LIFE

Changes at home may be therapeutic early in December and then in particular at mid-month and towards the 28th. If you've been unwell your home will represent a lovely healing sanctuary for you early in the month. Just ensure you gain a sense of cooperation from those you share space with. Mid-month is an excellent time to get your home shipshape for the festive season, and a small amount of improvement in your décor will work wonders.

♑

CAPRICORN

21 December – 20 January

January

WEEK 1: 1–8 JANUARY

Mercury in your sign from 8 January will increasingly bring out your chatty, communicative self and you'll enjoy the opportunity to get in touch with old friends and colleagues. A change of pace or a return to an old haunt could be beneficial for you. However, if a mystery arises or you are delayed or, at worst, feel lost, ensure you double-check information and look for facts to help you progress.

WEEK 2: 9–15 JANUARY

Significant meetings and communications will be heart-warming. You may experience an unexpected financial or ego boost but must avoid overspending or overindulging as a result, which you'll regret! a reunion will be fun, and if you're single you may gain the chance to reunite with an ex but you must ensure you're not seeing things through rose-coloured glasses.

WEEK 3: 16–22 JANUARY

This is a good time for romance. Singles may meet someone from your past and couples will enjoy rekindling romantic aspects of your relationship. You may be surprised by a change of circumstance or impromptu development that requires careful handling. The Aquarian new moon on 29 January will encourage you to think laterally about your life. Developments mid-week will bring to mind what your priorities really are.

WEEK 4: 23–29 JANUARY

You'll gain a great deal of clarity about where it's best to invest your energy and focus, especially regarding your home life, family and/or your personal life. You may enjoy being more spontaneous and upbeat, bringing a sense of fun into your everyday life. Consider how you might manage your budget in new and innovative ways to make your dollar stretch further on a daily basis.

FINANCES

Key financial developments are likely to put your mind to how best to budget and also share your assets such as joint finances with someone special. If you have a debt it may seem that it's slow to pay off, but rest assured you'll make progress if you stick with a plan of action. You'll know already early in the month if you exceeded your budget during December and will get the chance to remedy the situation.

HEALTH

Jupiter retrograde can contribute to feelings of being less energetic than you'd hope, and the stars between 9 and 12 January will encourage you to do something to improve energy levels. You'll gain the chance to put a practical schedule in place that may nevertheless involve an original or quirky approach to your health. A fresh diet or putting a curfew on couch-potato tendencies will work wonders for you.

LOVE LIFE

The full moon on 13 January points to a fresh cycle in a relationship. It'll be a good time to consider how you can express your appreciation for each other in romantic ways to nurture more of a sense of togetherness. If you're single and would like a partner this will be a wonderful period through to the first week of February to look for love. If you're happy being single this will be a romantic time, so be sure to take the initiative.

CAREER

The year 2025 is your chance to step into new territory if you've been itching to do so for some time. Pluto, the powerhouse behind much change in your life, will aspect Mars already in January, creating a sense of motivation to make changes in areas of your life you've outgrown. Just be sure to evaluate carefully where your priorities lie or you'll be prone to making rash decisions, especially at the start of the month.

HOME LIFE

The uncharacteristic feeling of restlessness may be annoying this month, so it's important to look for ways this can be a positive rather than a negative for you. The happy aspect between the sun and Uranus on 13 January will be particularly lucky if you wish to make changes at home or with family, so be sure to instigate positive change. You'll enjoy an unexpected visit or uplifting event that points to more change at the end of the month.

February

WEEK 1: 30 JANUARY–5 FEBRUARY

News or a trip will be important and could mean changes such as a fresh work or financial agreement or the chance to change your everyday routine. You'll enjoy being creative and upbeat and spending time with family or someone special, so be sure to make a date! Avoid feeling pressured by someone into a decision you're not yet ready to make. If necessary, obtain expert advice.

WEEK 2: 6–12 FEBRUARY

A new opportunity may knock at your door. You may gain the chance to view your finances and personal life in a new light that could, nevertheless, transform the way you do things. Focus on finding solutions rather than adding to problems. The full moon on 12 February suggests a fresh direction will appeal within a partnership or shared arrangement or collaboration. You'll progress more productively as a result.

WEEK 3: 13–19 FEBRUARY

You'll gain a deeper understanding of someone, which could transform a business or personal relationship. If you need the co-operation of a friend or organisation, ask for it; you may well get what you want, especially if you keep expectations real. Someone may prove to be a loyal supporter. A spending spree may create debt, so consider your purchases carefully.

WEEK 4: 20–26 FEBRUARY

It's a good week to research ways to improve finances. Shared duties and common ground may be in the spotlight, as it's time to renew or renegotiate an agreement. You must avoid seeing things through rose-coloured glasses and gambling, not only financially but also in your personal life. Be prepared to agree to disagree if necessary with someone close.

FINANCES

Considerable transactions could put you in an ideal place as long as you have made the necessary enquiries and done adequate research. Money could come your way early in February, but you must be careful to avoid spending as quickly as you earn or receive money because you could end up in debt rather than being streets ahead. You may receive money from an inheritance or from someone who is in debt to you.

HEALTH

Mars retrograde has been slowing you down health-wise, but it'll end its retrograde phase at the end of this month and that will enable you or someone close who has been unwell to gradually regain a sense of good health over the coming months. In the meantime, it will be important to ensure you don't burn the candle at both ends, but rather that you find ways to maintain your health and especially stress levels.

LOVE LIFE

The full moon on 12 February points to a fresh or unexpected development in your love life. For some Capricorns, though, news at this time will be more in connection with someone you share duties with such as a colleague. Be prepared to look at your joint duties and responsibilities in a fresh light. If you're single you may meet someone outgoing and upbeat but who may value their freedom above all else. Couples will enjoy doing something different this month.

CAREER

While financially you have opportunities this month, you may be more drawn towards maintaining the status quo in your career while you sort out various other aspects of your life. However, you may be surprised by opportunities that do arise and would be in a strong position to consider their merit very carefully, especially their financial value. As long as opportunities align with your values and big picture goals, February can be a go-ahead month.

HOME LIFE

Once again you're in the position to make considerable changes in your domestic life if you wish but, being an earth sign, stability and security at home are what help you recharge your batteries and stay on top of things. Some changes may be inevitable, and these will revolve around people or developments over which you have no control. You do have control over your reaction to events, and the more practical you are now the better for you.

March

WEEK 1: 27 FEBRUARY—5 MARCH

Domestic and personal peace and calm, stability and security will increasingly appeal. You may need to change some aspects of your life to ensure you gain these qualities. Talks, a trip or negotiations this week will set the ball rolling, so be sure to be proactive with your various plans and especially financially. Avoid financial and emotional gambling.

WEEK 2: 6—12 MARCH

You'll enjoy a sense of progress with your work projects or financially. You may at the least receive a promotion or a financial or ego boost. You may be ready to take on more responsibilities or feel the opposite: that you can safely offload some duties now. Make your decisions carefully, as a major decision or financial choice can be made so avoid rushing.

WEEK 3: 13—19 MARCH

Key news and developments will ask you to view a key commitment in a new light. How could you better share duties and responsibilities? You may be drawn to setting fresh boundaries in your relationships and expediting paperwork in a new way. This week's success will revolve around good communication skills and the wish to see value and fair play in your interactions and work.

WEEK 4: 20—26 MARCH / WEEK 5: 27 MARCH—2 APRIL

WEEK 4: a fantastic trip or visit could bring together all your favourite people and fun elements in life. Water may feature prominently, so a trip to the coast may appeal. This is a good week to concoct a clever budget. You may be in the position to recall a debt or repay a debt. There is a degree of fortune in the stars but you must avoid pushing your luck! **WEEK 5:** this is a good week to consider a fresh approach to your home or family matters, especially for December-born Capricorns. You'll find talks and a new arrangement will help you establish more peace and harmony. A financial circumstance is best tackled carefully and a personal or business agreement may seem predestined. Aim to build wealth and stability.

FINANCES

This is an important month financially, especially with regard to shared duties such as joint responsibilities at work or home. A key financial decision can be made but you must be very careful with this, as this month includes two eclipses that will have an impact on your business and/or finances. If you're already aware of considerable financial matters that need attention, be sure to avoid making large investments in other matters as this could distract you.

HEALTH

Being predominantly practical and methodical, you'll gain a sense of security in March by maintaining as well as you can a health routine you've already established. In so doing you'll gain the stability that enables you to thrive at work and at play. Just keep an eye on overexertion mid-month and towards the end of the month. If you do feel super tired at these times consider ways to work smarter, not harder.

LOVE LIFE

If your love life has been lacklustre, rest assured this situation will improve even if you need to undergo a minor soul-searching phase first. If you're single and have been in a complicated situation or disinterested in romance, this will change over the coming weeks and months and you'll enjoy a revitalised love life. For couples, where there has been a lack of communication this situation promises to improve despite a potential hitch at the start and end of the month.

CAREER

An eclipse month such as this invariably opens new doors, and there is every chance you can step into something new in your career if that's what you're looking for. If not, your every effort to focus on building wealth, stability and security will be rewarded and you'll gain a sense of motivation and success as a result. Suffice to say, this is the month to be outgoing and confident but you must avoid gambling on a future that is not yet secure.

HOME LIFE

You may receive unexpected news or undergo unusual changes at home. These are likely to be positive in nature even if there is some disruption or unsettling development in the process. You may be drawn to reconsidering how you share duties and responsibilities in the home and could better organise chores and domestic and financial commitments. Be prepared to think laterally about how to improve your home life and your efforts will pay off.

April

WEEK 1: 3–9 APRIL

A personal and, for some, financial circumstance will require your attention to ensure you are on top of things, as considerable commitments can be made now that will be long-standing. A domestic or personal circumstance is likely to head towards a positive if unexpected outcome. This is certainly a good time to take the initiative by laying careful plans for solid results.

WEEK 2: 10–16 APRIL

Important financial matters will catch your eye. For some these will revolve around important agreements or collaborations, and for others around domestic matters. It's a good week to focus on building a positive budget and review investments and consider whether some could be more profitable. The full moon on 13 April will highlight the chance to make a fresh agreement.

WEEK 3: 17–23 APRIL

Unavoidable decisions and developments will catch your attention, and with a little help from someone you trust or admire you could make a great deal of progress, especially financially and in your personal life. It's a good week to make a personal commitment and set a realistic budget as you may be prone to overspend, especially as a large outlay or investment is likely.

WEEK 4: 24–30 APRIL

Financial or personal transactions will require focus if they didn't already last week. Romance could flourish and a reunion will appeal. If you're single you may meet someone familiar but new. The Taurus new moon on 27 April brings the chance to establish more stability and security at home or with a domestic matter, but you must avoid arguments and a power play on that date.

FINANCES

April is a key month financially and you could make excellent progress. A fresh option is something to consider, but as you're likely to be moving into different territory financially it's important to research adequately. An expert or adviser will be indispensable. Both the full moon on 13 April and the new moon on the 27th point to fresh agreements that may be legal in nature for some and therefore not to be rushed.

HEALTH

This is likely to be a busy and varied month. You'll be drawn to bringing change with a view to experiencing more adventure and enjoyment in your daily life, and a sense of discovery and adventure will certainly improve your well-being. However, you may be prone to take on too much work, especially towards the end of the month, so be sure to maintain a balanced daily schedule including a fitness quotient.

LOVE LIFE

For some Capricorns the main focus in April will be on your personal life, as someone you feel you have a predestined connection with becomes centre stage in your life. The full moon on the 13th will spotlight the potential for misunderstandings, crossed lines or hasty decision-making, so if you've been planning a considerable investment in someone new you may do well to wait until the end of the month when you're more familiar with the relationship.

CAREER

The Libra full moon on 13 April will spotlight your need to find more balance within your career and projects and ventures, yet unavoidable commitments will mean you must stick with a certain schedule you're already on. It's nevertheless likely that someone close such as a colleague encourages you to take positive steps to advance your career, so be prepared to be adventurous and you may find that new agreements are possible.

HOME LIFE

You'll appreciate the opportunity to change various aspects of your home life, and this may involve fresh décor for example or a trip away. Absence makes the heart grow fonder, and this applies not only to relationships but also your home. You may find that an addition to your home such as a visitor brings unexpected joy, and if you do travel you'll experience the relaxation that comes from returning home.

May

WEEK 1: 1–7 MAY

You'll enjoy indulging in an activity you relish. A trip, music or catch-up with someone you love will appeal. Avoid being overly influenced by someone who doesn't have your best interests at heart, especially towards 7 May when conflict could erupt. Avoid travel delays by being well organised. A financial or personal matter will require careful analysis to avoid making mistakes.

WEEK 2: 8–14 MAY

The Scorpio full moon on 12 May will spotlight a group, friend or organisation that may be the focus of a developing drama. Perhaps you feel particularly passionately about a principle or have strong feelings that are best channelled into constructive plans that will deliver a happy outcome. Meetings and communications will be constructive and could lead to a financial boost.

WEEK 3: 15–21 MAY

A change of pace or place such as a trip somewhere beautiful will certainly feel therapeutic. You may enjoy a health or fitness boost this weekend. If you're concerned about your career direction this will become more pressing, and you may decide on a fresh path. A surprise or impromptu event at home with family or regarding property will buoy your mood.

WEEK 4: 22–28 MAY

You may experience a fresh incentive to make changes within your personal life or home or a shared situation. The key to making the correct decisions will revolve around good communication skills and the willingness to see other people's points of view. You may otherwise feel stuck within an existing situation you cannot move on from. You'll enjoy a trip or visit.

FINANCES

Key agreements and arrangements could be truly fortunate for you, but you must be sure to carefully research circumstances. You may receive an unexpected financial boost but must avoid gambling and overspending as a result, as otherwise your money could leave your hands as quickly as it enters. An arrangement towards the end of the month could be particularly transformative for you financially and within areas of your life you share.

HEALTH

This is a good time to consider the impact your work has on your health. If you've been considering something new in your daily life such as a fresh health routine, this may well be motivated by the need to place your energy into activities that actually motivate you as opposed to simply working for money day in, day out. Luckily, a meeting or news will boost your chance of creating a healthier lifestyle.

LOVE LIFE

Sharing and organising how you manage joint responsibilities in an existing relationship will involve discussion and the willingness to move into fresh territory so your love life remains an open book and communication lines are clear. If you're single, consider whether altering some of the methods you seek to spend time with others could improve, and as a result you may find by the end of the month that passion and romance really heat up.

CAREER

The Scorpio full moon on 12 May points to a fresh phase in your career and, for some, with certain groups or organisations you connect with. It's a good time to reinvigorate your career as you'll be ready to make changes, and the changes you make are likely to take. You may be surprised by news that spurs you on to turn a corner, and as long as new options align with your values and principles you're unlikely to go wrong.

HOME LIFE

You'll enjoy changing an important aspect of your home life and may be surprised by the results when you do. An impromptu guest or trip could be therapeutic, so consider going on a journey. People you invite into your home may contribute to a sense of excitement and joy. The new moon on 27 May could kick-start a fresh phase that will be personally invigorating and may involve a financial improvement.

June

WEEK 1: 29 MAY–4 JUNE

A family member or someone who is close will have news for you or vice versa. Where you're unsure of a decision, avoid gambling on your future and instead obtain specific and trusted advice. An expert can provide you with guidance, so get in touch with one. A therapeutic trip or get-together will boost morale, so be sure to reach out to those whose company you enjoy or admire.

WEEK 2: 5–11 JUNE

This is an excellent week to discuss matters that have been on your mind but you've been reluctant to broach, especially regarding health and work. For some Capricorns the full moon on 11 June will spotlight a personal or family matter that will require tact and diplomacy. News towards Monday could include a change of work or health routine. You'll gain the information you need but must avoid impulsiveness, which is likely to backfire.

WEEK 3: 12–18 JUNE

By adopting a healing and positive approach you could turn things around at home so they offer you more serenity and calm in life. You'll enjoy a get-together or trip. A change of routine will involve the need to dig deep and work out exactly where your loyalties and priorities lie. You may be ready to make long-range changes but must avoid impulsive decisions.

WEEK 4: 19–25 JUNE / WEEK 5: 26 JUNE–2 JULY

WEEK 4: a new chapter awaits in your work, health or daily life. If you're on holiday this promises to revitalise relationships but you will need to adapt to circumstances. Workers could experience a change in your usual routine or income. It's a good week to decide your priorities and find ways to negotiate your terms while also being flexible. **WEEK 5:** you may be surprised by some of the discussions or developments that arise as people you connect with are more expressive than usual. If disagreements arise consider whether these revolve around a difference in principles and, if so, you may have to agree to disagree. In this light, intense talks this weekend or early next week needn't be super disruptive.

FINANCES

Financial and work developments are likely in June, and you'll be drawn to formulating a fresh daily or health routine. For some lucky Capricorns this could mean an improvement in your circumstances, but for others the need to consider very carefully how you budget and invest your hard-earned cash. The full moon on 11 June will spotlight particular work arrangements that could flow better and your challenge will be to work smarter, not harder.

HEALTH

If you have health circumstances you'd like to investigate, June is your month! There is an extremely therapeutic aspect to the month, especially during the first week when a partner, expert or friend could help you establish a healthy daily work schedule and fitness routine. News towards 9 June could clarify a personal health situation, but if you still require more information you'll find ways to gain the information you need during the month.

LOVE LIFE

A relationship will have a therapeutic effect on you, which will revitalise your love life. A trip or change of environment could create a sense of passion and excitement; however, it's also likely that someone in your life behaves uncharacteristically erratically and you'll naturally lean towards re-evaluating the relationship. If you're single there's an adventurous aspect to the month that could lead to romance, especially around 10 June and from the 21st to the 23rd.

CAREER

News early in June will encourage you to be more communicative within your career, either through the way you collaborate with others or via improved communication skills in general. You may be drawn to updating your device, for example, or finding ways to broaden your skill sets. Someone helpful or an expert will be supportive if you need more information regarding finances and your career progress in the long-term big picture.

HOME LIFE

You may experience the need to change aspects of your home life, which would be because of someone you share the space with or due to the arrival of a visitor. While some of the developments may create a little upheaval, you're likely to move towards a positive change domestically or within your family so be prepared to take the initiative and work with changes in a creative, participatory way as opposed to working against them.

July

WEEK 1: 3–9 JULY

You'll enjoy a surprise, and an impromptu change of circumstances at home or with family will mean you must be adaptable. You'll enjoy an ego boost or compliment but you must avoid financial and emotional gambling. Get set to begin an exciting chapter that can boost your circumstances, and be prepared to assume more responsibility at work or ask for a promotion.

WEEK 2: 10–16 JULY

The full moon on 10 July will be in Capricorn and will spotlight your personal life, especially if you were born on or before 10 January. If you were born afterwards you're likely to begin a fresh work or health routine that could bring more stability your way. It's certainly a good week for all Capricorns to value your priorities, including who and what is most important to you now.

WEEK 3: 17–23 JULY

This will be a good week to really focus on good communication skills to avoid arguments when you feel under pressure. However, you'll experience an upbeat development this weekend that could smooth the way forward in many different respects in your personal life, so take the initiative. Romance could flourish. A surprise next week could buoy your mood at home.

WEEK 4: 24–30 JULY

Be prepared to turn a corner in a business or personal partnership as the new moon on 24 July helps you revitalise relationships and gain an increased sense of purpose. It's a good week to invest in your home life or property, and you may experience a financial boost. You'll enjoy a growing sense of clarity and the incentive to get things done, not only in your personal life but also at work.

FINANCES

This will be a good month to consider how to create a healthy and stable budget that works for you, especially in the first two weeks of the month. The remainder of July will encourage you to review and reconsider some of your investments and the way you earn money. You'll gain the opportunity over the coming months to establish a stronger position in the long term, so there's no need to rush. A positive financial opportunity is likely towards the new moon on 24 July.

HEALTH

The first two weeks of the month are ideal for investing in your emotional and mental well-being, principally by providing the peace and nurturance you require in your spare time from your home and/or family. Consider how much pressure you put on yourself. As the month progresses you may find ways to overcome stress while still maintaining healthy productivity at work. You'll feel encouraged to boost your appearance and treat yourself to a new look.

LOVE LIFE

You're likely to be entering fresh territory within a close relationship. Take note of developments early in July in your personal or domestic life, as these will give you a strong sense of where your attention is going to go in these two important areas of your life over the coming weeks and months. The first two weeks are certainly conducive to establishing arrangements and agreements that will enable your love life to thrive.

CAREER

Look out for new opportunities in your career. July is a good time to turn a corner in your life in general, and if your career has not been satisfying for a while this is the time to look for something fresh that suits you and therefore motivates you to work. The new moon on 24 July could bring a fresh business agreement that favourably impacts your finances, so this could signal an opportunity at work.

HOME LIFE

If you look at your home as a kind of a nest you'll gain the sense of its importance in July from a nurturing perspective. Be prepared to make changes to this important aspect of your life, especially if you feel that you've either outgrown it or are ready to fly the coop. You'll find that research and resources will come your way whether you wish to invest more in your current home or find something else.

August

WEEK 1: 31 JULY–6 AUGUST

Key news or a meeting regarding a shared project may take you to the past or require you to review certain arrangements. Be prepared to negotiate and use tact and diplomacy to avoid difficult conversations and/or being pressured. You may feel motivated to check details to ensure you're on the right track. If you're concerned about finances, consider seeking expert advice.

WEEK 2: 7–13 AUGUST

A business or personal partner has news for you that may take you by surprise. You have excellent stars this week for bringing something different into your shared business or personal relationships, so be sure to take the initiative. However, if some of your decisions involve finances be sure to research your options carefully or again engage the advice of an expert.

WEEK 3: 14–20 AUGUST

This is an excellent week for discussions and negotiations, both in your personal life and financially. You could overcome disagreements by adopting a sensitive approach, especially this weekend, and a close relationship could thrive as a result. Someone you have an unavoidable relationship with will be a focus. If you're working this is likely to be a busy week.

WEEK 4: 21–27 AUGUST

Avoid allowing restlessness to distract you from potentially wonderful developments this week. Key financial and personal decisions will open doors to a fresh chapter but you must do your research, especially if commitments are likely to be long term. When you do you may achieve a financial or ego boost. Important meetings and get-togethers with kindred spirits will lead to a lovely sense of belonging.

FINANCES

You may experience a positive financial development towards 9 August and again towards the 16th and the end of the month. The start of the month would be the time to consider broadening your horizons and using your money to fuel your projects and ventures. However, if you're required to make key financial decisions but are lacking insight into the outcome, be sure to engage expert advice. An expert or trusted friend may provide invaluable information.

HEALTH

Aim to devote time to some of your favourite activities to gain a sense of happiness, but you must also carve out time for yourself and those you love as you may otherwise forget to look after yourself. Venus will bring focus to your appearance and wardrobe at the start of the month, making this a good time to update both. Just be sure to be clear with any stylists you engage to avoid disappointment.

LOVE LIFE

Mercury retrograde may bring a nostalgic feeling to some of your interactions. If you have felt for a while that some of your relationships could be better or reconfigured so everyone is happy with the relationship, this is a good month to put some ideas on the table. However, things are likely to take off very quickly and especially around 8 August, so be sure the agreements you suggest and make are exactly what you want.

CAREER

Mars at the zenith of your chart will create a sense of progress but also of pressure, and while you prefer life to go ahead at a regular pace you may feel a little outside your usual comfort zone, especially towards 8 August. Be sure to consider your actions and words carefully to avoid landing in hot water. When you do this could be a motivational time to take steps forward in your career.

HOME LIFE

This will be an excellent month to make changes in your home and/or family and property, as the efforts you make are likely to improve your domestic life. Projects that involve collaboration or joint efforts are especially likely to succeed, so be sure to enlist people's help. Just be patient as Mercury retrograde until 11 August will mean that some projects will be slower to complete. You'll enjoy a therapeutic atmosphere at home or in a lovely environment towards the 19th.

September

WEEK 1: 28 AUGUST–3 SEPTEMBER

You'll appreciate the opportunity to get together with like-minded people, both socially and through work. Financially, you may need to review some of the arrangements you already have in place. You'll gain the opportunity to research your best options, so be sure to avoid making rash decisions. A change in the way you share duties or responsibilities at home or with family will merit patience.

WEEK 2: 4–10 SEPTEMBER

Get set for an inspiring week. That is, if you're ready to reset your beliefs and ideas. Fresh news and motivation will turn your mind towards new endeavours that could prove to be particularly invigorating and fulfilling. Keep an eye out also for who you meet this week, as socialising and networking could bring fresh inspiration your way. Singles could meet someone new who is mysteriously familiar.

WEEK 3: 11–17 SEPTEMBER

There is an element of the inevitable or of fate this week, especially in connection with people and money. If you've been putting off certain conversations or transactions you'll no longer be able to do so, and facing the music will be your best option. You may be surprised that getting on with things you've been putting off will be therapeutic or cathartic.

WEEK 4: 18–24 SEPTEMBER / WEEK 5: 25 SEPTEMBER–1 OCTOBER

WEEK 4: restlessness could distract you from some wonderful developments, so ensure you are focused. Get-togethers with kindred spirits will lead to a lovely sense of belonging. Domestic and personal developments by the end of the week are likely to raise spirits. It will be important beforehand to make valid agreements regarding shared assets or finances. **WEEK 5:** this is a great week to focus on good communication skills and negotiations, as you could make excellent progress in your collaborations and responsibilities, especially those in your personal life and at home. If you've been considering a move or fresh environment at work you're likely to enjoy pushing into new territory, but will need to manage potentially difficult communications towards 30 September.

FINANCES

This month's eclipses and the retrograde transit of Saturn will spotlight how important it is to reconfigure your financial circumstances so they better suit your current situation. If you're setting up fresh agreements with a business or personal partner, consider obtaining financial advice and avoid simply hoping for the best. The solar eclipse on 21 September will spotlight shared assets such as debt or joint finances. Aim to make a long-term agreement at this point that benefits you personally.

HEALTH

Peace of mind is the key to health and well-being, so the more you can infuse your activities with this in mind without compromising your beliefs and values the more productive and successful you'll feel by the end of the month. There are always irritations and frustrations, especially regarding collaborations and communications, so work on your ability to be patient, compassionate yet also diligent and resolute, as this will help you attain peace of mind.

LOVE LIFE

Jupiter in your seventh house of love makes a fortunate connection with the moon's nodes early in the month, potentially bringing you closer with someone you love. Be sure to make the effort to enjoy a treat and if you're single to meet like-minded people, especially around 3 September. However, there is also the likelihood that disagreements to do with shared arrangements or duties arise with a partner, and the better you handle this the better your love life will be.

CAREER

You may need to make a key commitment to a particular path within your career. Even if you feel vulnerable or sensitive about where your future lies be sure to take direct action, as in effect you'll be taking control of your future and could potentially propel yourself into fresh financial arrangements and agreements in your career. The art of negotiation and collaboration will be necessary to attain fresh ground.

HOME LIFE

You may be surprised by developments early in the month such as news from someone you share your home with or regarding finances. Be prepared to research your options and avoid knee-jerk reactions for the best results. The bigger picture is that your home, family and personal life will evolve into something new over time, and the better you handle smaller events at the moment the better the bigger picture will be.

October

WEEK 1: 2–8 OCTOBER

You can make a success of your activities even if you secretly fear your vulnerabilities or lack of skill sets will let you down. You may be pleasantly surprised if you give things a good go. Someone will help you if you ask for advice and you may be asked for help. Some communications may be difficult, so be tactful. Avoid minor bumps and scrapes and erratic drivers. Romance could blossom this weekend.

WEEK 2: 9–15 OCTOBER

A financial or personal commitment may be necessary for you to bring about the transformation you're looking for within a business or personal relationship. You'll turn a corner in a personal matter or at work, and this may concern a domestic-related circumstance. If a commitment seems restrictive, consider whether it provides security and weigh up your options.

WEEK 3: 16–22 OCTOBER

You'll enjoy a favourite activity or therapeutic trip. You're at a point where deciding how best to spend your spare time is a key to your happiness. You'll discover extra energy or momentum to invest in your career if you cannot take a holiday, and this will boost your self-esteem and potentially your finances. Avoid misunderstandings, especially at the weekend.

WEEK 4: 23–29 OCTOBER

This week you'll appreciate positive feedback from your career and those you depend on. You'll experience either a financial or confidence boost that will provide you with momentum moving forwards, both at work and financially. A domestic, property or family matter may surprise you mid next week. If you've been looking for a breakthrough, it's on its way.

FINANCES

There is a focus on shared finances at the start of the month and you'll be in a stronger position if you can organise finances rather than simply leave them to their own devices. Certain debts could come home to roost, and you'll need to find ways to pay these. A friend or family member may help. You may experience an improvement in your finances or at least a stabilisation of finances towards the second half of the month.

HEALTH

If you have not already organised a holiday, this will be a good month to consider a therapeutic break. Even if you simply book a holiday for the future it will have an uplifting effect. It's clear that a considerable amount of your focus goes to work and finances in October, so it will be important to manage your health and well-being or you may experience low energy levels that could impact negatively on your productivity.

LOVE LIFE

The month begins on a romantic note. You may be feeling nostalgic or experience memory overload about an ex. If you're single you may meet someone during the first weekend of the month, so be sure to organise a date. Your tact and diplomacy will be necessary in your love life, especially between 18 and 21 October when some of your decisions or actions could be misinterpreted by someone close.

CAREER

You'll gain a sense of momentum from mid-month onwards within your career that could move you into a different sense of status and improve your finances and self-esteem. Be sure to take the initiative with your various projects throughout the month and at the start of the month, even if they feel lacking in momentum. You're likely to see specific progress in the last week of the month if not before.

HOME LIFE

You'll appreciate the opportunity to infuse your home life with more beauty and luxury as you gain an understanding of the importance of investing in yourself and your home. You're likely to increasingly be drawn to making changes at home and especially within the areas you share such as common duties and joint space. You could make some invaluable long-term changes, so be sure to take the initiative. You may be surprised by developments towards 29 October.

November

WEEK 1: 30 OCTOBER–5 NOVEMBER

This will be an excellent week to focus on therapeutic ways to improve communications and relationships. This is particularly so as some developments are likely to proceed at a fast rate, especially regarding finances and your career. You may even be surprised by developments at home as the supermoon on 5 November spotlights developments there. Be sure to find time to take short breaks if necessary.

WEEK 2: 6–12 NOVEMBER

Venus will encourage you to reconsider how you spend your spare time and where you invest your time and money. A favourite activity or place will be a drawcard this week. You'll enjoy getting together with like-minded people. All of this will boost morale, so you mustn't allow a disagreement to detract from the good in your life.

WEEK 3: 13–19 NOVEMBER

This will be an excellent week to review some of your financial and work schedules, as you may discover there are more efficient or productive ways you could progress your projects and plans. Some communications and transactions are going to run extremely smoothly while others will be delayed or difficult, so be sure to use your communication skills for the best effect or you risk making needless mistakes.

WEEK 4: 20–26 NOVEMBER / WEEK 5: 27 NOVEMBER–3 DECEMBER

WEEK 4: the new moon on 20 November will revitalise your social life, so if you've had a very quiet time socially you'll enter the festive season celebrations early. If you've been enjoying an upbeat time you'll gain the opportunity to spend more time and energy with those you love. Working Capricorns are in line to boost your status, so take the initiative. **WEEK 5:** a reunion or trip and the consequent focus on a change in your domestic life will breathe fresh air into your environment. This could be an illuminating time for spiritual Capricorns, and students will enjoy taking the initiative with your various projects and holiday plans. Avoid disputes and taking people's random comments to heart, as someone close may be feeling a little out of sorts.

FINANCES

Some of your values and priorities in life are changing. As a result, you may find that some of your activities or friends no longer resonate. You're likely to gradually invest the money you used to invest in yourself and in your pastimes in different activities. Mercury and Jupiter retrograde from 11 November will provide ample time – several weeks, in fact, at the least – to consider your investments and take action accordingly when you're ready.

HEALTH

To some degree you're best equipped to navigate this month's developments, as you tend to take life one step at a time as opposed to rushing decisions and projects. Your ability to be diligent and patient will produce a positive mental and emotional outlook, this being important as there are likely to be considerable delays interspersed with very rapidly moving circumstances. However, people may be impatient so you must maintain positive interactions where possible.

LOVE LIFE

Focus on improving communication skills, especially in the first and last weeks of the month, as otherwise you may experience miscommunications or mistakes. Luckily, a change of environment or the wish to gain a stronger foothold within your relationship will be the motivation to gain more stability and security within your love life. Singles may find this a particularly adventurous and sociable, outgoing time, ideal for meeting a diverse group of people.

CAREER

Mercury retrograde will provide you with ample opportunity to rethink some of your career options over the coming weeks, so if you feel that you're under pressure to make serious decisions career-wise early in November rest assured you'll gain ample time to consider your true circumstances. The new moon on the 20th signals the chance to reboot your career. You'll also find that certain people who have your best interests at heart will be supportive should you need fresh perspective.

HOME LIFE

You may experience a surprise early in the month that will merit focus as you consider the best path forward both at home and within your general direction in life. Consider carefully what your long-term aims and goals are regarding your home. The full moon on 5 November will spotlight more clearly where your feelings and priorities lie, so it will be in your interest to avoid making rash decisions earlier in the month if possible.

December

WEEK 1: 4–10 DECEMBER

You'll enjoy socialising and connecting with family or friends. A therapeutic trip or reunion will raise spirits. Key talks to do with your work or finances will be productive, even if slightly challenging. Be prepared to de-stress when you can as the supermoon on 4 December may feel a little intense, especially in connection with family or those who demand your attention.

WEEK 2: 11–17 DECEMBER

You'll enjoy a get-together, reunion or trip somewhere beautiful, but if your plans are delayed avoid taking developments personally and look for therapeutic ways to bide your time and develop patience. If you're making considerable financial decisions, ensure you have all the facts: you may need to negotiate a work or financial matter and the clearer you are the better for you.

WEEK 3: 18–24 DECEMBER

A change of pace or place will be therapeutic despite the inconvenience of the change of routine. Some Capricorns will enjoy the festive season and social life that brings out the fun aspect of your personality. Some of your adventures may even surprise you. Be sure to keep a keen eye on your expenditure and financial transactions, as there may be confusion or mistakes could arise.

WEEK 4: 25–31 DECEMBER

It's a great week for a visit, socialising and a reunion. Take things lightly and boost your health when you can. A trip or at least a change of environment through visitors or fresh décor such as a splash of colour at home will raise morale. If you're in debt, however, you must avoid overspending and remember there are many ways to enjoy the festive season without spending money.

FINANCES

There are positive signs early in December that you could make true headway financially, especially if you've been careful with financial planning. At mid-month a financial transaction or negotiation will benefit from the full facts to avoid mistakes or a bad investment being made. You'll have access to an expert should complexities arise. A healthy approach to finances around Christmas will pay off in many ways than purely financially; finding the balance between overspending and making like Scrooge will be ideal.

HEALTH

You'll enjoy a boost in morale early in the month, and this could be through a group or organisation. It's important in December to avoid overdoing work and burning the candle at both ends, because this could lead to misunderstandings and mix-ups. An adventurous phase during the second half of the month will boost morale as long as you take things carefully. A change of place such as a holiday or trip will be therapeutic.

LOVE LIFE

The supermoon on 4 December will spotlight your love life, especially in relation to its romantic and fun aspects. If you feel that some of the joy has been lacking more recently, this supermoon will motivate you to zhuzh up your love life. Singles may decide there is a fresh path for you regarding the groups or organisations you frequent, and being adventurous and outgoing could lead to meeting fun people.

CAREER

The start of December is an excellent time to initiate talks and meetings with colleagues, employers, employees and business partners. You may receive unexpected news. It's a good time to sharpen your social and networking skills, as a dynamic approach to your career will certainly pay off. You'll enjoy being more outgoing with your activities of choice within your career and may be drawn to entering a fresh domain career-wise towards the end of the month.

HOME LIFE

You may be drawn to making changes at home, through a trip or by receiving visitors, especially around the Christmas week. Unexpected news around 10 December will already illuminate some of your options. Towards mid-month and at Christmas you'll enjoy changes at home, and bigger-picture plans such as a move could improve your bank balance as long as you do your research.

January

WEEK 1: 1–8 JANUARY

You'll enjoy some lovely get-togethers, and a reunion may be particularly poignant. Creative Aquarians will be especially productive. You may be surprised by news from family or regarding your domestic life. Avoid gambling and making assumptions; it's far better to work with the facts now. A financial or personal situation is best approached from a realistic and practical stance.

WEEK 2: 9–15 JANUARY

A significant link with your past will be relevant: you may return to an old haunt or will hear unexpectedly from someone. You'll enjoy hearing spontaneously from upbeat friends, but you must avoid a circumstance you know will cause disappointment. Financially, it's important to keep an eye on spending as you may otherwise find yourself in a pickle, especially regarding debt.

WEEK 3: 16–22 JANUARY

Developments could cause restlessness or the sense that change is coming. You'd be right: the Aquarian new moon on 29 January will bring a fresh situation for January Aquarians in your personal life and for February Aquarians in your work life or a change of daily schedule. Avoid feeling distracted and edgy; instead, find purpose in your activities and you could truly excel.

WEEK 4: 23–29 JANUARY

This is a great time to consider how to infuse your daily life with a more spontaneous and upbeat vibe. The new moon on 29 January will be in your sign and signifies the chance to revamp your personal life, so get set to let go of habits that no longer serve your higher purpose. Consider a new look or health routine. The current stars will help you attain your goals in many areas, including work.

FINANCES

A realistic and practical approach to finances early in the month will be productive, especially between 4 and 8 January. Avoid assuming everyone is on the same page as you are. If you have accrued debt, be sure to thoroughly research the terms and conditions of your lending arrangement and consider a fresh budget to avoid deepening debt. January is also a good month to consider whether you could earn more or find new income streams to boost your wealth.

HEALTH

Mars retrograde in your health sector may seem to slow you down, so be sure to find ways to boost energy levels or you may wear yourself out. Luckily, you'll gain the chance to indulge in favourite sports or fitness programs that will boost morale and energy. The full moon on 13 January may bring important information regarding your health or a work situation that is best navigated with good health practices in mind.

LOVE LIFE

Pluto in your sign has been encouraging you to revitalise your love life since 2023. This year you get the chance to put some of your ideas into practice so you feel your personal life is on track in ways you enjoy. However, this will involve some effort on your part even if you have a romantic notion that love will find its way to you. The new moon on 29 January could be particularly helpful in your love quest.

CAREER

You're adventurous by nature and will experience the motivation already early in January to alter your daily work life to create more purpose. If you feel that your current work is frustrating or really not you, you'll gain the impetus over the next quarter to change this for the better. It will involve a gradual process to build a solid foundation, and if you already enjoy what you do you'll enjoy investing increasingly in your work.

HOME LIFE

You may feel a need to return to an old haunt or reconnect with family. You'll enjoy receiving visitors and a sense of connection. However, you may discover that nostalgia has been driving some of your feelings about the past and as a result will gradually move forward into a refreshing phase that no longer requires you to feel so tied to the past. Some Aquarians will be drawn this month to making repairs to your home and/or relationships.

February

WEEK 1: 30 JANUARY—5 FEBRUARY

You'll appreciate the chance to boost your appearance this week and include more romance, art and music in your life. If you're contemplating a beauty treat, ensure you're clear about what you want. A work development may involve a new set of rules or fresh agreement, so be sure to be clear about your terms. Someone at home or a domestic matter may require special attention.

WEEK 2: 6—12 FEBRUARY

A reunion or draw to your past may bring out intense emotions or could prove transformative. Avoid resuming a bad habit. A fresh approach to health, your daily schedule and work will appeal. You're about to turn a corner in a key relationship or partnership, so think of innovative ways to move ahead. Just avoid crossed lines and misunderstandings, which could be rife this week.

WEEK 3: 13—19 FEBRUARY

A circumstance may seem more exaggerated than it need be so ensure you maintain focus, especially at work and with your bigger-picture plans. A personal or financial matter will enter fresh territory and merit a little research or closer attention to detail. The more organised you are the better for you! You may enjoy a surge in energy and could receive a boost at work or health-wise.

WEEK 4: 20—26 FEBRUARY

Talks are best approached with a philosophical view to avoid arguments. You may agree with someone and this will be motivating, but if not look for ways forward. Financial matters will deserve some focus and you must avoid overspending. Ask for advice with a difficult decision if need be. You'll receive key news that will merit careful focus, as a decision may be long-standing.

FINANCES

February is a changeable time for you, and if you've been working towards a considerable amount of change such as in your work or home life you're likely to undergo important financial transactions to effect these changes. However, if you're tempted by speculative investment and especially at the beginning of February you must be careful, as the possibility for gain is as strong as the possibility for loss due to exaggerated expectations.

HEALTH

If you've been experiencing health woes or a lack of energy you'll be pleased to hear that this situation will turn around at the end of the month. In the meantime, it will be important to find ways to conserve your energy and channel it in the best way possible to avoid an energy drain. The good news is that this is an excellent time to develop your spiritual and psychic abilities, and you may even surprise yourself.

LOVE LIFE

You may experience a strong draw to someone from the past such as an ex, but you must be careful to avoid resuming a relationship with someone purely out of nostalgia or a co-dependency you're unable to overcome. If you're single you may meet someone who seems familiar yet whom you've never met. This could be a cosmic relationship and one that would certainly be worth investigating. Couples will experience a particularly romantic beginning to the month, ideal for a holiday or short break.

CAREER

The new moon on 29 January kick-started a fresh chapter in your work or daily routine and this will be reinforced by the full moon on 12 February, which could bring a fresh arrangement or agreement your way. If you're looking for work the arrival of Mercury in your sign will certainly help you communicate well, making this an excellent time to circulate resumés and for meeting prospective employers or business contacts.

HOME LIFE

There is a progressive atmosphere regarding your home life this month that will enable you to move forward with your various plans and projects. This will be a welcome breath of fresh air, because in comparison with the previous few months you'll gain the chance to bring the kind of atmosphere you like into your home life. If you've been planning to find something larger or add to your family, the next few months look promising.

March

WEEK 1: 27 FEBRUARY–5 MARCH

The Pisces new moon on 28 February signals the chance to establish a strong set of values and principles to act as a guide regarding where to invest your efforts, time and money. You may enjoy an impromptu visit, trip or get-together. Domestic and personal agreements must be forged carefully to avoid arguments. The upcoming eclipse could signal long-term changes regarding someone you work with or rely on.

WEEK 2: 6–12 MARCH

You'll feel motivated to be innovative and adventurous and may appreciate the opportunity to travel somewhere different. If you're planning new ventures and ideas, this is the time to surge ahead. You'll enjoy a reunion. Try to get important financial matters or paperwork on the table before Mercury turns retrograde on 15 March. Key financial transactions and the option to improve finances will deserve careful focus.

WEEK 3: 13–19 MARCH

The supermoon on 14 March will kick-start a fresh phase for you in a personal or business arrangement and you may need to renegotiate a financial agreement in the process. Avoid making assumptions and be practical and realistic for the best results. Key meetings will be pivotal, yet a changing scenario suggests the more you can adapt as you move forward the more you'll appreciate events.

WEEK 4: 20–26 MARCH / WEEK 5: 27 MARCH–2 APRIL

WEEK 4: financially, events will point out where you may be able to budget better and whether you have over- or underestimated circumstances. This is a romantic week, and singles may be drawn to a charming person. You'll benefit by being realistic now even if you feel you're swept off your feet by circumstances. You may rekindle an interest, hobby or relationship. **WEEK 5:** you may see yourself or someone else in a new light. Your vulnerabilities may surface, so take things one step at a time. It's a good week to research your financial options. Love could blossom, so if you're single and looking for company it's a good week to find it! Romance should flourish for couples but you must avoid sensitive topics.

FINANCES

Be sure to get key financial considerations thought through before Mercury turns retrograde on 15 March. That is, unless you need the luxury of time to review some of your circumstances and in effect would like to slow some financial decisions down. If not, the beginning of March will be ideal for making financial decisions but you must avoid get-rich-quick schemes and temporary stop-gap measures.

HEALTH

As proactive and energetic Mars gains ground in your sixth house of health and well-being you'll gain a sense of revitalisation and improved energy levels in March. Be methodical and practical about scheduling activities aimed to boost your health and well-being as opposed to leaving fitness as something to haphazardly add to your timetable should the occasion arise. The end of the month is ideal for formulating a fresh diet that suits you.

LOVE LIFE

This month's eclipses are likely to alter how you share certain duties and finances in your life. A development in your personal life may be ideal but, if not, focus on building a solid foundation. Romance will certainly be a drawcard towards mid-month, when the eclipse could refresh your love life and bring a new understanding of someone close. Singles may meet someone new towards 20 March, and you may hear from an ex or feel nostalgic about the past.

CAREER

Developments in March will gather pace, so be sure to do regular progress checks to ensure you're on track career-wise as you may otherwise be easily distracted by considerable developments that risk leaving you in a position you hadn't necessarily planned. Mars in your work sector will boost your options, but you must be sure to negotiate circumstances as you will otherwise be giving up your free time at work for little or no remuneration.

HOME LIFE

Your home life will increasingly be in focus over the next few weeks and months. This will be a good time to consider investing more in your home life; for example, spending more time with those you love. If you're drawn to home improvements this is certainly a good time to put effort into some DIY projects. You may enjoy the company of a diverse group of people, being more sociable either within your own home or other people's.

April

WEEK 1: 3–9 APRIL

You may enjoy a trip or upbeat development at home. It's a good week to indulge in your favourite pastimes and in romance, the arts and music, but you must avoid daydreaming or being super idealistic as mistakes could be made. Ensure you allow the practical side of your nature to kick in, which will help you lay solid foundations for yourself and those you love.

WEEK 2: 10–16 APRIL

There are many positive aspects to this week, especially regarding your happiness in connection with a change of routine or schedule. You'll enjoy a reunion and the chance to engage in a different environment either via travel or receiving visitors. The full moon on 13 April will spotlight a shared responsibility or duty that is best handled carefully.

WEEK 3: 17–23 APRIL

You'll be drawn to making a considerable decision in your personal or work life. If you've been looking for work this is certainly a good time to make progress, likewise if you've been aiming to improve your health. It's also a good week to make a commitment to turn a corner in your financial agreements and arrangements to create more wealth.

WEEK 4: 24–30 APRIL

Ensure decisions you make at work will not adversely affect your income. If you're looking for work you may find something suitable, but you may need to negotiate adequate pay. A financial matter will deserve attention. For some Aquarians this week's developments will revolve purely around your love life. It's a romantic week, but you must avoid idealising someone.

FINANCES

Consider looking for ways to make your money work for you as opposed to you working harder to make money. It's a good month to improve your income, so make enquiries if you're looking for a new job or career that provides you not only with better pay but also more of a sense of purpose. Developments around 17 April and the new moon on the 27th will help you turn a corner financially.

HEALTH

A constructive aspect between Mars in your sixth house of health and Mercury will encourage you to boost your vitality and well-being. When Mars enters energetic Leo on 18 April you'll gain extra energy to get things done, and this will be a good time to manage your energy levels and channel excess energy into productive pursuits. If you've been suffering from health issues, the new moon on 27 April will help you construct a strong foundation for good health.

LOVE LIFE

Life is changing at a rate of knots and as a result your relationships will alter quickly, at least in the way you view others and in the way they see you. It will be practical to take things one step at a time at the full moon on 13 April, which could highlight aspects of your relationship that require fresh focus. If you're single you may meet someone new who seems familiar yet is a stranger.

CAREER

You can make a great deal of progress at work this month. To make the most of your opportunities be sure to invest in yourself, and remind yourself to believe in your own abilities. A reunion or the chance to reconnect with someone important in relation to your career is likely to boost your circumstances, so be sure to reach out to those you know who have your interests at heart.

HOME LIFE

The beginning of the month will be an ideal time to invest in your home life but also, coincidentally, to travel and visit other people's homes. You may invite someone to visit your home. If you're considering making changes at home you may find a financial investment makes sense, but you must be adequately sure to avoid making mistakes and especially around 13 April and the 27th, when you may tend to make rash decisions.

May

WEEK 1: 1–7 MAY

Finances may require some focus, especially if you're contemplating a large outlay. You may receive an unexpected financial boost. You may need to be tactful with someone you share duties or finances with, so be sure to work with the facts. If you've been considering a change in your daily work life or health schedule you'll gain the chance to put some of your ideas to the test.

WEEK 2: 8–14 MAY

You'll appreciate the chance to do something different this week, and travel, spiritual development, sports and the chance to learn something will all appeal. You may enjoy an impromptu visit or trip or will receive unexpected news that takes you somewhere different. You may also experience a financial or ego boost, so take the initiative.

WEEK 3: 15–21 MAY

Being a spontaneous yet generally grounded person you do enjoy impromptu get-togethers and will certainly appreciate the chance to spend time with favourite people, perhaps even on a whim. It will be in your interest, however, to keep developments in your personal life such as at home uppermost in your mind, as your priorities may otherwise clash. You may appreciate a flow of money going into your home or vice versa and coming from your home.

WEEK 4: 22–28 MAY

This is a lovely week to find the time to invest both in yourself and someone special, as couples will find romance can truly flourish and singles will enjoy meeting new and exciting people. A trip or return to an old haunt may be particularly exciting and will broaden your horizons, bringing fresh ideas into your daily life. Avoid gambling.

FINANCES

The key to building and maintaining wealth lies in good research early in May, as you otherwise risk making mistakes during the month. This aside, it's likely you'll receive a financial boost either early in the month or at the end of it. However, a personal or domestic expense will need to be offset, so if you're unsure about your options and how to manage your financial obligations then obtain expert advice.

HEALTH

You'll have a lovely opportunity to relax or recuperate in a soothing environment. For some this will be at home and for others somewhere different and exciting. You have the chance mid-month to boost your self-esteem and vitality through favourite activities and being with like-minded people, so be sure to organise events that warm your heart. A trip somewhere exciting will particularly appeal towards the new moon on 27 May.

LOVE LIFE

Mars in your seventh house of partnership will encourage you to be more outgoing and upbeat, and your partner is likely to be increasingly outspoken and proactive. Just avoid arguments in light of this newfound vitality! The lovely aspect to Venus at the end of the month will encourage you to invest more in yourself and your love life and partner, and romance could flourish. If you're single this will be a wonderful time to meet upbeat people.

CAREER

You'll be drawn to revitalising this important aspect of your life, and news or a change of pace or place will be inspiring. It's a good month to align yourself more closely in your career to your sense of purpose and activities you love, so be sure to take the initiative. However, if you've been clinging to an outmoded desire to work for the sake of security and stability, you risk losing interest.

HOME LIFE

You may be drawn to expanding your home life in some way, such as bringing more people into your home or creating extra space. To ensure a smooth process, be sure to research finances carefully to avoid a blow-out in costs. If you've been considering moving for some time but have been reluctant, towards the end of the month you'll regain a sense of potential and possibility even if only because you feel stuck.

June

WEEK 1: 29 MAY—4 JUNE

A domestic matter will deserve appraisal so you're best able to plan this key aspect of your life. You'll appreciate the chance to meet and socialise with informative and helpful people. A work meeting in particular may be constructive. If you require financial help or advice this will be available, so be sure to reach out. You may experience an improvement at work but you're likely to be busy.

WEEK 2: 5—11 JUNE

A fresh chapter in connection with a group, organisation or friend is about to begin. You may be drawn to turning a corner at work or beginning a fresh contract. A meeting or talk could be the catalyst to a fresh understanding in your personal life. You may need to negotiate towards Monday, so be sure to brush up your communication skills. Someone may ask for your help, and if you need help it will be available.

WEEK 3: 12—18 JUNE

You'll enjoy getting together with someone special. However, it is a rare relationship where you always see eye to eye, so if you experience a difference of opinion consider it as a necessary discussion that could lead you both somewhere productive. A business or personal partner has unexpected news and the way you react will determine the outcome. Avoid speaking without forethought for the best results.

WEEK 4: 19—25 JUNE / WEEK 5: 26 JUNE—2 JULY

WEEK 4: you'll appreciate the merit in adopting a new, more inclusive approach to those you see on a regular basis. In this way you'll enjoy sharing a supportive network. A lovely relationship can blossom, so be sure to take the initiative if you're single and looking for company. However, some communications may be more difficult to than you anticipated, in which case patience will be a virtue. **WEEK 5:** this will be a good week to stride ahead at work and with a solid health routine designed to boost energy levels. You may find you gain a sense of vitality that will help you complete chores and regain your joie de vivre. A change of routine or difficult talks early next week are best navigated optimistically yet realistically.

FINANCES

Be sure to avoid gambling in June, especially around the 11th and mid-month, as you may not be happy with the results. It's far better to rely on a stable or secure income and invest in sure-fire options. A positive development financially will certainly boost self-esteem, and this is likely mid-month. Money that is owed to you by a personal or business partner is likely to be returned, but it's best to avoid lending if possible.

HEALTH

Once Mercury enters Leo on 26 June you're likely to regain your vitality, so if you feel a little lacking in energy earlier in the month rest assured your energy levels will replenish. It will be in your interest to manage your health and well-being a little more carefully during the first few weeks of June, as important developments and talks will arise that require your full attention.

LOVE LIFE

It's a good month to build bridges with someone you've argued with or if you feel you've grown distant from them. The full moon on 11 June will bring out strong emotions but could also promote a healing process in a relationship. If you're single June is an upbeat time for meeting people, and if you're interested in finding a partner the second and third weeks and the new moon on the 25th could be productive.

CAREER

The full moon at the zenith of your chart on 11 June will spotlight your favourite activities and pastimes. For some Aquarians, June's developments spell a fresh chapter in your career as you are drawn to embracing more of what you love. For others the focus will be on your extracurricular activities, which will infuse your daily life with more variety and could as a result inspire you to alter your career.

HOME LIFE

You'll appreciate the opportunity to invest in your home and/or family. This may take the shape of a change of environment at home and, for some, a holiday or trip. Some talks may be a little complex, but if you avoid a battle of egos you could reach a solution to any issues that arise early in June. Venus in your domestic sector from the 6th is ideal for creating a sumptuous feel at home and improving domestic relationships.

July

WEEK 1: 3–9 JULY

Someone unpredictable will surprise you, so be sure to keep communications clear for the best results. You may enjoy a trip somewhere different. News at work or regarding your health or personal life signals the beginning of an exciting phase in which events could lead to adventure and more opportunities to indulge in your true interests. Avoid gambling and instead rely on the facts.

WEEK 2: 10–16 JULY

You'll appreciate the opportunity to turn a corner in your work or health routines, finding the time and space to configure a timetable that better suits you and creates a sense of stability and security. A change of pace or place will be refreshing and exciting, as will the sense of entering fresh territory either at home or in your relationships and communications.

WEEK 3: 17–23 JULY

A personal or business partner is likely to have important news for you that it's best to consider in your own time and with the benefit of expert help if necessary. Decisions this week may have longer-term consequences than initially apparent. As you head towards the new moon on 24 July you'll gain the momentum to make long-overdue changes in your daily routine that can benefit you personally.

WEEK 4: 24–30 JULY

The new moon on 24 July can facilitate improvements in your work and health life, so take the initiative in these areas as your efforts are likely to succeed. You'll enjoy an impromptu trip or get-together. Aim to build a strong foundation for yourself at work and health-wise. A lovely development should provide an ego boost, or at least the sense of being appreciated at work and/or at home.

FINANCES

If you need financial advice, experts will prove to be informative in the first two weeks of July so reach out. You'll gain the opportunity to look at your financial situation from an objective perspective, enabling you to mend any aspects of your finances you tend to overlook such as unnecessary expenditure. The new moon on 24 July will encourage you to turn a corner at work, and this is likely to have a beneficial impact on your finances.

HEALTH

You may discover you need to function more spontaneously and live off your nerves a little more than usual in July, so it will be to your benefit to find ways to unwind in a variety of fresh activities. Consider which sports and pastimes not only train your body but actually raise your spirits. The new moon on 24 July could open doors to something different health-wise and will have the simultaneous effect of boosting your self-esteem.

LOVE LIFE

July's developments will provide you with the insight you need to gain direction within your love life. A partner may appear more expressive than usual or may have key news that will require careful consideration. If you were born during the last week of January you're likely to begin a completely fresh approach to your love life, which is likely to be more outgoing and fun-loving.

CAREER

It's time for something new in your daily existence and you'll discover fresh ways to bring more of what you love into your career. You're very good at reinventing yourself, and where in the past you may have simply entertained exciting ideas, July will provide the opportunity to take action to enter different territory in your working life. For this reason, be sure to seriously consider opportunities towards the new moon on 24 July if not before.

HOME LIFE

For some Aquarians, July will involve changes at home that bring a degree of unpredictability into your environment. This may be due to influences such as a trip or visitor. For some Aquarians, however, there will be the need to make changes at home due to general feelings of restlessness and irritability. Be sure to avoid making changes purely for their own sake and investigate the financial repercussions of any actions you take.

August

WEEK 1: 31 JULY–6 AUGUST

Your hard work and diligence will show results. The key this week to progress lies in good communication skills and the ability to work under pressure while still being able to show care and support to others. For some Aquarians, developments now will revolve around finances and how to create a more stable and secure budget in the long term.

WEEK 2: 7–13 AUGUST

Discussions, meetings and ideas will flow this week, so be prepared to stay on top of fast-flowing circumstances. If you're travelling or receiving visitors you're likely to enjoy the change of environment. However, with Mercury still retrograde until 11 August, patience will be a virtue and especially with regard to a commitment. Romance, the arts and music will all appeal, especially towards Tuesday, a good day for romance.

WEEK 3: 14–20 AUGUST

This is a good week for get-togethers, both socially and in your work life, as you're communicating well. You may receive a boost in morale for hard work well done. If you have any relationships that have gone awry this is the week to mend bridges, especially towards 19 August. This is also a potentially romantic week, so singles should keep an eye out and especially this weekend.

WEEK 4: 21–27 AUGUST

Saturday's new moon suggests a new, more settled phase is about to begin in a key business or personal relationship. However, this may first involve a little soul searching or an eventful week. You may be surprised by an abrupt change of plan or development this weekend. Avoid taking developments personally and aim to welcome fresh dynamics into your life.

FINANCES

You may experience an improvement in your finances at mid-month and towards the end of the month but if the opposite happens be sure to enlist the help of an expert or adviser, whose information will be invaluable. A change of circumstances around the new moon on 23 August may precipitate the need to put in place a workable budget that better suits you and those you love.

HEALTH

Venus and Jupiter in your sixth house of health for most of August will encourage you to improve your mental, emotional and spiritual health. It's a good month to improve your looks, especially at mid-month, as your efforts are likely to succeed. Towards the new moon on the 23rd you may be drawn to improving your physical health or that of someone close. Be sure to take things one step at a time to avoid feeling overwhelmed.

LOVE LIFE

The Aquarian full moon on 9 August signals the opportunity to turn a corner in your personal life. If you were born after the first week of February you'll kick-start a fresh phase in your daily or health routine that could boost your personal life. The key earlier in August to an exciting love life lies in your ability to nurture yourself and your partner when needed. This will enable love to flow, especially at mid-month when romance can bloom.

CAREER

Mid-February–born Aquarians will be turning a corner in your career. All Aquarians will gain the opportunity to align yourselves more fully with aspects of your skill sets that you enjoy engaging in. You may be surprised by some of the opportunities that arise when you put your feelers out and may even be in a position to make a fresh agreement via negotiation towards the new moon on 23 August.

HOME LIFE

You may discover that some of your vulnerabilities emerge, and the more practical you can be about managing these, especially with regard to your home and relationships with those close to you, the better for you. A change of environment due to a visitor or trip will breathe fresh air into your domestic life and relationships, bringing a sense of variety and possibility into this important area of your life.

September

WEEK 1: 28 AUGUST–3 SEPTEMBER

Both your sign's rulers Saturn and Uranus are under pressure this week, so the more you pace yourself and look after your nerves and communications the better it will be for you. This aside, you'll relish a lovely get-together with someone close to your heart that will raise morale. You may also enjoy the therapeutic aspects of reliable and trustworthy people and prove yourself to be such to someone else.

WEEK 2: 4–10 SEPTEMBER

The total lunar eclipse on 7 September will feel romantic and even beguiling. If you were born in early February, prepare for a particularly romantic or mysterious weekend. You may experience a change of circumstance at work or financially during the week. If you've been single for a while, romance is on the horizon. A change in your daily routine or well-being could be ideal.

WEEK 3: 11–17 SEPTEMBER

Discussions and agreements you make may have longer-term implications than initially obvious, so be sure to make well-informed choices and avoid making snap decisions. Careful discussions in your personal life and at work could take you several steps closer to your desired outcomes. You may need to review or revise certain personal or financial arrangements.

WEEK 4: 18–24 SEPTEMBER / WEEK 5: 25 SEPTEMBER–1 OCTOBER

WEEK 4: the solar eclipse on 21 September will spotlight a key business or personal relationship. You could make a great deal of progress at work and in your personal life. However, this may involve a little soul searching first or an eventful week. News from a partner or a change of pace or a promotion could present fresh horizons to be conquered, which you will in your inimitable way.
WEEK 5: developments are likely to move forward at a relatively fast pace and you could make great progress in your health, personal life and the areas you share such as joint finances or shared duties at work. If you've been considering making changes in these areas this is a good time to do so. Just ensure you keep everyone your decisions affect in the loop to avoid misunderstandings.

FINANCES

September will be a memorable month regarding finances. Some Aquarians may experience a financial boost early in the month around the lunar eclipse on the 7th. A business or personal partner may have news that requires attention regarding your joint finances. Just avoid making shared financial decisions based on assumptions; it would be far better to first get professional or expert help if necessary.

HEALTH

You'll appreciate a wonderful opportunity both early in and at the end of the month to kick-start an upbeat health schedule. Consider approaching your health from a lateral perspective. A healthy mind will lead to the wish to look after your physical health, so consider seeking mental and spiritual sustenance as a priority. For some Aquarians, learning will revolve around self-knowledge, self-care and spiritual development and the net result will be improved energy levels.

LOVE LIFE

The first two weeks of the month are ideal for romance. If you're single you may meet someone who seems strangely familiar at the start of the month and get-togethers will have a therapeutic quality. However, care must be taken to avoid arguments during the first and last weeks of the month. The lunar eclipse on 7 September will spotlight a key shared circumstance and you'll gain the opportunity to discuss plans. Be optimistic about your romantic outlook.

CAREER

This is a wonderful month to socialise, network and boost your communication and negotiation skills, as you could make some wonderful new arrangements and agreements with colleagues, employers and business associates. There is an extremely fortunate aspect at the end of the month that in your case could open up a completely new horizon for you in your usual daily work or health routine, so be sure to work towards transforming this important aspect of your life.

HOME LIFE

Despite this being an eclipse month, which invariably involves a great deal of change, you are likely to discover that your long-term options regarding your home and/or family are positive. However, this will not be without experiencing some disruptions or disagreements early in the month that are best approached patiently and calmly. You'll see positive developments by the end of the month even though these are likely to involve long-term change.

October

WEEK 1: 2–8 OCTOBER

Shared duties may prove demanding, so ensure you're tactful while displaying your usual dynamic and optimistic approach. You'll succeed where others fail. Finances may require additional focus to ensure you avoid making mistakes with transactions. If you're drawn to making a large investment, ensure you check the fine print and avoid financial and emotional gambling. You'll enjoy a reunion. Romance could flourish this weekend, so plan a date.

WEEK 2: 9–15 OCTOBER

A key decision or commitment may be on the table. Decide how a personal decision may affect your work life and finances and vice versa. A deeper commitment to someone could open new doors. You'll enjoy finding fresh ways to boost your health and vitality and improve relationships. Romance could thrive, so be sure to organise a date. A trip or visit will feel energising.

WEEK 3: 16–22 OCTOBER

This will be an excellent week to reshuffle some of your commitments and duties, especially those concerning shared responsibilities at work. For some Aquarians financial matters will deserve a closer focus so that you're able to put in place a more advantageous and efficient budget. You'll enjoy a trip or favourite activity such as sports, so be sure to organise fun pastimes.

WEEK 4: 23–29 OCTOBER

Several processes will fall in place this week. You'll gain the opportunity to spend more time on the activities and people whose company you love. If you've been considering for some time revitalising your daily health or work schedule, this is an excellent week to do so as your efforts are likely to succeed. You may hear unusual news next week or have an unexpected get-together.

FINANCES

A financial transaction or focus on your finances early in the month will require attention to avoid debt or loss. If you're planning a considerable investment, be sure to double-check the terms and conditions. The full moon on 7 October will spotlight a shared or tax-related investment that requires a little more focus, and the new moon on the 21st points to the importance of keeping on top of shared finances that may again include taxes or debt.

HEALTH

This is an excellent month to invest your time and energy in your health and well-being, as your efforts are likely to succeed. You'll appreciate the feeling of improved energy reserves, which in turn will enable you to spend more time on your favourite activities and interests such as sports or travel. The final week of the month may be particularly energising, ideal for an outdoors adventure or trip.

LOVE LIFE

The first weekend of the month is particularly conducive to romance, so be sure to organise a date with a partner. If you're single you may meet someone desirable. Just be sure you're on the same page to avoid misunderstandings. If partners have been undergoing a difficult time you'll find the new moon on 21 October therapeutic, as it will help you reinstate a degree of harmony in your relationship. Singles may enjoy someone's therapeutic company at this time.

CAREER

Once Pluto ends its retrograde phase on 14 October you're likely to increasingly experience a more motivated outlook career-wise and will enjoy embracing change a little more. Beforehand, be careful with your communications to avoid arguments and misunderstandings. Jupiter in your sixth house of work will keep you busy, and as long as you avoid arguments and especially between the 17th and 21st you're likely to see good results by the last week of October.

HOME LIFE

A change of environment or routine will have a knock-on effect at home, where you're likely to be looking for some changes that reflect your personal scenario. In mid-September you'll be drawn to altering important aspects of your environment, which could involve a trip, visitor or the wish to change your immediate surroundings at home such as adding quirky personal touches to your décor.

November

WEEK 1: 30 OCTOBER–5 NOVEMBER

Developments concerning finances, work, travel or a relationship will merit careful analysis, as you could make a key commitment or boost your circumstances. Ensure you consider an optimistic plan in detail. If you receive disappointing news this week, bear in mind that sometimes for something new to begin then what is no longer required in your life must end. The supermoon on 5 November will spotlight fresh beginnings.

WEEK 2: 6–12 NOVEMBER

You'll appreciate an increasingly productive atmosphere and will enjoy a reunion or the opportunity to spend time with a favourite activity or person. You may also be drawn to travelling and entering fresh territory, either via a different environment or the activities you choose. Avoid arguments if possible at work on Friday and regarding shared duties, responsibilities or finances this weekend.

WEEK 3: 13–19 NOVEMBER

There is a sense of adventure and of fresh horizons this week, even if there's also a feeling that you're retracing your steps. Rest assured your experience will be put to good use and you'll gain the opportunity to move forward with the benefit of hindsight. For some Aquarians great progress is possible at work, and for others in your favourite projects and with family.

WEEK 4: 20–26 NOVEMBER / WEEK 5: 27 NOVEMBER–3 DECEMBER

WEEK 4: the new moon on 20 November will bring out your passion for various favourite activities. You may also find that your career, status and direction are in the spotlight this week. This is certainly a good time to boost your work and self-esteem. If you're already on holiday you're likely to enjoy yourself immensely, as the change of environment will boost energy levels. **WEEK 5:** the activities you love such as art, travel, movies, music and spirituality will all appeal to you now, and you'll enjoy indulging in romance involving dance, dinners and reconnecting with someone you love. A trip is likely to take you into unexpected or different territory. Just be careful around 29 November to avoid delays and plan ahead.

FINANCES

This is a good month to consider the best way forward financially, especially if you undergo changes in your career or income. An expert's advice will be particularly informative, so be sure to reach out if necessary. Above all, avoid feeling you must go with the general consensus in your financial planning, as your circumstances are unique and merit an individual and expert eye.

HEALTH

You'll appreciate the opportunity to explore and discover new pastimes and environments in the shape of a holiday or trip, which will have an uplifting effect on your health. If, however, you burn the candle at both ends this month you'll experience the necessity to take breaks. The new moon on 20 November is likely to encourage you to book a holiday if you haven't already. You'll enjoy bringing more variety into your daily life and sports.

LOVE LIFE

Venus in Scorpio from 6 November will add spice to your love life. However, it may also bring out fiery tempers, so be sure to avoid contentious topics and especially on the weekend of the 8th. Singles will enjoy a reunion during the same weekend and you may meet someone new who seems familiar yet whom you've never met before. A change of environment such as a short break may bring surprising fresh qualities into your love life.

CAREER

You'll feel drawn to expanding your skill sets and perhaps even to taking a fresh path in your career in November. You may receive unexpected news early in the month and again around the new moon on the 20th that will be surprising but also provides incentive to step into something different. Fresh negotiations could boost your self-esteem and you'll gain an increasing sense of passion and commitment.

HOME LIFE

As Uranus re-enters Taurus you may retrace your steps in November concerning certain developments in your home life. You may be surprised by news concerning a property or family member that will require you to recall experiences you learned from in the past and will enable you to take measured responses to unexpected developments. Expect a change of environment, either due to travel or visitors.

December

WEEK 1: 4–10 DECEMBER

You'll be in a position to help someone, and if you need advice or support it will be available. The full moon and supermoon on 4 December spotlights your family, home and creativity and suggests that the more adaptable you are the better it will be for you, especially in your personal life. Consider who and what are your main priorities at home and focus on them. The key to success is avoiding distractions.

WEEK 2: 11–17 DECEMBER

Important personal, work and financial matters will deserve careful focus. Avoid making long-term decisions based on other people's experiences alone and ensure you do your own research. Trust your gut instincts too, as these are unlikely to let you down. You may experience a financial or ego boost. You'll enjoy a change of environment, even if you need to adapt slightly to something new.

WEEK 3: 18–24 DECEMBER

The new moon on 20 December will contribute to an exciting and upbeat sociable week, coinciding with festivities. Some Aquarians will experience an ego or financial boost that will feel thoroughly uplifting. There will be reason to enjoy travel and get-togethers, but unless you plan your activities particularly well and especially towards Christmas, unfortunately there could be delays or misunderstandings.

WEEK 4: 25–31 DECEMBER

If you're working this week, a fresh approach to someone close such as a co-worker will ring in changes at work. The festive season will bring out the best in everyone. You may enjoy a boost in self-esteem, finances or ego but must be careful to avoid arguments and making rash decisions. Look for peaceful solutions and outcomes instead.

FINANCES

You have the equal potential in December to improve your finances dramatically but also to spend or gamble away a lot of money. It is therefore in your interests to set yourself a budget and stick with it. The adage about neither a borrower nor lender be applies this month, so if you do need to borrow money – for example, for domestic purposes – ensure the terms are manageable.

HEALTH

The start of the month is an excellent time for improving your health and well-being by indulging in your favourite activities such as sports, self-development, a deepening sense of spirituality and healing. At mid-month and towards the solstice you'll experience a therapeutic development that will be associated with a change of environment such as a holiday or through a favourite activity. If you're working during this time you'll appreciate the financial stability you obtain.

LOVE LIFE

As you have an analytical mind you may initially tend to evaluate circumstances in your love life intellectually. The pitfall here is that you then try to fit a relationship into a concept you have of what it should be. Certain expectations this month are best kept within the bounds of reality to avoid hasty decision-making, especially around the supermoon on 4 December. You'll appreciate a therapeutic and deeper sense of belonging with someone special during the last week of the month.

CAREER

You'll feel motivated and encouraged to stride ahead career-wise and an adventurous streak may see you entering fresh territory. The first week of the month is very good for discussing your options, such as attending interviews. Mid-month and towards 20 December you may experience a financial or ego boost related to your career, so be proactive. However, you must be sure of the facts if you're stepping into fresh territory to avoid misunderstandings and assumptions.

HOME LIFE

The supermoon on 4 December will spotlight your home and/or family and kick-start a fresh chapter in these areas. You may be surprised by developments, so if you're blindsided consider where your true loyalties lie and follow that train of thought. A change of environment may have its fair share of surprises around Christmas, but with attention to detail you'll enjoy investing in this important aspect of your life.

♓

PISCES

18 February – 20 March

January

WEEK 1: 1–8 JANUARY

You'll get a commitment from a friend or group such as a work arrangement. You may be surprised by unexpected news or an impromptu get-together this weekend and may receive deserved praise or a pay rise. A trip or visit will be enjoyable, as you'll appreciate time spent with someone you admire or love. If you're uncertain about where you stand, find out more.

WEEK 2: 9–15 JANUARY

You'll revel in the chance to indulge in the aspects of life you love. A sociable time will strike a nostalgic chord. You may enjoy the chance to prove yourself at work or network. Just be sure to avoid overextending yourself financially and circumstances where you feel like a fish out of water. If you're on holiday prepare for a fabulous event, but avoid overindulgence as you'll regret it.

WEEK 3: 16–22 JANUARY

A lovely aspect between Venus and Mars spells romance, and it's a good week to indulge in music, the arts and favourite activities. Links with your past due to a reunion or return to an old haunt may include surprising developments. A group, organisation or social setting could bring something new and exciting into your life. Mid-week next week may feel intense but will help you turn a corner in a favourite area. Think laterally for the best effect.

WEEK 4: 23–29 JANUARY

Key decisions that involve a practical stance on your behalf will ask that you be logical, yet you may feel far more inclined to be emotional. A get-together or romantic tryst will be uplifting but you must avoid being impulsive. The new moon on 29 January will help you let go of the past in a different and perhaps unusual way. A change in connection with a group or organisation may arise.

FINANCES

This year your finances are likely to fluctuate, so be sure to keep them on an even keel by placing the intention and configuring a budget to keep things even. Otherwise, you may find things a little topsy-turvy. You may already discover now at the start of the year that certain expenses, while what they've bought have been enjoyable, will require repayment and prospectively more than you'd hoped.

HEALTH

You'll be drawn to improving your appearance, wardrobe and fitness in January and your efforts are likely to succeed. Venus in Pisces from the 3rd will certainly be a motivator to seek to improve not only your looks but also your happiness, as this is what creates the luminosity that projects true beauty. January is certainly an excellent time to develop your interests in spirituality and such modalities as yoga, meditation and self-development.

LOVE LIFE

The moon's north node enters Pisces on 12 January, putting focus on your love life over the next 18 months. This brings the very real opportunity, especially towards the end of January and early February, to make considerable changes to this key part of your life. If you've been single and are looking for a partner you're likely to find one. Couples can ramp up romance, but if trouble has been brewing then changes are likely within the upcoming year.

CAREER

Developments may present a stop-start sense or of having to navigate at the least a fresh landscape that means you must be on your toes. Luckily, communications with a group or organisation are likely to go well but you must avoid intense talks and discussions early in the month and around 9, 13 and 20 January for the best results. Aim to look for practical and reasonable results on these days in particular.

HOME LIFE

You'll gain the willingness to imbue your life with more of what you love, which will include the company you keep. Those you love will have their own courses of action to take and it'll be up to you to provide the stability and security you prefer. Venus will joint Saturn and Neptune in your sign from 3 January, enabling you to do just that, but you must avoid seeing certain people and developments idealistically.

February

WEEK 1: 30 JANUARY–5 FEBRUARY

The conjunction of Venus, Neptune and the moon's north node in your sign spells a romantic, even spellbinding, week. If you're single you may meet someone special, especially if you were born towards 20 March. If you're making key financial decisions ensure you have all the details before launching head first into something you're unsure of. Avoid simply following trends: consult your inner principles and decide your priorities.

WEEK 2: 6–12 FEBRUARY

You will be drawn to adventure, yet if your plans are unclear this could be a frustrating week as your head is likely to be somewhat in the clouds. If a change of circumstance or unexpected development feels disorienting it's vital you maintain focus and plan ahead. The full moon on 12 February will shine a light on the benefits of a fresh approach to your work and health and an upbeat daily schedule.

WEEK 3: 13–19 FEBRUARY

You may feel particularly romantic but potentially also a little idealistic, so be sure to keep your feet on the ground. A work duty will benefit from more clarity to establish parameters. You may uncover deep secrets. Spiritual Pisces may feel inspired and a lovely friend or organisation will raise your mood. A reunion or return to an old haunt may boost morale. It's a good week to clear debts.

WEEK 4: 20–26 FEBRUARY

The ideas of someone close or a colleague may differ from yours. Make the effort to collaborate, as you may otherwise butt heads. A debt or bill will need to be paid or cleared. A project or idea that may be at work, via a key decision regarding future options or a health matter will entice you. If you feel your options are limited, hard work and dedication could lead to a breakthrough.

FINANCES

Expect key financial changes at this time. The conjunction of Venus, Neptune and the moon's north node on 1 February set the tone for the month. For some Pisces this will be a super ideal time for you, with money coming your way. However, for others there will be the need to reassess past expectations that may have been unrealistic or you'll need to reassess current circumstances if you've gambled in the past on a hunch, especially around the 10th.

HEALTH

If you've been suffering from a long-standing illness you'll gain the opportunity to improve circumstances through hard work and diligence. You may discover that certain modalities that seem left of field could be of use, such as spending time in nature and visualisations. Keep an eye on health around 4 February and the full moon on the 12th. The new moon on the 28th will be ideal for kick-starting a fresh health routine.

LOVE LIFE

This is one of the most romantic times of the year, so make the most of opportunities. Some Pisces may be drawn to an ex or to rekindling a past relationship, but on both sides you must be certain this is due to true love and not nostalgia. Such a romantic signature for all Pisces will be delightful, but you must keep your feet on the ground as you're likely to see life through rose-coloured glasses.

CAREER

Your daily work life and routine are likely to change and you'll gain a deep understanding of the exact parameters at mid-month, around the full moon on 12 February and the new moon on the 28th. Key news will be decisive and may be somewhat unexpected at mid-month. You'll gain the opportunity to steer a fresh course in your career as long as you keep your feet on the ground and communications clear.

HOME LIFE

You'll notice a sense of positivity return to your home life if things have been a little slow or have stopped more recently that will take place towards the end of the month. The majority of February will be ideal for being patient at home, showing compassion for yourself and others in the anticipation that things will improve. The full moon on the 12th could bring a fresh phase with unexpected aspects.

March

WEEK 1: 27 FEBRUARY–5 MARCH

The Pisces new moon on 28 February signals the chance to boost your appearance, profile, well-being and romance. You'll find out whether you've been unrealistic about someone or a venture and, if so, you'll get the chance to focus on building more security in your life. This is a good week to put many things in perspective for yourself, as the eclipse season this month is likely to shake up your personal life.

WEEK 2: 6–12 MARCH

You're creative at the moment, which people will respond to positively. You'll feel motivated to connect with someone upbeat and may be inclined to make a commitment to a person or project. If you must invest more than time into ventures, such as money, ensure you do adequate research to avoid making mistakes. A reunion or news from your past will be inspiring for mid-March Pisces.

WEEK 3: 13–19 MARCH

Friday's lunar eclipse signals a fresh commitment to an agreement, especially if it's your birthday on Friday. If you were born later in March you'll begin a fresh work or health schedule. You may discover a new way to approach a personal or work relationship, such as being more practical as opposed to idealistic. A meeting will be key to your progress and may involve surprising news.

WEEK 4: 20–26 MARCH / WEEK 5: 27 MARCH–2 APRIL

WEEK 4: the sun–Neptune conjunction will bring out the best in you, as you'll feel inspired to enjoy your interests such as art, spirituality, romance, film or dance. However, if you tend to be absentminded, idealistic and non-committal these aspects may become stronger, so be sure to focus at work! Nevertheless, you may be pleasantly surprised by developments. **WEEK 5:** be prepared to discuss work or daily logistics. If you avoid squabbles you could reach a positive arrangement in your personal life or financially as the eclipse on 29 March brings fresh arrangements. Meetings and communications may resonate deeply, especially if you were born mid-March. You'll meet someone or hear from someone you have a predestined connection with. Singles may meet a lovely character.

FINANCES

Key developments are possible in March, so if you've been considering making certain changes to your investments, earnings and budget then this month circumstances are likely to motivate you to take action. The solar eclipse on the 29th will be in your finance sector and will bring important developments, unless you've already experienced these earlier in the month. Be sure to investigate options carefully to avoid making mistakes and avoid gambling.

HEALTH

It's likely considerable developments in your personal life will be exhausting, even if exhilarating. You may be particularly prone to experience a past or niggling health situation towards the end of the month, so be sure to make efforts earlier in the month to boost your constitution. The eclipses will mean mid-March–born Pisces must adjust to a fresh daily work or health routine, so be sure to find ways to gain extra energy to put into your activities.

LOVE LIFE

This month's eclipses are in Virgo on 14 March and in Aries on the 29th. Both eclipses signal considerable changes in your personal life that cannot be underestimated; they could be life changing. Relationships can highlight your approach to yourself. The lunar eclipse on the 14th will spotlight whether you're sacrificing your life for someone else or whether your relationship is fulfilling you personally as well. If it's the former, it will be important to attain a more balanced outlook.

CAREER

You'll increasingly find throughout March that your communications improve, and this will doubtless improve your outlook at work. Because so much of your focus is going to be on your personal life it will be important to maintain a professional stance at work. If you were born after mid-March you're likely to see considerable changes in the workplace and could experience a boost in self-esteem and finances, so be proactive with your work initiatives.

HOME LIFE

Family and those you love will gain your attention and you may need to alter some of your usual routine to accommodate their demands or wishes. You'll be wearing many different hats at once in March and this may initially be disorienting, as you prefer to take life in a more intuitive and less proactive, hands-on and demonstrative way. Your communication skills will be tested, so be sure to be patient and also gain a sense of balance.

April

WEEK 1: 3–9 APRIL

This stands to be a fairly intense week for you unless you're lucky enough to be on holiday! To relax you'll appreciate the opportunity to indulge in romance, the arts, film and dance. It's certainly a very good week for spiritual self-development and to make a personal or work commitment. You may receive uplifting news from a group or organisation or regarding finances.

WEEK 2: 10–16 APRIL

Expect key developments in your personal life. You're stepping into new territory, even if you reconnect with an old friend or work situation or an ex. Circumstances have moved on over the years. However, you'll appreciate a lucky or unexpected boost that will improve your finances, personal life or morale.

WEEK 3: 17–23 APRIL

The conjunction of Venus, Saturn and the moon's north node in your sign points to important and unavoidable decisions and developments in your personal life, and especially if you were born after mid-March. You're likely to experience upbeat developments in your life, but if you find the opposite occurs rest assured this is a clearing of the past so a better future may arise.

WEEK 4: 24–30 APRIL

You'll enjoy a get-together or good news, especially if it's your birthday at the end of February. March-born Fish are likely to receive key work news that may involve a degree of negotiation. This is a transformative week, where your values will determine the decisions you make. These will be long-standing, so ensure you're clear about the outcomes.

FINANCES

It's certainly a very good month for you to work towards prosperity. You may be surprised by financial developments, as some projects you've been working on will bear fruit while the outcome of others may be unexpected. Particular arrangements at work and with family will improve your financial options. The final two weeks of the month will involve the need to make shrewd financial decisions regarding your personal life or work.

HEALTH

This is a good month to seek the advice or expert knowledge from a professional with regard to any niggling health or personal issues, as their help will be invaluable and especially if you were born after mid-March. As there is such a lot going on this month for all Pisces it's most definitely in your interest to take things one step at a time and to avoid making rash decisions, especially towards 27 April.

LOVE LIFE

For most Pisces this is a super romantic month. There is also a karmic aspect to developments, where past actions clearly lead to present developments. It's a super-romantic beginning to the month, so make the most of it! It's all go for you in your personal life, especially if you were born before mid- to late March. If you were born afterwards, the focus is more likely to be on work commitments.

CAREER

As there is a fair amount of focus in April on your personal life you may find work takes less focus, yet your career will require attention as it is a changing scenario. You may be particularly busy if you work in property, such as in construction or real estate. An important career decision towards the end of the month will require a patient and shrewd response, with a key emphasis on income and budget. Avoid selling yourself short.

HOME LIFE

The first week of April will be an excellent time to put energy into your home life and those you share it with. You'll enjoy visitors or will visit someone else's home. A trip or change of environment will be enjoyable and will offer the sense of freedom while you're away, but also the pleasure of coming home. If finances have been tough you'll find your home life becomes a centre for planning ways to make more money.

May

WEEK 1: 1–7 MAY

This is a good week to improve your appearance, health and well-being as your efforts are likely to be successful. Ensure you research your ideas and avoid making snap decisions; you may be tempted to cut corners, especially at work and home. You may enjoy unexpected praise or a financial boost. An agreement or key new arrangement will require tact.

WEEK 2: 8–14 MAY

Good communications skills will be the catalyst for a successful week, as circumstances will demand that you change your usual approach to people. A fresh agreement or arrangement in a key relationship or shared project will be productive, as you may find that a balance of power will need redressing. Be tactful and precise in your speech and you could accomplish a great deal this week.

WEEK 3: 15–21 MAY

An unexpected yet mostly welcome development will improve your self-esteem and could also boost your finances. You may receive a compliment and the chance to prove yourself. The key to your success now depends on your being super clear about your long-term goals, especially with family, friends and work colleagues, otherwise misunderstandings will arise.

WEEK 4: 22–28 MAY

This is a good week for discussions and negotiations, including those to do with work and finances, as your efforts are likely to pay off. Some Pisces will be lucky enough to receive a financial or personal boost. The Gemini new moon on 27 May will kick-start a fresh chapter for you that will encourage you to be more outgoing and adventurous both financially and at work.

FINANCES

This is a good month to consider how you might invest your hard-earned cash more wisely and also consider how you might share joint finances more equally, such as those you have with a family member or organisations such as the tax department. You may experience a surprise development financially towards the full moon on 12 May. Financial progress is possible, so be sure to look for better investments and consider reconfiguring your budget if necessary.

HEALTH

It's a good month to gain energy through an upbeat exercise routine. Be sure to consider taking up a new class or fitness schedule as you'll appreciate the outcome. If you've been feeling under the pump at work, avoid relegating your health and well-being schedule to second priority in the belief you have no time for it. On the contrary, if you can maintain a solid fitness regime you'll gain energy.

LOVE LIFE

Someone special will merit more time and energy from you. As a result you could make a fresh commitment to them and a cherished project or arrangement that will benefit you both. Couples will appreciate the chance to indulge in romance, especially in the first week of May, and singles may meet someone with whom you appear to have a predestined link, especially if you were born in mid-March.

CAREER

There is a wonderful opportunity towards the end of the month to boost your work circumstances and potentially your finances. This will encourage you during the previous three weeks to work harder towards certain goals in the knowledge that you can attain them. Some Pisces will be in a position to negotiate a fresh agreement or contract, so if you've been considering a new job be sure to take the initiative.

HOME LIFE

Your home life will gather focus, especially from the perspective of where you see it going and whether your financial and emotional investments in your home life still support your big-picture goals and provide you with a sense of deep purpose. If you feel you need to make a change at home, ensure you adequately research the vital financial aspects as otherwise you may be surprised by news at mid-month that could be disappointing.

June

WEEK 1: 29 MAY–4 JUNE

The key to a successful week lies in good communication skills, as you may find yourself put on the spot. Be prepared to show just how strong you are, and if necessary find an expert or adviser who can provide you with the facts you need to gain traction at work or financially. If you are an adviser yourself you're likely to be busy at work.

WEEK 2: 5–11 JUNE

Your activities and interests will grab your attention, and the more adventurous you feel the more likely you will be entering fresh territory at work or in your free time. A health or sports event will catch your eye and there are certainly therapeutic aspects to the week that could improve your well-being. News from family or regarding your home or property is best approached matter of factly.

WEEK 3: 12–18 JUNE

You may feel more spontaneous and wish to make changes at home or work. Your efforts are likely to succeed with the right information. You may be surprised by a meeting or news and must avoid misunderstandings. An unexpected disagreement or change of schedule needn't ruin your week; it could be the opportunity to mend bridges. A talk with a work- or health-related expert will boost your mood.

WEEK 4: 19–25 JUNE / WEEK 5: 26 JUNE–2 JULY

WEEK 4: the new moon on 25 June will usher in a fresh chapter that will stimulate improvements at home, in a property and, for spiritual Fish, in your beliefs and self-development. A meeting or friendship could mark a turning point. If you have felt stuck in a personal or financial situation, circumstances are likely to bring things to a head that will nevertheless help move things along. **WEEK 5:** if you have experienced challenges you'll be happy to hear that you'll gain a sense of progress, as you get the information or the green light you've been waiting for. Be optimistic at work and home that your efforts will pay off, especially those you've been very diligent with. You may be pleasantly surprised by a financial or personal boost this weekend or early next week.

FINANCES

Financial matters are best approached diplomatically in June, as certain expectations you've had in the past versus current developments will require your full attention. If you have lent or borrowed money you may need to review how you'll clear the loan. Therapeutic aspects in June suggest you could overcome financial complexities, but you must avoid making impulsive decisions. It would be far better to seek the advice of an expert if needed.

HEALTH

You'll appreciate the opportunity to consider fresh avenues, be these via travel or study or a change in your daily routine. All of the above can contribute to improved health and well-being this month, so be sure to look for ways to boost your feel-good factors as your efforts will succeed. The second week of June may be particularly therapeutic, although you'll need to avoid stress and especially in relation to finances, home and/or family.

LOVE LIFE

Mars will contribute to a livelier love life from 17 June on throughout July. However, a partner may seem feistier than usual even if they seem surprised when you point this out. The new moon on the 25th could help you turn a corner if you have felt your love life has been in the doldrums, so be sure to take the initiative. Singles may meet someone who is strangely familiar around the 25th and who may become significant.

CAREER

In a changing world and potentially busy month your career can go from strength to strength, as long as you stay on top of a fast-moving schedule. You may experience an ego or financial boost associated with your work early in June already. The full moon on 11 June will encourage you to move into fresh territory work-wise. If you're on holiday your time out will be inspiring career-wise.

HOME LIFE

News and developments at home will take a considerable amount of energy and emotional investment, so it would be in your interest to be patient in this area. When you are you'll enjoy a change of routine or schedule that could really buoy your mood and health. If you're considering a move, the attendant upheaval is likely to lead to a better circumstance as long as you undertake adequate research and prepare well.

July

WEEK 1: 3–9 JULY

You'll enjoy a sociable atmosphere, as it will bring you in touch with like-minded people. You may be surprised by a financial or personal development. Avoid travel delays by planning ahead, although some unexpected delays will be out of your hands. You may be asked to take your responsibilities at work or health-wise more seriously, and it may be time to consider a more efficient schedule.

WEEK 2: 10–16 JULY

You'll enjoy socialising this week and may meet a new group of people or be drawn to signing up for fresh activities that bring you closer to like-minded people. The full moon on 10 July will spotlight your social life. If you've been super sociable over previous weeks you're likely to wish to slow down. If you've been a hermit you'll enjoy being more outgoing.

WEEK 3: 17–23 JULY

Developments will highlight your true values and principles, and for some these will be reflected in your relationship decisions and for others in your work and health arrangements. It will be to your benefit to consult experts if need be regarding finances and health and maintain an even keel with your communications to avoid arguments. You'll enjoy a lovely trip or get-together this weekend.

WEEK 4: 24–30 JULY

The new moon on 24 July will help kick-start a fresh chapter that may initially feel a little overwhelming or confronting, but if you pace yourself and are open to something you're likely to find that stepping into new territory or accepting a challenge will be productive. Intense conversations needn't be a spanner in the works if you maintain perspective.

FINANCES

You'll appreciate the opportunity to look at your finances from a fresh perspective, especially with regard to making your savings and earnings work for you so you have money to spend on activities you enjoy such as travelling and socialising. You'll gain the opportunity to turn a corner in your career or usual daily routine, which could also improve your finances, so be open to new opportunities and especially towards the new moon on 24 July.

HEALTH

You'll enjoy devoting more time and effort to your health, and a lovely opportunity for a trip or fun development in the third week of July will provide you with the motivation to bring fresh and uplifting practices into your daily life that can only benefit you. Be prepared to consider a fitness program that may seem more physical than you would usually undertake but that with expert guidance could in fact improve your energy levels.

LOVE LIFE

It's time to bring a little bit of variety and spice into your love life, and for some this will involve a trip or the chance to alter your usual routines so you can spend more time with each other. If you're single and looking for romance you're likely to find it around the full moon on 10 July, so be sure to socialise then. Emotions are likely to run high between the 23rd and 25th, so avoid conflict.

CAREER

Do you have the balance you deserve between job security and an interesting, exciting daily life? This will be a good month to consider ways you could satisfy both these desires by adding more aspects you enjoy to your career. The new moon on 10 July will be ideal for networking and researching fresh options. The final week will be ideal for proactively infusing your daily life with more qualities you want to have in it. Be sure to reach out and meet people!

HOME LIFE

July is an excellent time to focus on your home life and specifically its capacity to nurture you and sustain your well-being. The beginning of the month is conducive to improving your environment through such activities as DIY projects or gardening. You'll also enjoy adding mood-enhancing décor such as fresh cushions or lamps. The entry of Uranus into Gemini may produce restlessness, so gauge whether changes you consider at home are due to this or whether they merit considerable effort.

August

WEEK 1: 31 JULY–6 AUGUST

A trip, news or get-together towards Friday will be significant. This is likely to be a productive if quirky week, with news coming that opens your eyes to different options and opportunities in your personal life and career. If a minor hurdle arises, rest assured you'll overcome it. A constructive approach to your relationships, especially your home life, will be fruitful and well received.

WEEK 2: 7–13 AUGUST

You'll enjoy an upbeat and varied week, and if you like to socialise you'll appreciate getting together with like-minded people now. A business or personal partner is likely to have important news for you. It's certainly a good week to begin a fresh daily work or health routine. The Venus–Jupiter conjunction next week will bring romance, music and beauty front and centre in your personal life.

WEEK 3: 14–20 AUGUST

This is an excellent week to reach out for what you want in life because the stars will support your efforts, so whether you wish to gain kudos at work or boost your romantic life, now is the time to take action. You may experience a therapeutic development in your life. If you wish to improve your health this week is ideal to take the initiative.

WEEK 4: 21–27 AUGUST

A fresh incentive may catch your eye in a work context or with a favourite project. The new moon on 23 August will help kick-start a fresh daily routine such as a different health schedule. Some late February–born Pisces will be turning a corner in a personal relationship. You may be surprised by some developments this week, and if you work towards a solid outcome you'll succeed.

FINANCES

You may need to undertake a delicate financial discussion with someone in your household or close to you. The more methodical and practical you are the better will be the outcome. If spending has been too high in your family or domestic zone it will be necessary to discuss better ways to economise. Be sure to avoid gambling, especially during the final week of August, as you may be surprised by unexpected financial developments at that time.

HEALTH

The sun in your sixth house of health is shining a light on your health practices. Are you doing enough to support your body in all aspects: physical, mental, spiritual and emotional? This is an excellent month to get on top of your health routine as the stars will support your efforts, especially around 19 August. Every small step you take will add up, and by the end of the month you'll see improved health and vitality.

LOVE LIFE

Mars in your seventh and eighth houses throughout August will bring feistier aspects of a partner to the surface. This may initially feel disorienting, especially around the 8th, but if passion has been lacking in your love life it's about to make a return! You may need to approach a personal decision very carefully around the full moon on the 9th, and if in doubt be sure to seek the advice of a loyal friend or organisation.

CAREER

August is an excellent month to draw on your social and networking skills to build a stronger profile in your career. The sun will bring out your more proactive and dynamic aspects, creating the ideal opportunity for you to make positive changes in your career. Communications will improve after the third week of the month, so if some communications are still complex earlier on be patient. The new moon on 23 August could bring a fresh opportunity work-wise.

HOME LIFE

The start of the month will be ideal for adding a little zhuzh to your home life in the shape of refreshed décor and a constructive approach to interpersonal differences. You may need to negotiate certain terms or agreements during the first week of the month. Potentially surprising developments will ask you to embrace something new at home but which at the same time will bring you closer to someone you love or admire.

September

WEEK 1: 28 AUGUST–3 SEPTEMBER

Saturn re-enters your sign, bringing a nostalgic tendency with your thoughts going to the past. It's a good week to review finances and a work or health routine. Keep an eye on communications, especially next week towards Wednesday, as you may receive unexpected news or must contend with a busy or delayed schedule. You'll enjoy a lovely reunion or the chance to review domestic priorities.

WEEK 2: 4–10 SEPTEMBER

The Pisces lunar eclipse on 7 September spells a fresh chapter in a key business or personal relationship if you were born on or before 7 March and a fresh daily or health schedule if you were born afterwards. You may enjoy a particularly creative or romantic week. Communications are likely to go well as long as you steer clear of hastily spoken words or reactions.

WEEK 3: 11–17 SEPTEMBER

Someone close has important news, either in your personal life or at work or both. This is a good time to discuss your options and make well-informed decisions, but you must be wary of succumbing to other people's pressure and putting too much pressure on yourself. Give yourself the space and time to make informed choices at work and in your personal life.

WEEK 4: 18–24 SEPTEMBER / WEEK 5: 25 SEPTEMBER–1 OCTOBER

WEEK 4: a fresh incentive may catch your eye in a work context or involving a favourite project, interest or venture. This week's solar eclipse may feel particularly invigorating as you gain the chance to make fresh arrangements that will keep your work and health schedules upbeat and varied. Keep an eye on your energy levels to avoid fatigue, as you're likely to be busy. **WEEK 5:** it will be to your benefit to be patient with those who have been a part of the change in your life recently, and of course to be patient with yourself as you move forward into fresh territory. Communications and negotiations will go particularly well or move quickly this week, so be sure to be precise about your wishes to avoid misunderstandings further down the track.

FINANCES

As Saturn re-enters your sign, where it will be for the next five and a half months, you'll gain the opportunity to reconfigure, rethink and restructure your finances. Keep an eye on developments towards 16 September, as these will bring clarity to certain financial arrangements that may need to be renegotiated.

HEALTH

The first and second weeks of the month, including the lunar eclipse on 7 September, will kick-start a fresh chapter in your health and wellness schedule. You'll gain the opportunity to discuss clever and practical ways to bring more joy to your health practices and also your personal life through more energy. Take steps to manage stress so you don't succumb to making impulsive or rash decisions.

LOVE LIFE

September will be a key month for you in your love life. If, for example, you've been considering altering your status from single to a partnership or from married to single this month is likely to hasten you along your path of change, especially if you were born around 7 March. You may enjoy a reunion early in the month that brings a degree of nostalgia your way. Be sure to base your decisions on current circumstances as opposed to memories.

CAREER

You'll appreciate positive indications at the beginning of the month regarding your work and daily schedule. If you've felt in the past that some aspects of your work have been overlooked you'll gain a deeper understanding of the appreciation for your hard work.

HOME LIFE

Seeing your home as a nurturing provider of stability will encourage you to focus on this important aspect of your life in September. It may as a result gain more prevalence as you realise its value. You may experience a particularly busy home or family life this September, so good planning will be to your benefit.

October

WEEK 1: 2–8 OCTOBER

A health matter will benefit from research and an optimistic approach. You'll get well ahead this week with a sensitive approach to others. A particular get-together should feel uplifting, but if it doesn't consider whether someone has your best intentions at heart and whether you're feeling super vulnerable. If it's the latter, consider finding ways to boost your self-esteem and self-confidence.

WEEK 2: 9–15 OCTOBER

A choice concerning finances, work or a close relationship will merit careful consideration, as you're about to begin a fresh chapter in one or all of these areas. Avoid emotional and financial gambling, because when you do you could broaden your horizons in your personal and professional lives, breathing fresh air into both, and enjoy a romantic, productive and enriching week.

WEEK 3: 16–22 OCTOBER

You'll gain the opportunity this week to make an important personal or financial investment that could in essence be therapeutic. If you've been preparing to make a commitment in your personal life or financially, the results of your efforts are likely to bring the peace or harmony you desire. However, financial transactions merit a careful approach to avoid making unnecessary mistakes.

WEEK 4: 23–29 OCTOBER

Creative and artistic Pisces can make a great deal of progress this week. This is also a good time for self-development and investment in your skill sets and abilities. Romance could truly thrive, so be sure to organise dates. A partner may have important news for you. A degree of tension in communications is best approached carefully to avoid misunderstandings. You may be surprised by news mid next week.

FINANCES

Consider taking a careful approach to finances early in the month, as you may discover an anomaly in an invoice or accounting that will deserve rectification. If you tend to be reckless financially this will be a good month to change that tendency, as you may discover needless spending. Nevertheless, a positive financial option at mid-month could truly boost your finances, so be sure to keep an eye out for opportunities then.

HEALTH

A health or beauty treatment early in the month will raise morale. To truly feel that you're on track health-wise and gain a sense of purpose in October, consider where your true priorities lie. This is a good time to invest in self-improvement, not only physically, mentally, spiritually and emotionally but also in the skill sets that enable you to feel you are of use in the workplace. This would also boost your self-esteem and therefore contentment.

LOVE LIFE

Good communication skills grease the wheels of sound relationships. A case in point will be the first week in October, when care and attention to carefully chosen words will smooth over a sensitive phase. The full moon on the 7th points to the chance to kick-start a fresh chapter in your personal life. If you've been uncertain about whether to make a commitment to someone, consider waiting until the new moon on the 21st, which will be revealing and potentially healing.

CAREER

This is an excellent month to sharpen your social and networking skills and make a splash with those people who could potentially help you gain ground in your career. It's a case of friends and influential people helping you move forward. Be prepared also to negotiate and make serious commitments that could improve your career outlook. Most importantly, consider the skill sets you'd like to use more frequently in your daily life and look for avenues to do so.

HOME LIFE

Your sign's ruler Neptune enters your sign on 22 October, where it will stay until the end of January 2026. You'll gain the opportunity to retrace some of your steps in your story so far throughout 2025, and may even experience a nostalgic time and the need to recalibrate during the last quarter of 2025. Your home life will provide adequate opportunity for self-reflection, much of which will take place during quiet hours.

November

WEEK 1: 30 OCTOBER–5 NOVEMBER

A personal matter or relationship will benefit from focus. A father or authority figure may play a central role in your decision-making. A clever plan will bring rewards. The supermoon on 5 November will spotlight your finances, negotiation skills and values. You'll gain the opportunity now to clarify where you stand.

WEEK 2: 6–12 NOVEMBER

The entry of Venus in passionate Scorpio will encourage you to be more outgoing in your personal and business relationships. Romance could certainly thrive this week, but so too will arguments and especially at the weekend, so it's best to avoid contentious topics. You may be drawn to planning a holiday, and if not to taking a trip to reunite with a person or activity you love.

WEEK 3: 13–19 NOVEMBER

This week is all about connections and people you would love to deepen your relationship with and those you're moving away from. You'll gain the opportunity to discover more about each other, and this will enable you to make important decisions towards the new moon next week about which collaborations and associations you'd like to continue and which you're ready to let go of.

WEEK 4: 20–26 NOVEMBER / WEEK 5: 27 NOVEMBER–3 DECEMBER

WEEK 4: the new moon on 20 November will revitalise your interest in esoteric studies, travel and meeting new people. You'll also be drawn to reconnecting with those you love on a deeper level. Collaborations at work could thrive, and you may enjoy a reunion. You may experience an unexpected development concerning finances, especially those you share with someone such as a mortgage lender or partner. **WEEK 5:** personal and financial developments will be a focus this week, and you may need to make decisions regarding unusual circumstances. Some Pisces will need to be focused on how to respond to developments involving someone close. An intuitive, gentle and sensitive approach to your feelings and those of others will help you navigate this week's events. Romance and the arts could flourish, so take the initiative.

FINANCES

Unexpected or surprise developments early in the month and at the end of November will place considerable focus on finances. You may discover you have overestimated a circumstance. The good news is you'll gain the opportunity to rectify the situation. You may be surprised by developments towards the 19th and the new moon on 20 November will enable you to consider how you wish to move forward, especially regarding shared finances such as joint family responsibilities and taxes.

HEALTH

The health of yourself or someone close such as a family member may be on your mind. If you experience feelings or vulnerability you'll gain the opportunity to improve health and well-being as a result. A lack of self-esteem may be at the root of some of your reluctance to be more assertive, and if this is so then developments this month will leave you in no doubt that building stronger resilience and self-confidence will create a more robust mindset.

LOVE LIFE

The path of true love rarely runs smoothly, or so the adage goes. The supermoon on 5 November will spotlight tension in a relationship but will also highlight therapeutic ways forward. The entry of Venus in Scorpio on the 6th will spice up your love life but could also bring an argumentative aspect out in yourself and a partner, especially around the 8th. The last week of November could see romance thrive, and if you're single a reunion is possible.

CAREER

An outgoing approach to your career will work. A change within your focus or a surprise at work will encourage you to be bold and enter fresh territory. The pace is likely to be slower during the last three weeks of the month, which in fact may work to your benefit as you'll gain the chance to catch up on work and review your progress. Misunderstandings are likely during the last three weeks of the month, so be super clear.

HOME LIFE

With five planets retrograde for much of the month you may find that your home becomes a place you increasingly use for rest, because you're going to need to catch up with yourself. Some Pisces will be taking a holiday or experiencing a change of address and will thus spend a little more time than usual on feathering your own nest. It will certainly encourage you to spend more time there.

December

WEEK 1: 4–10 DECEMBER

You'll feel drawn to freedom or to a sense of possibility through travel, study and self-advancement. Be prepared to be spontaneous but avoid impulsiveness, as it could backfire. The supermoon on 4 December will spotlight agreements and contracts, enabling you to gain insight into where you stand financially and work-wise. If you require expert help it will be available. Your expertise may also be in big demand this week.

WEEK 2: 11–17 DECEMBER

Are you seeing life through rose-coloured glasses? If so, you'll find out this week via a reality check in your personal life or career. Your plans may be based in reality but others may see them differently, and you'll get the chance to adjust your perspective. A trip or another fun activity will certainly raise morale, and you'll enjoy reconnecting with those you love.

WEEK 3: 18–24 DECEMBER

This week features many of your favourite activities, but if you don't take the initiative and attend events you may get swept up in the chaos of the festive season. However, if you make time for your interests such as healing activities, self-development, spirituality and the arts you'll find this a therapeutic week. That is, as long as you steer clear of mysteries not of your making.

WEEK 4: 25–31 DECEMBER

You'll enjoy spending time with someone special and revelling in favourite activities in your spare time, and if you're working you'll appreciate immersing yourself in that environment even if there is the inconvenience of working at this time of year. A trip or visit will prove to be therapeutic; just ensure you plan well ahead to avoid too many delays. Avoid financial and emotional gambling.

FINANCES

Early December has excellent potential for obtaining expert help financially that could take you into calmer seas. It's important not to gamble, as this is unlikely to work in your favour. In mid-December you may experience a financial boost or another unexpected financial development. The expert help of an adviser will be invaluable, so if you're unsure of your circumstances then reach out at this time.

HEALTH

This is a good month to consider how far you've come so far this year with regard to health, and if you realise you've let your attention to health slip it's a good time to reorganise your daily life so health once again becomes a priority. Otherwise, you may discover health issues resurge. The phase around the solstice has a therapeutic quality, so be sure to take the initiative and engage in healthy endeavours guaranteed to boost your mood.

LOVE LIFE

The supermoon on 4 December will spotlight the way you communicate and could also highlight the dynamics of certain relationships. Initially in December you may find you need to work a little harder than usual at good communication skills, but as the month goes by you'll increase your understanding of someone close. Mid-December may be a particularly complex time, so be sure to pay extra attention to communications then to avoid confusion and arguments.

CAREER

A great deal of focus on your favourite pastimes and people may distract you from your career in December, yet important groundwork is being laid for 2026. Try to maintain a steady flow at work to pave your way ahead, as 2026 will include the opportunity to boost your career. An outgoing approach to your activities could involve a career improvement around the new moon on 20 December if you've already prepared the way.

HOME LIFE

This will be an excellent month to invest more of your time and energy in the smooth running of your domestic life, as you'll gain the opportunity to feel more in sync with those with whom you share space. During the last half of the month you may be drawn to travelling and your favourite pursuits, so your home may take second place to adventure. Nevertheless, your activities will inspire you to take time out at home.

ALSO BY PATSY BENNETT

SUN SIGN SECRETS
Celestial guidance with the sun, moon and stars
ISBN: 9781925946352

This comprehensive, ground-breaking astrology book is for everyone who wants to make the most of their true potential and be in the flow with solar and lunar phases. It includes analyses of each sun sign from Aries to Pisces and pinpoints how you can dynamically make the most of your life in real time alongside celestial events. Work with the gifts and strengths of your sun sign in relation to every lunar phase, zodiacal month, new moon, full moon and eclipse.

Look up your sun sign to read all about your talents and potential pitfalls, and discover how to express your inner star power during the various phases of the sun and moon throughout the days, months and years to come.

Available at all good bookstores.